Highland Sanctuary

Ohio University Press
Series in Ecology and History

James L. A. Webb, Jr., Series Editor

Conrad Totman,
The Green Archipelago: Forestry in Preindustrial Japan

Timo Myllyntaus and Mikko Saiku, eds.,
Encountering the Past in Nature: Essays in Environmental History

James L. A. Webb, Jr.,
Tropical Pioneers: Human Agency and Ecological Change in the Highlands of Sri Lanka, 1800–1900

Stephen Dovers, Ruth Edgecombe, and Bill Guest, eds.,
South Africa's Environmental History: Cases and Comparisons

David M. Anderson,
Eroding the Commons: The Politics of Ecology in Baringo, Kenya, 1890s–1963

William Beinart and JoAnn McGregor, eds.,
Social History and African Environments

Michael L. Lewis,
Inventing Global Ecology: Tracking the Biodiversity Ideal in India, 1947–1997

Christopher A. Conte,
Highland Sanctuary: Environmental History in Tanzania's Usambara Mountains

Highland Sanctuary

*Environmental History in
Tanzania's Usambara Mountains*

Christopher A. Conte

OHIO UNIVERSITY PRESS
ATHENS

Ohio University Press, Athens, Ohio 45701
© 2004 by Ohio University Press

Portions of this book appeared in a slightly different form in Christopher A. Conte, "The Forest Becomes Desert: Forest Use and Environmental Change in Tanzania's West Usambara Mountains," *Land Degradation and Development* 10 (1999): 299-307. © John Wiley and Sons, Limited. Reproduced with permission.

Printed in the United States of America
All rights reserved

Ohio University Press books are printed on acid-free paper ∞ ™

12 11 10 09 08 07 06 05 04   5 4 3 2 1

Library of Congress Cataloging-in-Publication Data

Conte, Christopher Allan.
  Highland sanctuary : environmental history in Tanzania's Usambara Mountains / Christopher A. Conte.
    p. cm. — (Ohio University Press series in ecology and history)
  Includes bibliographical references and index.
  ISBN 0-8214-1553-0 (cloth : alk. paper) — ISBN 0-8214-1554-9 (pbk. : alk. paper)
  1. Human ecology—Tanzania—Usambara Mountains—History. 2. Mountain ecology—Tanzania—Usambara Mountains—History. 3. Geographical perception—Tanzania—Usambara Mountains—History. 4. Landscape assessment—Tanzania—Usambara Mountains—History. 5. Usambara Mountains (Tanzania)—History. 6. Usambara Mountains (Tanzania)—Colonization. 7. Usambara Mountains (Tanzania)—Environmental conditions. I. Title. II. Series.
  GF729.C66 2004
  333.7'09678'22—dc22

2004002991

For Sabine and Marcus

Contents

List of Illustrations	ix
List of Tables	xi
Acknowledgments	xiii

Chapter 1. Forming the Highland Sanctuary
*Natural and Human History in the
Eastern Arc Mountains* — 1

Chapter 2. Humanity's Imprint
Mountain Forest, Garden, and Pasture — 17

Chapter 3. Colonial Science and Agricultural
Development at Kwai and Amani — 41

Chapter 4. Seeking the Good Forest — 68

Chapter 5. Transforming the Agricultural Landscape — 96

Chapter 6. Agriculture and the State
*Imposing a Landscape Makeover
in Insecure Times, 1946–1961* — 126

Chapter 7. Preserving the Usambaras in
Independent Tanzania — 148

Notes	161
Bibliography	201
Index	211

Illustrations

Maps

1.1.	Eastern Arc Mountains	xiv
1.2.	East and West Usambara Mountains	2

Figures

1.1.	Diagrammatic section of the Usambara Mountains	6
1.2.	View of the West Usambara massif from southeast	7
1.3.	View of South Pare mountains from Pangani Valley highway	8
2.1.	Small farmstead, West Usambara	21
2.2.	Iron worker, Nyassa	23
2.3.	Irrigation furrow	26
2.4.	Mlalo old town site	34
3.1.	Former colonial estate, Mkuzi	56
3.2.	Amani post office	61
4.1.	Forest boundary near Mkuzi	69
4.2.	Eucalyptus	77
4.3.	Pit-sawing platform, Magamba	85
5.1.	Rice farming, Kitivo	99
5.2.	Sisal fields below Usambaras	100
5.3.	Maliki Kinyassi in front of ceremonial hut, Mlalo	119
6.1.	Market ladies, Kwemakame	136
6.2.	Stall feeding cattle	143
7.1.	Palms, near Muheza	160

Tables

Table 5.1. Census data for Mlalo Basin   122

Table 5.2. Acreage devoted to major crops on average holding, Mlalo   123

Table 6.1. Acreages devoted to major crops, old system and new system, Mlalo Basin   133

Table 6.2. Extract of monthly exports from Native Authority markets, W. Usambara Mountains 1955–57 (in kilograms)   137

Table 6.3. West Usambara, population by ethnicity, gender, and age, 1931   138

Table 6.4. West Usambara population by gender, age, and location, 1957   138

Table 7.1. Forest loss in the Eastern Arc Mountains   151

Table 7.2. Change in land use in the West Usambara's Shume Ward, 1957–76   154

Acknowledgments

I began the field research for this book in 1991 with the help of generous fellowships from the I. I. E. Fulbright Program and Michigan State University's College of Arts and Letters. I continued work on the project in 1996 and in 1998 with financial support from Utah State University and the American Philosophical Society.

During my stays abroad in the U.K., Germany, and Tanzania, I was greatly assisted by a number of organizations and people. My informants, all of them elders from the West Usambara Mountains, took me into their homes and generously shared their pasts with me. Without their kindness and openness, this book could not have been written. Nor could I have collected their testimony without the assistance of Peter Mlimahadala and Sufian Shekoloa, who helped locate informants, conduct the interviews, and translate testimony from Shambaa, Pare, and Vamaa into Swahili. In Tanzania, the staff at the Tanzania National Archives, the Lushoto Silvicultural Research Center and the offices of the East Usambara Conservation Management Area Programme also facilitated my research. I would also like to acknowledge the hospitality of Stig and Tia Johansson, David Scheinman and the all the folks at Grant's Lodge in Migambo.

I found writing this book to be an extraordinary challenge. The text's transformation from dissertation to manuscript benefited greatly from the comments of Harold Marcus, David Robinson, and David Campbell. Greg Maddox and Jim Giblin also contributed with commentary on several sections. James Webb, Jim McCann, and Tom Spear all read the manuscript and made valuable comments. Finally, Sabine Barcatta worked with me throughout the ten years it took to complete this work, carefully editing my flawed prose and always massaging my vulnerable psyche. While the book is better for the help I have received, I bear full responsibility for its flaws.

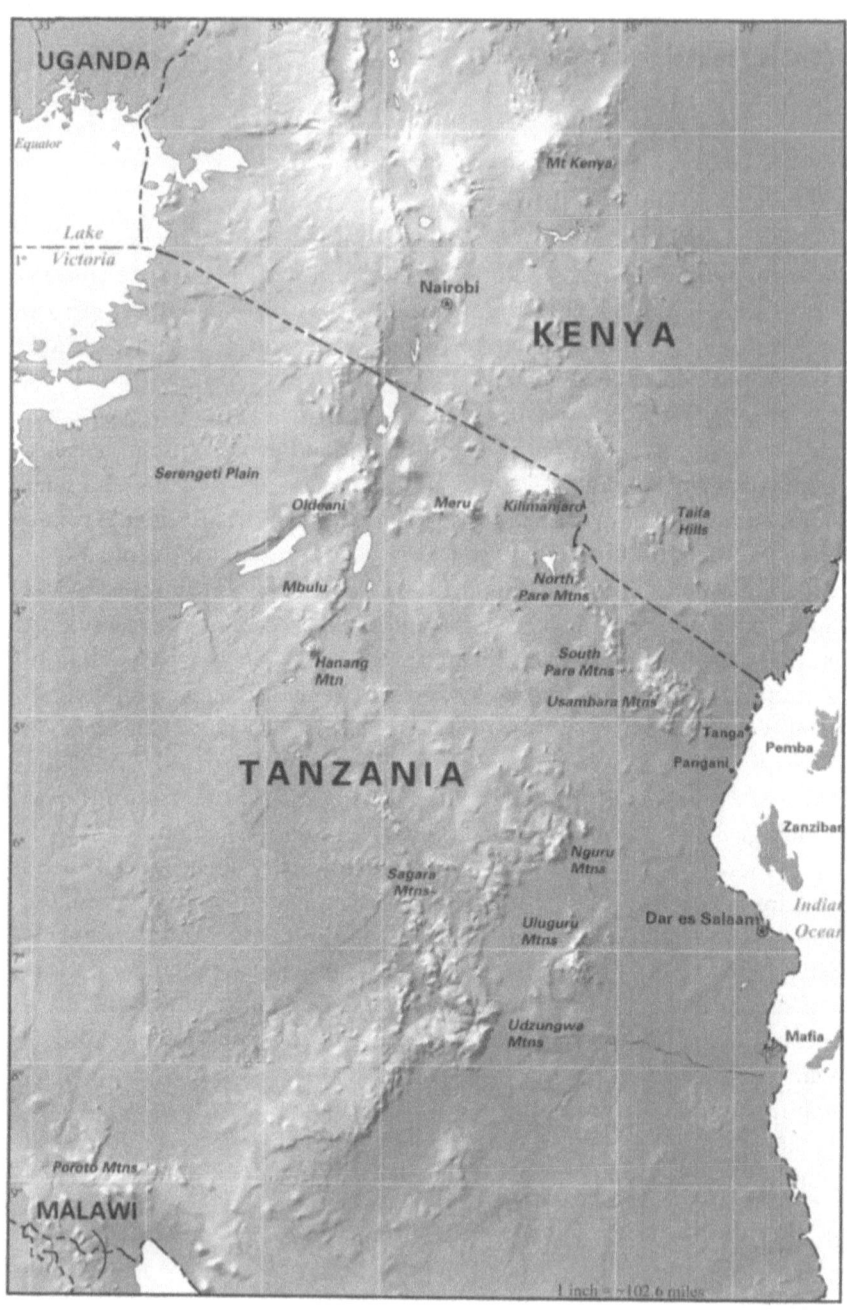

Map 1.1. Eastern Arc Mountains

CHAPTER ONE

Forming the Highland Sanctuary

Natural and Human History in the Eastern Arc Mountains

IF YOU CATCH THE EARLY morning flight from Nairobi to Dar es Salaam, the weather may permit an unobscured view of Mount Kilimanjaro's magnificent volcanic peaks, which rise to almost six thousand meters just south of the Kenya-Tanzania border. As the jet's flight path veers to the southeast toward the coast and Tanzania's capital, Dar es Salaam, more mountains come into view. From the air, these granite massifs appear much smaller and more worn than Kilimanjaro. Indeed, their highest peaks reach just above two thousand meters. They lack Kilimanjaro's stunning alpine tundra and glaciers, and therefore its reputation. Yet, in stark contrast to the browns and yellows of the surrounding plains, the weathered uplands appear particularly verdant. These ancient mountains, with names like Taita, Pare, and Usambara, form the northern part of the Eastern Arc, a group of massifs that lie relatively close to the East African coast. Geologically speaking, at two hundred million years of age, they are ancestors to Kilimanjaro, formed only a million years ago.[1]

The Eastern Arc Mountains appear as green islands scattered in a brown savanna sea because their cooler mountain temperatures condense

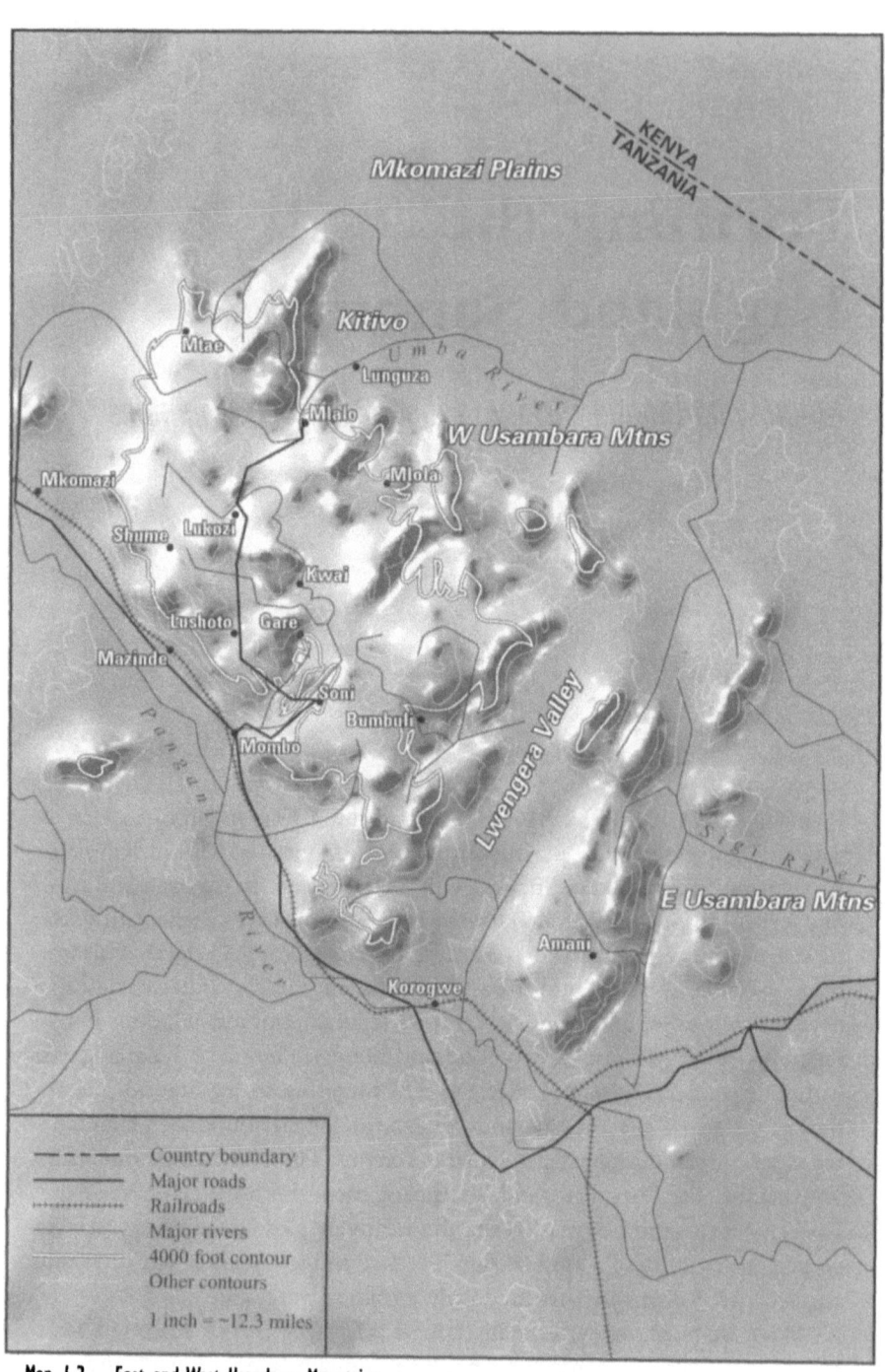

Map 1.2. East and West Usambara Mountains

the moisture-laden air wafting over them from the nearby Indian Ocean, keeping them far wetter than the surrounding plains. Throughout much of their natural history, then, the mountains have formed islands of climatic stability when other East African environments experienced fluctuating moist and dry phases. Thus, a peculiarity in physical geography helped to foster the evolution of biologically diverse forest flora and fauna on these ancient weathered inselbergs. Although tourists seldom venture into them, the Eastern Arcs have attracted their share of human attention. For millennia, African farmers in search of a place where they could survive East Africa's capricious climate have cultivated their soils. During the past century, the forests' ecological magnificence has drawn scientists and conservation advocates who seek, like their African counterparts, a strong measure of environmental control in East Africa's highlands.

This book compares the strikingly different environmental histories of two groups of these ancient mountains, the East and West Usambaras. Today, even to the casual observer, West Usambara's mountain landscape suggests a history of ecological degradation and decline. Most hillsides appear heavily used by small-scale agriculture. Of the remaining forests, most consist of monoculture plantations of exotic cypress and pine, and almost all of West Usambara's forests bear the scars of heavy wood extraction. Only a few miles to the southeast, across the Lwengera Valley, the massifs of East Usambara stand in stark contrast. Many of these uplands still carry large patches of indigenous forest, filled with endemic species, in addition to plantation groves. Cultivated fields of tea divide the forest patches, covering the landscape in characteristic light-green hues that set off the darker swatches of the rain forest canopy. The impact of small-scale agriculture appears more localized here. The chapters that follow ask what led these places, standing side by side and linked so closely by natural history, along such disparate ecological pathways.

In my interpretation of Usambara's environmental history, I call upon a number of sources that tell very different stories. The insiders—those who live in the mountains and who have inherited from their ancestors a complex social memory of the place—represent the land's history from the perspective of their labor and their community life. Outsiders—colonial bureaucrats, settlers, and scientists—also provide interpretations of mountain history, which, like those of their African counterparts, reflect particular cultural and ideological leanings. Of course, the mountains have produced their own history through their changing physical and biological manifestations. The interpretation I present seeks both to unravel and to integrate those stories in order to demonstrate the paradoxes and contingencies of Usambara's complex and changing environmental situation.

Throughout my analysis, I argue that the various historical interpretations assign value to elements of the mountain landscape in ways that continually reshape people's and institutions' stances toward the land.[2] Colonial-era interpretations of environmental history, for example, have tended over the past century to portray the Usambaras as divided in a conflict between forest and field. Whether a forest's value derived from its ecological complexity, its economic value as a timber source, or its soil's suitability for plantation crops like coffee or tea, the landscapes that indigenous people created invariably represented, to the colonial mind, a threat to the forest. African stories about mountain life, which grow out of experience and the transmission of memory, suggest a more integrated mountain history in which myriad environmental and social elements overlap in integral ways that sustain communities materially and ideologically. The Western and African views are largely incompatible and their clash has led to a series of conflicts that reshaped the Usambaras' mosaic of ecological communities. That conflicted past is vitally important to the current debates raging over conservation in the Usambaras and the rest of East Africa's highlands.

Nature's Sanctuary

Historians and scientists have yet to fully integrate their interpretations of environmental change.[3] The historical sciences separate human and natural history. Despite this tendency, natural history, a holistic scientific interpretation of the prehuman past, remains integral to humanistic interpretation precisely because it breathes life into nonhuman actors. The natural history that emerges from the cumulative scientific work on the Eastern Arc Mountains highlights the forest ecosystems' central role of evolutionary engine. As a result, forest remnants have become exceptionally important as centers for the scientific study of species endemism and biological diversity. Ongoing forest conservation projects and numerous studies of the Eastern Arc's endemic flora and fauna help to keep the forest-centric view in the limelight, and the forests' increasing fragmentation leads scientists to call ever more stridently for strict forest conservation.[4] This natural history is compelling; it provides us with ecosystems worth saving because they stand undiminished by human hands.

The scientific interpretations agree that the flora and fauna in Usambara's remaining forest patches speak to a natural history of stability on a continent generally accustomed to dramatic alterations in climate and geology. Natural history also links the Usambaras biogeographically to the other massifs of the Eastern Arc Mountains in Kenya and Tanzania. The unity extended even farther during the early course of African forest evolution, when forest species from East Africa's forests mixed and maintained affinities with their cousins in Central and West Africa. However, the geologic forces of the Mesozoic era (less than sixty-five million years B.P.) severed these evolutionary contacts by raising the Central African plateau. Once isolated from their ecological cousins in West and Central Africa, the rising Eastern Arc massifs' location fostered the evolution of an abundant but now spatially restricted biological diversity.[5] Forests have flourished in the highlands for the past thirty million years because elevation allowed the mountains to condense the regular moisture regime that the Indian Ocean low pressure pumped twice yearly across East Africa. The wet conditions at high elevation nourished forest growth even during the Pleistocene epoch's glacial episodes, when cooler and drier conditions depressed forest vegetation over much of East and Central Africa. The warmer and wetter periods between the ice ages saw the expansion of forest species into the savanna.[6] Thus, the Eastern Arc Mountain forests served as the regional hubs of forest expansion and contraction.

On the local scale, forest ecology in the Eastern Arcs reflects the historical interplay of geology, climate, and weather across each massif. Differences in elevation and aspect have scattered rainfall unevenly across the mountains and created a corresponding mosaic of forest communities. On the West Usambaras, for example, the main faults, and thus the escarpment faces, travel north-northwest with complementary faults diverging to the north-northeast. The heavily bisected mountain terrain creates a complex of rain shadows.[7] Rainfall volume and intensity therefore depend heavily on location and on the time of year. The rains of April and May, also known as the "long rains" because of their intensity, move in from the southeast and fall heaviest on the southern and eastern slopes, whereas the lighter "short rains" ride the northeast monsoon and fall more readily on the northern slopes. This pattern distinguishes the forest's ecological communities of the relatively dry rain-shadow climate of the central plateau (1,000 mm annual rainfall) from those of the well-watered southeastern slopes of the massif only thirty or so kilometers to the southeast (2,000

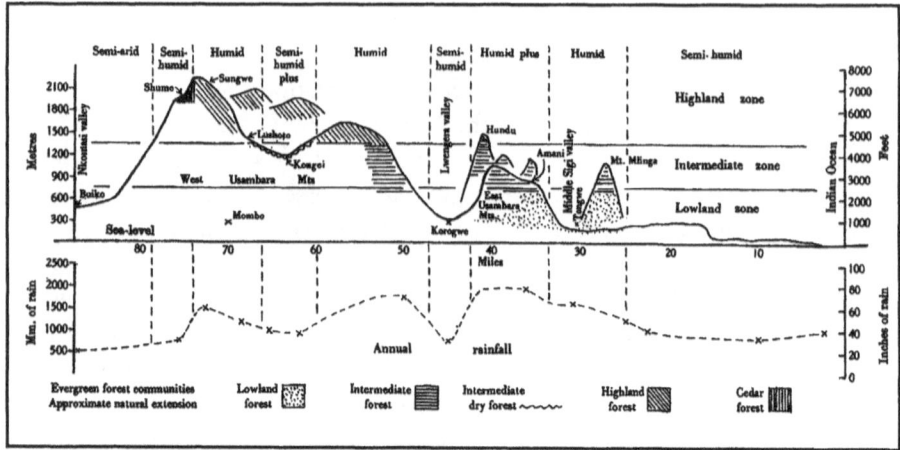

Fig. 1.1. Diagrammatic section of the Usambara Mountains, south-east–north-west. Reproduced from R. E. Moreau, "A Synecological Study of Usambara, Tanganyika Territory, with Particular Reference to Birds," *Journal of Ecology* 23.1 (1935): 6, by permission of Blackwell Publishing.

mm annual rainfall).[8] The mosaic of temperature and rainfall conditions offers plants and animals a variety of mini habitats where they can fend off competition.

From a natural history perspective, the Eastern Arc forests represent remnants of the prehuman past, and the ideal forest, the landscape most worthy of conservation. Plant inventories that count over three thousand species of vascular plants substantiate the old-growth forests' biological diversity. Jonathan Kingdon argues that the Eastern Arc forests now shelter animal species that learned to take advantage of the varied forest ecology when arid climatic episodes shrunk their lowland forest habitats and greatly restricted their range. Climate change thus accounts for the fact that the Eastern Arc Mountains now shelter the remaining populations of the tree hyrax, a once regionally widespread mammal. They also host a number of highly specialized bird species dependent exclusively on forest habitat. The forests have likewise protected the evolutionary processes of numerous amphibians and reptiles. The East Usambaras contain fourteen unique species of lizard, while tree frogs occur in eleven genera and seventeen species. The mountains are home, moreover, to as many as thirty-five species of millipedes, archaic diplopods that can survive only in particular moist habitats.[9]

Although hyraxes, passerine birds, amphibians, and millipedes might not match the worldwide popularity of the large mammalian flagship species of East Africa's "living Pleistocene" savannas, the Eastern Arc's biological

Fig. 1.2. View of the West Usambara massif from the southeast, looking across the Lwengera Valley. Photo Christopher Conte

diversity has nonetheless received the attention of *Nature*, which recently designated them as "biodiversity hotspots," marking them as critical centers of forest protection.[10] As important as forest preservation has become to conservation biology, East and West Usambara's forests remain the site of bitter contests over natural resources. *Homo sapiens*, admittedly a relative latecomer to Usambara's forest natural history, has nonetheless been resident in East Africa for tens of thousands of years, and its hominid ancestors used forest resources for millions of years before that. A more inclusive natural history, one that continues into the present, must both insert our species into the natural history of forest evolution and define the biological legacy that has emerged from humanity's interactions with East African forest environments.[11]

Subsequent chapters draw much from science's construction of Eastern Arc forest history. I argue for the forests' centrality to Usambara's environmental history, but also identify humanity's influence on even those seemingly pristine forest remnants that have garnered conservation biology's careful attention. Chapter 2, for example, takes a long view of human patterns of forest use. Just as natural history links the Eastern Arc Mountains' regional biogeography, human history argues for powerful links in the ways agricultural communities used and understood these mountain forests whose ecology they influenced. In the twentieth century, the forests' history changed course radically, and chapters 3, 4, and 7 examine the lines of conflict that conservation biologists and ecologists argue have laid siege to the precious forests that have survived.

Fig. 1.3. View of South Pare mountains from the Pangani Valley highway. Photo Sabine Barcatta

The Mountains as a Human Sanctuary: Forming a Cultural Landscape

In contrast to the scientists who observe and analyze mountain biology, ecology, and biogeography, generations of farmers and herders have come to know the Usambaras over the past two millennia through their work and their social lives. Archaeological and oral sources, as well as historical and anthropological studies, all suggest that, in the Usambaras, indigenous peoples' mountain home appears to them as a haven safe from unpredictable and even dangerous surroundings. Such understandings are not unique but form a motif in East Africa's highland history. The peoples who now inhabit the Usambaras therefore share a regional history that binds them culturally and economically to their neighbors on mountains and hills of the East and West Usambaras, North and South Pare, Taita, and Nguu. In this context, the upland farming and herding communities have come to understand their environment as a place that provides for cultural reproduction. The regional history also demonstrates that they have evolved similar strategies to enhance agricultural productivity and to mitigate the capriciousness of climatic uncertainty.

With this in mind, chapter 2 ties Usambara environmental history into its regional context in order to examine land-use patterns over the long term. Historical and archaeological studies of ancient life in the Eastern Arc Mountains and their surroundings indicate that environmental changes such as deforestation, forest regeneration, soil erosion, and biological simplification all coincide with the growth of East Africa's iron-using agricultural communities.[12] The linguistic and archaeological data for agricultural expansion and ecological change point to an association among the spread of Bantu languages and culture, the introduction of iron smelting and forging, and change in highland forest ecology, beginning by the first millennium A.D. The Usambaras were simply one of several mountain environments experiencing, roughly contemporaneously, these transformations. Archaeological research also suggests a particular cultural and technological unity among highland farming communities, sometimes dubbed the "*Mwitu,*" or forest, tradition.[13] Ancient highland farmers in Upare, Taita, and Usambara irrigated their gardens and planted the same crops (and crop varieties). They imitated each other's pottery styles, and, where possible, they smelted and forged iron. Mountain farmers tended to settle in and to farm the wetter montane or submontane woodland and forest areas, and from this base, they tended to extend their cultivation down the hills onto the drier plains.[14] Ancient Bantu culture underwent a number of permutations as it spread to different environments across East Africa, but its penchant for complex adaptation allowed mountain farmers to remain in one place over centuries. Through their labor and environmental knowledge, Usambara's residents successfully built and reproduced a community life that political and social discord occasionally threw into chaos. Nevertheless, the notion of a mountain sanctuary remained an integral part of their language, their oral history, and their sense of place.

Above the agricultural regions on the high plateaus of the Usambaras, low relative temperatures and aridity limited agriculture's possibilities. This environmental niche of relatively dry highland forests dominated by conifers became the realm of a predominantly pastoral people now referred to as the Wambugu, distinguished from their neighbors who speak Bantu languages by their Cushitic language and their historical associations with East Africa's Rift Valley.[15] Although their oral traditions place their ancestors with their herds on East Africa's open savannas, they, too, adapted to the mountain forest and grew to understand it as a sanctuary. When, in the twentieth century, colonial foresters and timber concessions invaded their homeland and transformed the landscape, the Wambugu lost their forest base and their way of life.[16] To one elder who knew the Usambara forested grazing lands as a youth, European foresters sterilized his land with exotic pines and cypress: "People preferred the indigenous forest more than the exotic forest. Indigenous forests are better because they allow grazing inside them. When exotic species are planted, grass does not grow below. Look around when you go into the exotic forest and what do you see—nothing, it is sterile like a desert."[17]

Several chapters in this book touch on the rapid series of economic, cultural, and ecological transformations that these pastoralists made in response to larger upheavals in East African history.[18] Theirs is a story of unlikely cultural survival in the face of the immensely powerful forces that practically eliminated Cushitic speakers across much of East Africa. Mbugu oral traditions recall how the Maasai forcibly evicted their ancestors from Kenya's Laikipia Plateau, causing them to wander as vagabonds the Rift Valley plains, where they survived from their herds and their ability to develop social relations with highland farmers. Eventually, the Wambugu found their promised land, not on the open savanna pastures, but in the Eastern Arc forests of Upare and Usambara. The story's motif jibes with historical trends in the history of conflict and accommodation in East African pastoralism. Although they compete over grazing territory in an effort to maintain a purely pastoral economy, herders also depend upon their ability to forge relations with neighbors who practice agriculture, in order to mitigate the loss of animals or pasture during devastating droughts or epidemics.[19] The Mbugu transition to the forest marks a shift, not so much in a mode of production, but to a sense of security removed from their difficulties in the Rift Valley.[20]

Although the ecological conversions necessary for farming and herding altered the forest, human survival still depended upon a landscape's long-term resiliency, and people developed strategies to maintain it. Steven Feierman's study of the ethnic and political history of Usambara's Shambaa people, Usambara's most populous ethnolinguistic group, examines the environmental imagery present in a cultural idiom that expressed a leader's responsibility for "healing the land" with gently falling but steady rainfall, which limited soil erosion.[21] For the Shambaa, these soft mists symbolized political tranquility and resulted in productive agriculture. The antithesis—violent storms, devastating floods, or drought—resulted in political unrest and led to famine. The forest, meanwhile, existed on the Shambaa cultural periphery and beyond the borders of their gardens. It offered room for expansion, fuel for the iron forge and cooking fire, and a hunting ground. Forest lands in this way supplemented agricultural life, but they acquired greater cultural and economic value when transformed into productive gardens. Mbugu herders, on the other hand, linked the forest's health directly to pastoralism's viability. In the end, land-use patterns across the Usambaras constantly altered ecological relationships of the forest complex, but exploitation patterns differed greatly in time and space.[22]

Over millennia, the selective use of Usambara's forests created a markedly humanized landscape. A mid-nineteenth-century aerial observation of Usambara would have likely revealed a massif largely clothed with primary and secondary forests, with open patches of several square miles surrounding permanent settlements. Smoke rising from the fires in ironsmiths' furnaces, farmers' fields in preparation, and herders' pastures in formation marked the mountain landscape. This place inscribed itself on peoples' memories, and its image lived through the elders I interviewed for this book. Their history forms an important part of this analysis.

A New Mountain View: Science, Forestry, and Colonial Bureaucracy

European imperialists came to understand the Usambaras not in terms of what the mountains had provided the indigenous inhabitants, but for what they promised. First Germany (1890–1914) and then Great Britain (post–World War I) ruled in succession the part of East Africa now known as mainland Tanzania. The imperial agents who reconnoitered the Usambaras before Germany's colonial conquest and occupation tended to portray a place and a people frozen in time. The stasis, be it cultural, economic, or ecological, veiled a kind of potential energy that they believed colonialism could release. In the West Usambaras, the hubris of colonial natural resource policy helped to throw the area into a maelstrom of conflict and dramatic ecological change. In contrast, the same ignorance and failed land-use policy eventually pushed the East Usambaras into Tanganyika's economic backwaters, with serendipitous results for forest preservation.

In 1852, Johann Ludwig Krapf, a German missionary employed by the British Church Missionary Society (CMS), visited the Usambaras in his attempt to extend CMS influence beyond the East African coast. As far as we know, Krapf was the first European to traverse the mountains. He compared them to Switzerland and to Germany's Black Forest, a descriptive theme that subsequent observers would often repeat.[23] Although the mountains almost certainly presented Krapf with a bucolic scene slightly reminiscent of temperate mountain environments, the Usambaras do not resemble the European Alps either environmentally or culturally. He simply squinted hard enough to see something familiar while he planted the seed of alpine imagery in the minds of those who followed.

A generation after Krapf's 1848 and 1852 expeditions, the German East Africa Society, the organization charged by the German imperial government with initiating colonial economic development, sponsored a more professional cadre of observers—geographers, economists, and botanists—to scout out the possibilities for the colonial project. They described temperate highlands, free of malaria, which could theoretically support a healthy settler population and a forestry industry. With their proximity to the coastal ports of Tanga and Dar es Salaam, the Usambara Mountains in particular presented a prime attraction early on in the process of colonization.

The publication of Oscar Baumann's article "Usambara," appearing in the 1889 volume of *Petermanns Geographische Mitteilungen*, represents the first systematic description of the Usambaras. Baumann's expedition in 1888—from August 22 until October 18—followed established paths that skirted East and West Usambara's most heavily forested sections.[24] Based on his limited observations, Baumann divided the mountains into three zones: the forest, the settled regions, and the high grazing areas.[25] The *Kampinenzone*, or settled farming region, appeared to Bauman overworked, eroded, and largely deforested, except for the gallery forests he encountered in stream valleys. But, in northwestern Usambara, he found the alps: high pastures surrounded by tall mountains and cool, luxuriant forests. Perhaps recalling Krapf, Baumann's description compares the high alpine valleys to the Austrian Tyrol.[26] Here, Baumann also observed the Wambugu living what he believed to be a carefree life removed from the drudgery of cultivation, a place where cattle and goats provided subsistence. Baumann's divisions, the pristine *Urwald,* the idyllic, partially forested, alpine region, and a heavily settled and environmentally degraded farming zone, actually envisaged much of the colonial imagery to follow.[27]

Once fully under way in the late 1890s, Germany's East African colonial project attempted a broader and more scientific landscape reading of the Usambaras. Since German economic success would depend on plantation crops such as coffee, rubber, and sisal, the colonial enthusiasts logically turned from geography to botany for guidance. Chapter 3 examines Germany and Britain's attempts to impose upon East and West Usambara an economically viable botany. It presents the history of two scientific research stations, Kwai Farm and the Amani Institute for Biological Research (later called by the British the East African Agricultural Research Station). Early in its administration, the German government abandoned Kwai, situated on 1,300 hectares of West Usambara's plateau grazing lands, turning it over to a private owner, and the farm remained in various settlers' hands until the 1950s. Its story speaks both to the failure of estate agriculture across the Usambaras and to the tensions fomented among indigenous peoples by colonial land alienation. At Amani, which the German colonial government built in the far wetter rain forests of Eastern Usambara, colonial scientists undertook an ambitious program of botanical research designed to serve colonial agronomy throughout the tropics. The experiments continued until after World War II, but continual ill will between Amani's research scientists and the colonial agricultural bureaucracy led to the station's abandonment. Amani's mission statement called for equal attention to pure research in botany and to applied research that would immediately facilitate settler agricultural production. However, the station's scientists failed to find a balance that satisfied its financial contributors. Amani's failure to become a font of quickly applicable knowledge oriented toward production for the international market exposed its scientists' work to suspicion among bureaucrats concerned with bottom-line agricultural productivity.

Activities at Kwai and Amani fit into the larger context of colonialism's program of agricultural reform in European-style tropical plantation agriculture and in indigenous horticulture. Chapters 5 and 6 document the broader interplay among deteriorating environmental conditions, science, African husbandry's long-term history, and bureaucratic imperatives under both German and British colonial administrations. These chapters show just how poorly informed and ill conceived the colonial state's venture into tropical agriculture turned out to be. Britain's colonial Agriculture Department, consumed by worries of soil erosion, tried to institute drastic alterations in land use and land-tenure arrangements in the West Usambaras. The resounding failure of the project echoed for decades in subsequent development projects carried on in independent Tanzania. In East Usambara, conflicts over land use occurred, but they were muted by the pattern of colonial land alienation. The German administration, mistakenly believing in the fecundity of forest soils, alienated the vast majority of the East Usambara Mountains and designated them as private holdings earmarked for coffee production. When coffee production failed in the first decade of German colonialism, many of the estates remained dormant for lack of a substitute crop. Therefore, much of the old-growth tropical forests that the Germans believed held so much economic promise remained unexploited until the 1950s, when estate owners and foresters butted heads over the direction of the forests' management.

Measuring the Landscape: The Forester's Vision

> Left unattended, the [indigenous] forest will renew by its own force, be it via seeds, coppices or root suckers. This new "urwald" with its mass of trees and bushes, vines, tree fern and other weeds allows for a pictorial image, but does not make any profit. The goal of forest administration must be to make profit out of existing woods and to increase it in the future; therefore this virgin forest, after using up all the usable old woods, has to make space for a planned, profitable artificial forest.[28]

Although this quote from Siebenlist refers to German East Africa's forests, it speaks for the nineteenth- and twentieth-century forestry ideology prominent in the colonial tropics and, for that matter, across Europe and North America. Given the uniformity of forestry's vision, the divergent forest histories of East and West Usambara demonstrate just how variable forest policy and its implementation proved to be. In its zeal to transform the forest into tree farms via silvicultural science, the Forest Department predictably alienated indigenous forest peoples such as the Wambugu in West Usambara. In response to their expulsion from their range, Mbugu communities completely transformed their economic status from herders to farmers over the course of a single generation. On the forester's ideological landscape, the forest was a colonial treasury that Africans robbed, wasted, and destroyed.[29]

Inside West Usambara's forest, the ideological and ecological transformation continued apace. Foresters sought to create a rational, quantifiable, and exploitable forest, bereft of indigenous land-use systems and indigenous trees. In their view, research should focus not on the complex natural history of plant adaptation and evolution, but on fostering and maintaining a minimum diversity of those tree species whose presence secured a reliable and sustained timber yield.[30] As chapter 4 points out, despite the implementation of colonial forestry principles in West Usambara, a sustained yield was never attained.

A different scenario played out in the East Usambara's forests. The Amani station attracted a number of scientists who placed an indelible stamp on modern interpretations of the Usambara's ecological and natural history.[31] I trace that naturalist tradition from its inception under Adolf Engler, head of the Berlin Botanical Museum during the late nineteenth century, down to the present. A strong preservationist bent has distinguished the recent additions to this tradition, and helped convince the Tanzanian government to establish the East Usambara Nature Preserve.

The Modern Landscape: Restoring the Forest Sanctuary

> In all their beauty and variety wild Saintpaulia are a vivid expression of quite exceptional biological interest in a few very confined and precise localities in Tanzania. Now that their climatic, geological and historical basis has been recognized, the boundaries of these highly localized communities can be drawn with some precision and the result has been considerable alarm at their imminent extinction. The world has suddenly begun to look to a small nation to take on responsibility for a series of freak enclaves where millions of years of evolution are on show.[32]

This popularized scientific portrayal of Usambara's "natural" environment focuses on the forest as something to be preserved for its inherent botanical and zoological values. Contemporary scientists agree with their predecessors that the mountain forest's functions in water condensation (clouds and mist) and conservation are extremely important for downstream users, but they now argue, in addition, for the exceptional value of the forest as a refuge for endemic species. Moreover, the biological interest in Usambara is part of a wider interest in the entire Eastern Arc Mountain range as a distinct bioregion.

With the forest at the landscape's ideological center, agricultural land and its inhabitants still represent a threat to the forest's ecological integrity.[33] Since colonial times, moreover, conservation and development specialists who focus on agricultural lands have argued that an environmental crisis extends to the agricultural landscape surrounding the forest fragments. Chapters 5 and 6 examine colonial conservation projects on such agricultural lands that began in the 1940s and extended into the late 1950s. The schemes' legacy is apparent both in contemporary approaches to development and community responses to them.

Independence did not bring an end to Usambara's environmental problems or the struggle for control over natural resources. Chapter 7 traces the shifts in the conservation and development paradigms, which now increasingly stresses an ideological and rhetorical stance toward conservation among international donors, the state, the scientific community, nongovernmental organizations, and local leaders. Agrarian communities know well the organizational slogans about tree planting, fire prohibition, zero grazing, and erosion control. Their parents knew them, too, in the 1940s and 1950s. Chapter 7 asks how much has changed since independence and how much environmental control local communities have garnered since their liberation from the colonial state. It questions how the seemingly incompatible goals of economic development and environmental conservation have been reconciled on the physical and biological landscape.

The theme of a mountain sanctuary runs through Usambara's environmental history. With this in mind, Bantu-speaking farmers like the Shambaa, the Mbugu herders, colonial officials, scientists, and development specialists all built interpretations of how ecological relations have functioned and how they should operate in the future. Despite their ideological differences, all interested parties still seek some sort of environmental control, and the potential for conflict remains as real now as it did half a century ago when peasant resistance killed soil conservation projects across East Africa. Today, the intense competition for scarce mountain resources continues apace, and people continue to shape nature's succession as they learn to live with the consequences.

CHAPTER TWO

Humanity's Imprint

Mountain Forest, Garden, and Pasture

OUR EVOLUTIONARY ANCESTORS FORAGED IN East Africa's mountains and savannas for four million years. Their food gathering helped to shape particular ecological niches. In the more recent past, *Homo sapiens* used tools to create particular ecological conditions, at first to sustain the wild animals and plants they hunted and then, increasingly, to supplement the hunting economy with herds of domesticated animals and grains. This chapter traces the most recent phase in that progression by examining how agriculture and pastoralism shaped the Usambara landscape tapestry over the past two thousand years. In husbandry's formative phases, people experimented with systems of resource exploitation and exchange patterns that tied together forest, garden, and pasture. Some arrangements failed, others succeeded, but they always changed in response to natural processes and human initiatives. Sometime between 800 and 1100 A.D., the pace of adaptation and local interaction began to accelerate as successes in production led to population growth and to a broadening scope of interaction.[1] While in the time scales of human evolution these changes appear very recent, the landscapes that European colonists encountered upon their arrival in the final decades of the nineteenth century had nonetheless seen a thousand years of fine-tuning.

During the relatively brief moment of colonial and postcolonial rule, imported Western ideas regarding land health and degradation have become a powerful currency in East Africa's highlands, often as part of coercive state-sanctioned attempts to reshape indigenous horticultural and animal husbandry practice. The imposition has focused as much on the ideology of land use as it has on the actual practice of environmental conservation. It has also been steeped in ignorance about the agricultural past. Farmers whose cultural history stressed local adaptability and survival in a difficult environment have often resisted the state's prescriptions, which, for the most part, derive from attempts to impose an inequitable agricultural system. Modernization, in its guise of economic development, has posed economic challenges and offered opportunities, but it has also shaped the ways individuals present their own and their ancestors' notions of a properly husbanded landscape. Recovering that history presents problems of interpretation, however. Rather than a comprehensive agricultural history, what follows seeks to tease out from the perspectives of oral tradition, historical linguistics, and archaeology the central elements of both the continuities and the changes in land use, as well as the ecological changes, that preceded the twentieth century.

The Evolution of Usambara's Land-Use Systems in Their Regional Context

Agriculture's evolution in East Africa was largely a highland phenomenon. Although the mountains provide a generally regular rainfall regime, its spatial distribution depends upon location, elevation, and aspect, a pattern that successful agriculturalists would have to know intimately. Soil fertility differs markedly between mountain ranges. Unlike the younger, more fertile volcanic soils on Mount Kenya and Mount Kilimanjaro, for example, the Eastern Arc Mountain soils derive from ancient granite bedrock and therefore have a different chemical makeup. Although their acidity and low humus content do not favor agriculture, neither do they rule it out.[2] Despite the highlands' favorable geographic situation, droughts do periodically occur, and Usambara's agricultural history, like that of the larger region, bears the imprint of annual climatic variability. Farmers in the Usambaras have shown the ability to shift into and out of different production regimes when need be, and to develop techniques to mitigate environmental capriciousness. Under these conditions, an agricultural community's survival required sophisticated levels of environmental knowledge, as well as social and economic relations that operated beyond the mountains' ecological boundaries.[3]

As scholars across the disciplinary spectrum have endeavored to piece together the specific manifestations of agriculture's development in eastern and southern Africa, the cultural and economic transformation from foraging to plant and animal husbandry has come to constitute a vitally important theme in African historiography. Most of the discourse revolves around three interrelated historical processes: the spread of Bantu languages; the development of ironworking; and the adoption of agriculture as the main mode of subsistence production. Linguistic research established in the 1950s and 1960s that the majority of languages spoken in eastern and southern Africa stem from the Bantu subgroup of the Niger-Congo language family. The genealogy of Bantu languages further suggested that their differentiation occurred over the course of the past two millennia, which means that they spread into the region recently. Until the past decade or so, archaeologists often attempted to neatly integrate their roughly contemporaneous archaeological evidence for ironworking into a theory that argued for the migration into eastern and southern Africa of a superior culture-group: speakers of Bantu languages. The historical interpretation placed Bantu-speaking farmers in a West African cradleland in what is today northwest Cameroon. From there, they migrated both through and around the Central African forest basin into eastern and southern Africa, displacing and absorbing autochthonous people as they went. Their superiority lay, it seemed, in their technological package, which included iron and agriculture, and their superior social organization.[4]

As more evidence has piled up, increasingly complex explanations have emerged.[5] Recent interpretations agree that agriculture and herding largely replaced foraging in eastern and southern Africa south of the equator over the past three thousand years. The regional transformation coincided with the spread of Bantu languages from west to east and south over roughly the same time span. However, the consensus view has abandoned the argument for a direct correlation between a particular people and these processes. Jan Vansina, who has devoted a large part of his distinguished career to these questions, argues that there was no single migration event, but successive spreads in waves of a single *language*, followed by linguistic differentiation and then further spread of some of the new languages.

Population movements, where they occurred, operated on local scales and among groups of related people who maintained contact with one another. Furthermore, agricultural successes and language spread created their own dynamic; as people settled, more or less permanently, populations of both autochthonous and immigrant people increased. Population growth, in turn, pushed people at the margins of fertile land, or of political power, further afield into new exploitable environments. Vansina argues that Bantu cultural prestige flowed from a settlement's stability and its size rather than its technological prowess.[6] During this rudimentary early phase, autochthonous people no doubt played a large role in the overall process because they understood the limitations and possibilities of local environments. In East Africa, autochthonous peoples had successfully reared livestock and cultivated millet and sorghum, and perhaps smelted and forged iron, some centuries before Bantu languages began to appear.[7]

As agricultural societies learned what East Africa's environments had to offer, they fine-tuned their farming techniques. They also manufactured iron tools and pottery, industries that led to environmental transformation. In fact, the accumulation of evidence from linguistics, archaeology, and paleoecology has revealed a pattern of large-scale deforestation in the interlacustrine highlands beginning about two thousand years ago, a process tied closely to ironworking.[8] As the agricultural complex moved eastward into new environments, it drew from its Great Lakes origins a proclivity to seek out places that offered abundant moisture and forest resources, which in northeastern Tanzania meant the highlands.

Sometime early in the first millennium A.D., agricultural settlements appeared in the forested highland regions of northeastern Tanzania and southeastern Kenya. Because of their clear preference for living near forests and on the highland ridges overlooking the plains, Christopher Ehret has dubbed these peoples the "Upland Bantu," while archaeologists often refer to the process of environmental exploitation as the "Mwitu," or forest, tradition. Both names fit. Ehret argues for the earliest Upland Bantu settlements in North Pare and on the southern slopes of Mount Kenya. From there, satellite communities apparently emerged on the hills of Mount Kilimanjaro, South Pare, Taita, and the Usambaras.[9]

Whatever languages the first agriculturalists spoke and the exact geographical sequence of highland settlement, the archaeological remains of distinct pottery and iron furnaces from West Usambara support a case for population growth in forested highland environments. At Nkese, an archaeological site on the southern side of the West Usambara massif dated to the second century A.D., pottery styles and iron furnaces show close affini-

Fig. 2.1. Small farmstead colonizing the forest's edge in West Usambara.
Photo Christopher Conte

ties with those found as far afield as the East African Great Lakes and as close as the Taita hills.[10] The Nkese settlement site, close to the escarpment edge, also closely resembles agricultural colonies of similar antiquity in Taita. The steep elevation gradient made available to Nkese's horticulturalists a variety of temperatures and soils all the way down to the valley floor, while the nearby forests provided fuel for their iron furnaces. During the remainder of the first millennium A.D., the historical evidence points to changes in language and pottery styles, but the practice of settlement in close proximity to a number of microenvironments has persisted in highland settlement across Usambara, Taita, and Upare.[11]

Beginning in the second millennium A.D., the highland agricultural system entered a phase of profound change that began to shape the contemporary mountain landscape. By narrowing the analytical scale to West Usambara's Mlalo Basin, some of the transformation's specific consequences become apparent. Mlalo's agricultural history spans the evolution of upland farming systems. Early settlements at Mlalo are contemporaneous with Nkese's. Its location near the escarpment's edge and its environmental endowments allowed for the flexibility in production systems and the intercommunication with other highland peoples characteristic of the early phases in the highland agricultural system. From the hill above present-day Mlalo town, the landscape's diversity and its potential for horticulture are striking. The mountain basin to the south of town, a large, bowl-shaped depression surrounded by high hills, covers about twenty-five square miles. The Umba, a large, perennial stream that rises in the mountains south of Mlalo, meanders through the basin and the center of Mlalo town before dropping to the plains beneath. Over a thousand meters below, a swath of riparian green marks the river's northeasterly passage through the savanna to the Indian Ocean. Beyond the river's lowland course, to the northwest, lies the broad, flat, brown Mkomazi Plain, which spreads out to the horizon. Kasigau, the southernmost of the Taita Hills, breaks the plain's visual monotony as it rises, island-like, one hundred kilometers to the north. Shifting focus from the horizon to the plains directly below reveals more greenery. Local people call this place a *kitivo* (pl. *vitivo*), a generic term for a depression holding the alluvial soils deposited from the floods of Usambara's mountain streams as they debouch onto the plains. Vitivo occur at several places around the base of the Usambaras and generally hold both prime agricultural soils and malaria-carrying mosquitoes. Consequently, mountain people today consider them a good place to farm but not necessarily a good place to live.[12]

While Mlalo's location and varied environments favored it as an early agricultural and industrial site, its long-term cultural vitality and economic productivity still depended on its inhabitants' ties with their mountain neighbors in Taita and Upare, places referenced often in Mlalo's oral history. Informants note, for example, the exceptional importance of a group of ironsmiths from Upare, referred to as the "Washana," whom they credit with immense and secretive power.[13] Such claims are at least partially confirmed by the archaeological evidence for the ubiquity of ironworking in South Pare, as opposed to its paucity in the Usambaras. Pare smiths, or at least Pare iron products, have likely served people at Mlalo and other parts of the Usambaras for centuries.[14] Oral histories also link the Usambaras and the Taita Hills through migration stories. In fact, many Mlalo elders claim Taita ancestry.[15]

Fig. 2.2. Iron worker at Nyassa in the Mlalo Basin. Photo Christopher Conte

Taken together, the archaeological and linguistic evidence make a strong case for long-standing links among mountain peoples from southeastern Kenya and northeastern Tanzania. Highlanders also forged links with coastal settlements beyond the mountains. Ehret argues that coastal connections to Usambara date from the fifth century A.D., when coastal Bantu languages (Seuta in Usambara) began to supersede the older Upland Bantu tongues. Archaeological digs at Gonja on the northern side of South Pare unearthed cowry shells and glass beads, which signals its inclusion in regional trade with the coast dating at least to the ninth century.[16] The economic repercussions of the luxury trade notwithstanding, the East African coast's inclusion in the Indian Ocean world transformed highland life in even more profound ways.

Bananas, an Asian import, revolutionized highland agriculture. When and exactly how bananas and plantains (*Musa spp.*) arrived in East Africa remains unclear, but the plant's wild progenitors occur only in Southeast Asia and their domesticated varieties likely traveled to the Swahili Coast well over a thousand years ago. Banana cultivars thrived in the Eastern Arc Mountains, which served as one set of stepping stones for the crop's eventual dispersal into the lake district and on into Central Africa.[17] Highland farmers developed an expertise in banana propagation.[18] The horticultural skill is particularly evident in the Usambaras, where approximately sixty banana varieties have been identified that are exclusive to the mountains.[19] The warm and wet ecological conditions surrounding Usambara's agricultural settlements suited wonderfully banana cultivation and propagation. In an impressive taxonomic and linguistic study of bananas and plantains in Africa, Gerda Rossel ties the introduced crop's rapid cultural acceptance to the presence in the mountain zones of *ensete,* or "false banana," which closely resembles the true banana in appearance, though not in its fruit-bearing characteristics. Banana trees therefore looked familiar, had similar utility (leaves for wrappers, leaf fibers for weaving, medicinal oils), but also bore edible and versatile fruits.[20] In addition to its nutritional fruit, the banana tree's wide leaves mitigated the erosive effects of heavy rains. Banana horticulture had become so important that, by the late nineteenth century, German observers recorded that the trees' leafy canopies completely dominated the Mlalo Basin landscape.[21]

Their ties to the Indian Ocean complex also provided highland peoples with access to taro, yams, rice, and sugar cane, and when, in the sixteenth century, the Portuguese began to actively trade on the East African coast, three American exotics—cassava, maize, and potatoes—became horticultural options.[22] As with bananas, these crops suited the well-watered highlands; after all, they had evolved in a wet tropical climate, and all, except maize, could be propagated through plantings rather than seeds. The increasing variety of crops would prove important to Usambara's agricultural history, as shifting ecological conditions forced changes in the farming system. The new crops allowed cultivation to expand into new ecological zones and to intensify production on more established locations. When farmers added irrigation technology to their expanding farming system, the diversity of horticultural arrangements must have seemed almost limitless.

East African "hill-furrow irrigation systems" impressed nineteenth-century European observers unfamiliar with African agricultural practice, yet, placed in context, irrigation technology represented only one of a number of indigenous adaptive practices designed both to secure subsistence and to produce surplus.[23] Although its antiquity is debatable, irrigation in East Africa predated European contact by at least several centuries. The remains of an impressive precursor to the Usambara works are still evident at Engaruka, a now long-abandoned settlement characterized by grids of irrigation channels, stone-edged canals, and stone terraces.[24] Engaruka's location on the Rift Valley floor below the escarpment required farmers to channel stream flow in a region where dry-land agriculture is practically impossible without artificial means. The more sophisticated and specialized the system of terraces and furrows became, however, the greater the potential for soil exhaustion, and the more precarious its owners' subsistence situation. Ultimately, the Engaruka works proved unsustainable and their failure forced its inhabitants to migrate.[25]

At Rift Valley sites like Engaruka (less than 500 mm annual rainfall), irrigation made an agricultural life possible, but in East Africa's highland environments, where rains fell more reliably, similar technological arrangements may well have represented a response to the environmental problems associated with population growth and, at times, a conscious investment in surplus production. Irrigation required larger labor investments than rain-fed agriculture in a long-fallow system. Moreover, a cadre of specialists had to maintain dams and furrows. Farmers would therefore not have taken lightly the decision to initiate irrigation works, especially if surplus land were available.[26]

Thomas Hakansson has argued that in South Pare, irrigation, as part of a larger trend toward agricultural intensification, did not represent a response to population growth or to scarce land resources. Rather, Pare cultivators pumped the surpluses realized by irrigated gardens into the regional exchange system throughout the nineteenth and early twentieth centuries. In the Pare case, exchange, specifically for cattle, drove the investments in labor and expertise that irrigation required.[27] Hakansson's analysis demonstrates further that in Upare, nineteenth-century agricultural intensification was not an innovation but followed a well-worn trajectory in which regional patterns of exchange figured prominently.

In the West Usambaras, permanent streams and springs presented farmers with similar possibilities to irrigate the landscape in order to enhance subsistence and to produce agricultural surpluses. Just below Mlalo town, for example, farmers tapped the perennially running Umba in order to extend cultivation to the steep slopes along the northern escarpment face.[28] Farming communities in other parts of the Mlalo Basin and across the Usambaras also built irrigation complexes to increase food supplies and therefore meet their own needs during dry years. However, the substantial annual investments in furrow maintenance support Hakansson's argument that the production and redistribution of agricultural surplus would occur in years of adequate rainfall. Farmers who had produced surpluses

Fig. 2.3. Irrigation furrow draws the Umba's waters to gardens below Mlalo.
Photo Christopher Conte

could reinvest their wealth in livestock or, by the nineteenth century, in the caravan trade that passed below the mountain escarpment.

Even with the agricultural system's growing diversity in Usambara, exploitable environments were limited. At its point of greatest versatility, the model production regime required that villages locate around the 1,400-meter contour near the escarpment edges. From there, men and women traveled to fields that could lie anywhere along the elevation and ecological gradient, depending on season and weather. From Mlalo, farmers still make the two-hour journey down the mountain to grow rice on the alluvial soils at the mountain base, where their ancestors grew sorghum and maize. Above, in the mountain basins, men and women tended their gardens, which they intercropped with a mixture of native and exotic plants. The decisions about what to plant—beans, maize, sugar cane, bananas, tobacco, yams, taro, or sweet potatoes—depended upon their knowledge of soil and weather conditions. They avoided, however, the relatively cold and dry forested plateaus; nothing in their repertoire could flourish there. That pastoralists found a niche in these environments attests to the versatility of another of East Africa's central modes of production.

Oral traditions in the West Usambaras maintain that sometime during the middle of the second millennium A.D., lineages of a pastoralist society entered the mountains and took up residence on the relatively cool and dry plateaus, which could not support agriculture.[29] There, the Wambugu developed a land-use system eminently suited to the mountain environment. Despite the cultural separation between the Bantu-speaking farmers, known today as the Shambaa, and their new neighbors, whom they called the Wambugu, the relationship that emerged between the two societies nonetheless proved mutually beneficial.[30]

Mbugu history is largely an enigma. Its heyday belongs to an era that predates East Africa's linguistic drift toward Bantu languages, when speakers of Southern Cushitic and Southern Nilotic languages dominated East Africa's landscape. The few Wambugu who still know their Southern Cushitic language refer to it as Maa'a and to their ancestors as the Vamaa. According to Ehret's interpretation, Southern Cushites introduced livestock raising and cultivation to East Africa, although their herding activities provided them with much of their subsistence. Their territorial preferences lay in the eastern extension of the Rift Valley, which extends through central Kenya and eastern Tanzania and places them on the savanna grasslands adjacent to a number of highland zones.[31] Given the well-known transhumance patterns of Maasai pastoralists who today occupy these areas, the Maa'a must have similarly moved their herds into mountain pastures to take advantage of dry season water sources and grazing. In the light of their long tradition among East Africa's pastoral environments, their eventual dispersal into the suitable grazing zones of the Upare and Usambara plateaus appears to have been more gradual than the oral traditions suggest. However, droughts that struck in the 1780s and 1790s, followed by even more severe rainfall deficits in the 1820s and 1830s, may well have hastened their dependence on a mountain base.[32]

Mbugu oral traditions emphasize the group's cultural separateness, their pastoralist tradition, and a shared experience of hardship as they wandered the East African savannas looking for a home. According to their stories, the Vamaa occupied Kenya's Laikipia Plateau until Maasai pastoralists pushed them southward and eastward across the Rift Valley. Their wanderings eventually found them living near, or at times among, the Bantu-speaking farmers—the Pare, the Shambaa, and the Zigua—of what is today northern Tanzania. This historical tradition also explains the close social and cultural ties the Wambugu have maintained with the Pare people and the ritual importance of certain places in the South Pare hills just to the northeast of Usambara.[33] Mbugu residence on the neighboring West Usambara central plateau fits this Pare model of contact, where the cool cedar and Podocarpus forests presented immigrant herders with an immediately secure social, political, and ecological situation.

The migrations into the Usambaras appear in oral traditions as a well-organized series of movements by affiliated lineage groups that purchased with their cattle their right to reside in the mountains.[34] The oral traditions function, in effect, to assign usufruct rights to particular forest pastures, while they draw a sharp distinction between the Wambugu, as itinerant herders, and their neighbors who worked the land. In Mbugu cultural history, the mountain plateau forests became a refuge around which they forged a dual identity that included a long-held pastoralist ideal and an increasing appreciation for what the forest offered.

At least by the early eighteenth century, the Mbugu migrations began to have political repercussions for the Shambaa farming villages. According to Steven Feierman's analysis of Shambaa political history, prior to the Mbugu immigration, farming communities lived in a decentralized setting of loosely affiliated neighborhoods. The ties of family and marriage cemented social relations at a local scale, while their cultural ancestry bound them to the other Eastern Arc highlands like Pare, Ngulu, and Taita. Feierman argues that the Mbugu cultural separateness unsettled the decentralized organization of Shambaa politics and helped unify Shambaa communities under a single dynasty, called the Kilindi.[35] Certainly, the Wambugu were different. Their status as immigrants, their Cushitic language, their origin myths, their pastoral economy, and their forest seclusion could well have alienated them from the Washambaa. The Shambaa perception of an Mbugu fifth column may also have been enhanced by the latter's regular travels to the South Pare, where the Wambugu met in secret with their Pare relatives for adolescent male initiation ceremonies.

How did Mbugu communities adapt to the highland forest environment? If West Usambara's high plateau offered less immediately available pasture than the plains' savannas, oral accounts note that pastures nonetheless existed in the forests at Shume and Magamba.[36] Although testimony is contradictory on the subject of pasture creation, the herders probably fired the edges of these glades and other suitable areas to expand the pastures.[37] Councils of elders regulated access to pastures in their respective settlement regions, though they renegotiated these arrangements, especially during droughts when grazing conditions could vary markedly over relatively short distances.[38]

The demands of grazing required that herding families live in dispersed homesteads, where each small settlement maintained exclusive rights to pastures close to its houses (*mvera*).[39] The Wambugu hid their dwellings among the trees and built them to accommodate their families and their livestock. Away from the homesteads, sturdily built fenced cattle enclosures (*boma*) also dotted the landscape. The bomas protected the animals under ordinary circumstances, but when cattle raiders threatened, leaders sanctioned the construction of large defensible enclosures called *heiboma*, which, hidden in the forest, served as animal sanctuaries and hideaways.[40]

The immigrant herders altered the forest ecology, particularly through the use of fire for pasture creation and conditioning. Yet the Wambugu also implemented social mechanisms to limit human and animal population densities, which in turn helped to maintain a largely forested plateau environment. The Wambugu prohibited premarital intercourse, delayed marriage, and spaced their children in ways common to other East African pastoral societies.[41] They regulated their herds' size through the ritual slaughter of animals and through exchanges with the Washambaa, who sought livestock, hides, and dried meat in return for farm produce and iron implements.[42] When the Kilindi asserted their rule in Shambaa neighborhoods, the Wambugu cultivated relations with the new ruling clan by paying regular tribute in livestock, labor, and women.[43] Inside their territory, herders wealthy in cattle spread their animals across several localities by marrying several times and by distributing their livestock among their wives' sons. These marriage patterns fostered unity across the plateau, while the dispersal of livestock limited overgrazing and mitigated the effects of localized rainfall failure.[44]

> Although the Mbugu herders moved their animals, during droughts, we'd hear that there grazing was abundant and here was a desert[45] ... [T]here would be a cousin there who would take the animals. In fact, all over the Usambaras we had relatives with animals. People sometimes moved with their families, sometimes not, if they expected to return. People had their clan areas so that when they came back they had their place that they own.[46]

Temporary movements (*urang'a*) were usually no more than a day's walk from the home camp, so family members could bring herders food and news of home.⁴⁷ During severe droughts, however, entire families might migrate out of their forest enclave in search of pasture and food. Playing on their ties with Shambaa farmers, they sought out areas on the edges of farmlands, where agricultural produce was readily available in exchange for labor or for livestock.⁴⁸ Despite their claims to a cultural propensity toward reclusiveness, the Wambugu could not avoid periodic contact with the havens of agricultural production ringing the massif, a common motif in the history of East African animal husbandry.⁴⁹

The relationship between herding, honey, and the forest environment illustrates this paradox. Through fire and pasture creation, forest-based pastoralism facilitated environmental changes that suited honey production, and informants drew a very clear relationship between honey production and honey's cultural significance to pastoralist identity.⁵⁰ Honey holds powerful cultural importance among many East African pastoralist communities, since it has served historically as the main ingredient for the beer brewed for most ritual and social occasions.⁵¹ Honey also served the Wambugu as an important dietary supplement, especially during seasons of hunger. While honey helped define the Mbugu cultural separateness, it also linked them with their Shambaa neighbors, from whom they purchased their hives.⁵² Moreover, honey linked the Wambugu to the plains below the Usambaras, where they sold honey to Maasai pastoralists.

In response to a number of social, economic, and environmental challenges, these Cushitic-speaking pastoralists from the savannas had transformed themselves from clients and refugees into an independent mountain people. Yet, they could not escape the fact that pastoralism's economic viability still depended on reciprocal relations with their neighbors. What appeared to be a stable mountain production system broke down under the perturbations of a series of social and ecological disasters that struck Eastern Africa during the latter half of the nineteenth century. The same trade patterns that had introduced bananas, maize, and cassava to the region earlier in the millennium now fostered a burgeoning trade in slaves and ivory and introduced an economic transformation that would eventually eliminate Mbugu forest pastoralism.

In the context of East African history, Usambara's precolonial settlement and exploitation fit with trends in other neighboring highland environments. Agriculture in East Africa became in large part a highland phenomenon, where collective experience and knowledge helped Bantu-speaking communities carve out a viable agricultural system centered at particular points along massif edges. Patterns of deforestation and regeneration in the long-fallow system they employed eventually gave way to intensified land use and permanent forest loss around settlement sites. A series of crop infusions from the Indian Ocean basin reinvigorated agriculture during the second millennium A.D. Bananas (*Musa spp.*) proved extraordinarily suited to the mountain environment, eventually dominating the agricultural landscape and spurring population growth. Immigration also swelled mountain population from time to time as impoverished outsiders sought the stability offered by the highlands. The Usambaras, like their neighboring massifs, had presented for at least two millennia a viable environment for extensive and intensive husbandry, though one not uninfluenced by deforestation and accelerated soil erosion. By the mid-nineteenth century, cracks appeared in the works and a series of crises shook the system.

To what extent was environmental degradation part of the evolution of land use in the Usambaras? If one measures degradation as a disturbance of the optimal bioproductivity of the forest ecosystems that largely covered the mountains before Iron Age agriculture began, then yes, Usambara's farming systems have degraded the mountain environment and they continue to do so. Forest loss is part of East Africa's Iron Age agricultural history; it affected environments from the Great Lakes to the littoral. However, over the long term of indigenous management in the Usambaras, biological productivity continued both on the plateau rangelands and in the farming zones. The retooled landscaped consisted of a variety of ecosystems that included productive pastures and gardens, interspersed with forests. In terms of the process leading to ecological stress and crisis, the important questions become not how much forest disappeared, but how changing modes of exploitation affected the sustainability of bioproductivity, and how successfully the agrarian communities responded to preserve it or to restore losses. In this context, land degradation becomes a function of the dynamic relationship between biological productivity and exploitation, rather than a departure from a particular type of vegetation community.[53] Furthermore, in this conceptualization of degradation, population growth is not necessarily a degrading influence, especially if societies intensify land use to increase outputs without long-term damage to the soil. Likewise, famine episodes, while they may reflect a collapse in exploitation systems and losses of environmental control, may or may not signal a landscape's descent into a state of irreparable damage.

Farming's Temporary Collapse in the Late Nineteenth Century

The second half of the nineteenth century was a time of general political, economic, and ecological crisis in East Africa.[54] In the Usambaras, the calamities stemmed in part from the region's intensifying participation in the global commodities markets, where boom and bust cycles predominated. In East Africa, trade between the coast and hinterland had a checkered history. During the eighteenth and early nineteenth centuries, demand for agricultural slaves and ivory in both the Atlantic and Indian Ocean trading zones had fueled a particularly violent era of slave raiding in what today are southeastern Tanzania, Malawi, and Mozambique. Further north, the geographic idiosyncrasies of the trade had largely spared East Africa's coastal hinterland, until the boom in another commodity, cloves. Clove production in East Africa began on Zanzibar, probably during the first decade of the nineteenth century. As prices rapidly rose over the next three decades, so did the amount of acreage devoted to the spice trees, first on Zanzibar and then on Pemba. The wildly successful plantation economy created a related spike in the demand for slaves from central and northern Tanzania. By the mid-nineteenth century, clove trees so dominated the island landscapes that they displaced land formerly devoted to food production. In response to the growing local demand for food, grain plantations, also worked by slaves, sprung up along the mainland coast opposite Pemba and Zanzibar. Around the coastal towns of Pangani and Tanga, a slave system of agricultural production and a related hinterland slave trade flourished during the nineteenth century's second half. Because of its proximity to the central production areas, the Pangani Valley became one of several conduits of this particular manifestation of coast-based caravan trade and therefore of slave production.[55] The process reconfigured political and economic life in the region. Agrarian communities in East and West Usambara were increasingly drawn into the violence associated with trade. Slave raiding and warfare created refugees, who gravitated to population centers, where powerful men, many of them directly involved in the regional commerce and violence, offered protection. The displacement of thousands of people undermined their sophisticated systems of environmental control and ushered in an era of hunger and hardship.[56]

Not surprisingly, oral traditions in Mlalo recall a series of famines that struck the region during the nineteenth century's second half. Elders recall them as *njaa ya kijankingo* (when people ate the skins of cattle), *njaa ya pato* (the hunger of greed, or rapacity), *njaa ya kigogo* (when there was no food at all and people ground banana tree roots to make flour), *njaa ya mnyime afe* (when one treated one's neighbors as if they were dead).[57] Between midcentury and the end of German colonial rule in 1916, bracken vegetation invaded the once carefully tended horticultural and pastoral lands.

In the early phases of the hard times, ancient demographic patterns played themselves out in intraregional migration, and many refugees sought sanctuary in the Usambaras. Refugee settlements ringed the massif along the 400–450 meter elevation gradient and were usually located in vitivo.[58] Kamba and Taita colonists from southern Kenya settled at Lunguza and Mngaro below the Mlalo Basin.[59] Other Kamba settlers occupied cultivable sections of the Lwengera Valley that separates East and West Usambara. On the southern side of the massif, Iloikop Maasai established a settlement at Vuruni, near the Zigua trading town of Mtaarwanda.[60] The mountain-base sites received an annual average rainfall of less than 500 mm and therefore depended on groundwater and surface stream flow from the mountain watershed, where rainfall averaged at least three times that amount.[61] Although seasonal rainfall usually proved too scant for most crops, sorghum could thrive there, and irrigation furrows leading from streams flowing down the escarpment provided enough moisture for maize and rice farming along stream courses and their immediate flood plains. The growth of these plains settlements seems to have been supported by a sustained period of normal or surplus moisture.[62]

Despite their productivity, or perhaps because of it, some of the valley settlements proved unsafe. In the 1840s, slave raids scattered immigrants in the Lwengera Valley, which separates the East and West Usambara massifs. When this spate of slaving episodes ceased, settlers returned to the valley in large numbers and remained until 1865, when, once again, its inhabitants evacuated in response to a new round of attacks. By 1890, this important and productive lowland agricultural area with a permanent water source became an impenetrable thicket of secondary forest.[63]

The violence that depopulated the Lwengera Valley, as well as other parts of the Usambaras, helped to destroy Kilindi rule. When the Kilindi monarch, Kimweri ya Nyumbai, died in 1862, a succession dispute broke out and quickly devolved into a civil war between rival claimants and their respective supporters. Much of the impetus for the conflict derived from the wealth introduced to Usambara by the Pangani Valley caravan trade. Where, traditionally, Kilindi dynasts had claimed ritual power over rain charms and based themselves in the mountains, the new economic

Fig. 2.4. Mlalo old town site poised on a hilltop. Photo Christopher Conte

conditions had shifted the locus of political and military power to the plains. At Mazinde, a hot, dusty trading town in the plains below the West Usambara massif, Semboja, the town's appointed Kilindi chief and self-styled warlord, took full advantage of the new regional trade patterns and gathered around himself the military and political power necessary to lead a successful coup against his rivals. Semboja's mercenaries and their enemies exposed almost every community in the East and West Usambaras to the regional violence that increasingly covered East Africa's hinterland.[64] The shift in regional political economy transformed the Usambaras into a repository of plunder for slaves, foodstuffs, and livestock. Hill settlements like Mlalo became fortresses surrounded by heavily guarded thorn-hedge walls. Where they could, people moved to the relative safety of the heavily fortified towns, abandoning the agricultural sites that left them exposed. The less fortunate, or the more independent-minded, hid themselves in isolated mountain glens and eked out a living as best they could. The warfare and hunger continued for a generation and led to pronounced depopulation in several mountain regions, where abandoned homes and fields covered the landscape.[65]

In the mountain district of Bumbuli, for example, a center of dense Shambaa settlement, Oscar Baumann, a geographer employed by the German East Africa Society, found its fields neglected and much of the town abandoned in 1890.[66] Another German account confirms Baumann's findings and claims an extensive depopulation of most of the area between Bumbuli and the former Kilindi royal settlement of Vuga. That would include most of the productive agricultural areas on the southern side of West Usambara.[67] On the more isolated western side of the massif, Baumann found in 1888 refugee families living in hidden valleys tucked in along the escarpment wall above the Mkomazi Valley. At Mbaru, for example, he visited a hamlet where the inhabitants had built their ten "poor" huts on the edge of a cliff and had surrounded the entire community—gardens, pastures, and homes—with a thick fence of interlaced thorn bushes that measured "one-half hour's walk in circumference." Traps designed against human intrusion (*Fussangeln*) covered the fields in an additional effort to deter raiders.[68] Similarly fortified settlements ringed the massif's northern side at Mtae, Mabaramo, Mlola, and Mlalo.

Some communities adapted more successfully than others. Mlalo and Mlola, neighboring mountain basins on the northern side of West Usambara, demonstrate the differential. Mlola, historically an important Kilindi subchiefdom and population center, experienced the periodic rainfall deficits associated with its location in a rain shadow of both the northwest and southeast monsoon rains. During the occasional droughts, Mlola's continuing viability as a settled agricultural community depended, therefore, upon its access to the riverine soils of the plains below the escarpment and trade with its neighbors in other parts of the mountains. That Baumann, in 1888, should find the people of the basin living in intense poverty, fear, and hunger signals a breakdown in the function of its agricultural system.[69] The crisis seems not so much tied to Mlola's inherent environmental marginality, or to drought, but to the threat of political violence that limited free movement up- and downslope.

Shambaa traditions place Mlola squarely in the regional violence caused by the Kilindi war. Sometime in the late 1860s, Taita mercenaries in Semboja's hire attacked Mlola in a tactical feint designed to draw fighters out of Vuga while another Taita force attacked the Kilindi capital from the west.[70] Several years later, in the 1870s, a squad of mercenaries from East Usambara again attacked Mlola and killed the rival Kilindi chief.[71] As the struggles continued, Mlola's inhabitants, like those of Bumbuli to the southeast, found themselves caught in a vortex of terror and uncertainty that crippled production and trade. In this militarized context, where war captives constituted a major medium of exchange, travel to the plains gardens left farmers liable to kidnapping. So it happened that in September 1888, Baumann, a well-armed outsider, found them unwilling even to open village gates to discuss provisioning his caravan. Everything about the village spoke to its poverty: "There lay the miserable hamlet of Uandani at the foot of a steep slope [near present-day Mlola] surrounded by miserable, half-dried crops. The people, shy and dirty, were as unfriendly as their surroundings. When we approached, they closed the village gates.... It was so sad and barren that we must ask ourselves if such a land is even worth exploring and exploiting."[72] Baumann's party nonetheless needed provisions, and when villagers quoted high prices, members of the caravan fired off a mortar round, whereupon the price dropped. To the people of Uandani, Baumann must have seemed like another in a long line of violent and predatory visitors.

In contrast, observers described Mlalo's late-nineteenth-century landscape as a haven of surplus production in a sea of violence and poverty.[73] Baumann marveled at the basin's fertility and observed a variety of crops under both swidden and intensively irrigated arrangements, which he claimed produced surpluses even in the middle of the September dry season. Mlalo's market looked to him to be the only operational one in the West Usambaras.[74] His discussions with the Mlalo chiefly authority, Kinyassi, also revealed that Mlalo's location on the northern side of the massif had buffered it somewhat from the war's epicenter in the Pangani Valley. In the late 1880s and early 1890s, Mlalo's agroecology appeared to be stable.

Three years after Baumann's reconnaissance, German Lutherans from the Bethel mission set up their station, Hohenfriedberg, on a hillside overlooking the basin from the northwest. During 1891 and 1892, the mission gardener, Carl Hölst, collected important information regarding local weather and farming practices. His observations are invaluable to the reconstruction of Mlalo's agricultural landscape.[75] Like Baumann's, Hölst's Mlalo appears to be a densely populated center of intensive agriculture, where irrigation furrows and reservoirs still stood out on the landscape. Banana plantations surrounded the numerous villages and carefully fenced and bounded fields covered the basin.

In fact, Hölst found eleven varieties of banana trees planted in freshly cleared forest fallow, and in well established fields where farmers intercropped maize, beans, pumpkins, sweet potatoes, cassava, taro, yams, melons, sugar cane, and tobacco. This great variety notwithstanding, Hölst observed that bananas dominated up to four-fifths of the cultivated landscape. Depending on type, they were eaten raw, cooked, or dried and pounded into flour.⁷⁶ Intercropping choices and timing depended on the long-term store of cultural knowledge regarding soil fertility, the timing of the three agricultural seasons, and past use of the field. At Kitivo, two hours' walk from Mlalo, Hölst found that both resident farmers and peripatetic basin inhabitants planted, irrigated, and harvested rice three times in good years.⁷⁷ Even when the weather failed to cooperate, with too little, too much, or poorly timed rainfall in the basin, Mlalo could draw food supplies to its market from Kitivo or from other mountain areas like Tewe, Mbaramo, and Mtae. Each of these neighborhoods lay within walking distance, but soil, temperature, rainfall, and agricultural specializations differed. The market linked the diverse products of the mountains' agroecological zones. In addition to agricultural produce, the locally manufactured items of the ancient highland agricultural tradition, iron and pottery, also found their way to Mlalo's thriving market.⁷⁸

While the intensity and complexity of agriculture at Mlalo suggested stability to Baumann and Hölst, the system showed the strains of success. Because of its productivity, refugees had swelled a population already confined by regional violence to the northern side of the West Usambaras. The immigrants placed pressure on land reserves and in turn helped to ratchet up the level of intensification by providing the surplus labor for canal and dam construction and maintenance. Over the short term, the combination of banana culture, heavily intercropped and irrigated fields, and cultivation on the plains helped Mlaloans to weather the nineteenth-century disasters.

Mlalo represented in microcosm both the successes and vulnerabilities of Upland agricultural tradition. The town's market functioned as a regional conduit of commodity exchange, while an expansion of the hill-furrow irrigation cultivation along the Umba River and in their kitivo on the plains below the town helped support the increasingly dense population. In addition to the system's economic and technological components, Mlalo depended upon all of its environmental endowments, especially its soils and the forested upper Umba watershed, which in turn sustained the irrigation lifeline both in the hills and in Kitivo. However, over the longer term, intensive agricultural practice would shorten fallow periods and increase soil exhaustion and erosion. While the European observers noted with admiration the extent of irrigation works, their ubiquity arguably signaled vulnerability to perturbation of their component parts.⁷⁹

On the central plateau, the regional chaos that disrupted the lives of their neighbors also forced the Wambugu out of their regular pattern of ecological and social relations.[80] The crisis in pastoral life intensified during the early 1890s, when the Wambugu, along with practically every other herding community in East Africa, experienced a spate of animal diseases that devastated their economy. The rinderpest epidemic, which killed animals from the Horn to southern Africa, destroyed pastoral life across East Africa. It struck in Usambara before the Germans arrived (at Mlalo in 1892), killing cattle in large numbers.[81] A desperate race to restock from the animals that survived became a general priority for pastoralists. Some Mbugu herders negotiated for animals with their relations in the Pare hills, while others simply stole them.[82] For the Maasai who had grazed their stock on the plains below Usambara, this desperation fueled a series of raids into the mountains in search of cattle.[83] Raiders harassed Mbugu herders around Shume on the western side of the massif, forcing them to flee to more inaccessible areas around Malibwi, Kwai, and Mshangai.[84] In what informants recall as a last-ditch effort to save their animals, they gathered their remaining livestock and constructed stockades (heiboma) where young men of the warrior age-set could protect the community's remaining wealth.[85] Although pastoralism survived, the difficulties forced many families to leave the mountains altogether.[86]

Some of the ecological repercussions of these difficult times on nineteenth-century pastoralism in West Usambara appear in a 1935 forest botany survey in which C. J. W. Pitt-Schenkel describes in great detail the forest communities in Magamba forest reserve, once a center of Mbugu pastoralism. Pitt-Schenkel discovered on the uninhabited forest lands near Kwai on the eastern edge of the Magamba forest clear signs of a former cultivation regime. From his analysis of the botanical composition of the secondary forest, he figured that about 10 percent of his survey area had been cultivated over one and sometimes two fallow cycles.[87]

Although oral histories emphasize the Mbugu defense of their pastoralist ideal at Malibwi and Kwai, Pitt-Schenkel's survey implied that herders had adjusted to the East African ecological disasters in practical, if mundane, ways. The cumulative effects of the breakdown in Shambaa agriculture, along with their livestock losses due to disease and raiding, led the Wambugu during the nineteenth century to increasingly depend on growing their own crops in a regime of shifting cultivation. Certainly, by the mid-1890s, the Mbugu communities around Mshangai and Malibwi regularly planted maize and pumpkins.[88]

While the Wambugu had suffered through a very difficult period in their history, uninitiated observers saw Mbugu life and their lands in idyllic terms, as shown by this description of the central Usambara landscape in the vicinity of Kwai and Malibwi in 1896:

> [T]raveling in a northerly direction, I arrived at the highland plateau of Kwai, a true paradise for the German farmer. All of the vegetation and mountain formations were as if transformed. Between the hills there were large grassy plains, broken here and there by small or large stands of trees. On the mountains one sees, in places, thick, beautiful primeval forest, which, as one climbs higher, loses its tropical character and at 1600 meters and above is mixed with numerous conifers, podocarpae, falcata, and Juniperus procera. The plains are cut by many small streams, which, due to the slight gradient, have a swampy appearance and are surrounded by thick stands of reeds and rushes. The inhabitants of this land, as well as of the bordering regions with the same vegetation, are the Vamaa, exclusively cattle herders, who cultivate their luxuriant shambas only for their own needs.[89]

Although Eick paints a wonderful, bucolic portrait of pasture, forest, and luxuriant gardens, his failure to realize the strain under which the Wambugu lived would have dramatic repercussions when he tried his own hand at agriculture at Kwai. Ultimately, Mbugu survival as a community of pastoralists depended upon recolonization of abandoned areas and rebuilding of social relations with their neighbors.

The Mbugu lineage (Ombeji) leader at Malibwi, Mlimahadala, summed up their difficult circumstances in a conversation with Ernst Johanssen, a missionary who visited him in 1897. The young chief spoke to Johanssen of his peoples' recent bad luck. He further complained that the elders had taught their charges nothing about agriculture or the medicinal herbs, an ignorance that made them dependent upon Shambaa expertise. Pastoralism, he believed, had made them vulnerable to cattle diseases that destroyed their herds and led to starvation.[90] Mlimahadala understood that the Wambugu would have to adjust to the new epidemiological, economic, and political forces entering the mountains. Perhaps this is why he had repeatedly asked the German missionaries at Hohenfriedberg (Mlalo) for a teacher. He could not have predicted just how dramatic that transformation would have to be.

Even with the intensification of land use, large pockets of central Usambara's turn-of-the-century landscape remained the domain of high forest. Eick's description of Kwai points to a patchwork of forest and pasture, a paradise, he thought, for German settlement. Eick's view carried the day and he headed a colonial experiment in agriculture at Kwai beginning in 1896. Moreover, by 1895, the Department of Natural Resources and Surveying had already sent forestry "experts" to reconnoiter and assess the commercial worth of Usambara's timber resources.[91] As German settlers and the colonial forestry service moved into these forests, the heyday of the Mbugu monopoly on forest use ended abruptly.

In terms of land use, colonialism presented Usambara's farmers and herders with an ideological and practical challenge at the very moment they began to recover from a disastrous half-century. In some areas, carefully husbanded lands had been abandoned. In others, such as Mlalo, late-nineteenth-century intensification threatened to run up against the limits of soil capability on the ancient granitic massif.[92] Ecological stress had likely played itself out in other regions of the Usambaras many times, on a smaller scale, over the course of centuries. What was different about the nineteenth century was the speed and extent of the disturbances to the land's resilience. In some places like Mlola, the landscape never again recovered the capacity to support agriculture. Usambara's agricultural history therefore reveals an ongoing historical tension between the landscape's colonization and recolonization by both people and nature. As the nineteenth century ended, German colonizers entered this world intent on imposing their own style of ecological transformation and control.

CHAPTER THREE

Colonial Science and Agricultural Development at Kwai and Amani

As German colonialism ensconced itself in northern Tanzania's hinterland during the 1890s, its forestry and agricultural institutions initiated yet another in the ongoing series of economic and ecological transformations in the Usambara Mountains. The ad hoc and intensely violent phase of coast-based entrepreneurial exchange in commodities gave way to colonialism's more systematic, though often violent, push for economic development through agricultural production. German colonial agents constructed a plantation system in and around the Usambara Mountains, where crops like sisal, timber, and coffee might prosper.[1] This chapter examines two settings where German and British colonialists attempted to spur plantation agriculture in the mountains before World War II. The men who ran Kwai Farm in the West Usambaras and the Amani Institute for Biological Research in the East Usambaras engaged in a program of agroecological transformation that ultimately failed. Their stories offer instructive lessons about the limits of colonial power to shape ecologies and the unintended consequences of its application.

Confident in their own ability to steer agricultural development, the colonialists chose not to consult the collective experience of their colonial subjects, who understood Usambara's environmental limitations and possibilities. Colonial planters and scientists had their own ideas, which they implemented with the arrogance that stemmed from a perceived superiority of European industrial society.[2] Ignoring the rights conferred by indigenous investments in the land, the colonial states codified their land claims based on nothing more than their putative technological superiority. Colonial confidence notwithstanding, the histories of Kwai and Amani presented here demonstrate a decidedly ambivalent relationship among scientists, colonial bureaucrats, and plantation managers. From 1902, Amani served these groups in its roles as Germany's foremost center for biological research into tropical plantation production. It replaced the failed attempt at Kwai, where five years earlier the colony's chief concession had built an experimental station not in a tropical rain forest, but in a more familiar setting among the conifer forests and pasturelands on West Usambara's central plateau.

When asked about Kwai, the elders will tell stories about its local historical significance in the heyday of Mbugu pastoralism and as a livestock research center under the Germans. Visitors to Tanzania's National Museum will likely see the display about the processed meat products from Kwai's German-era butchery. Despite its local history and well-known wurst, Kwai is today an obscure place. The Catholic mission in the valley below the town of Kwemekame is called Kwai, so most outsiders simply conclude that that was where the Germans built the farm. On an October day in 1996, when I asked informants to take me to the old farm site, I found myself led not to the mission, but to a valley south of it. I saw no sign of the handsome stone buildings I had read about in the archives, their timbers and foundation stones having been long ago removed for pressing construction needs in Kwemekame. The only evidence of a former homestead appeared in the tall palms and lines of eucalyptus trees and sisal plants that mark, respectively, the farm's old boundaries and now overgrown roadways. Still, my informants easily pointed out the house site and the flattened earth floors of what had been one of Kwai's livestock barns. We found what were once hillside pastures now covered with a collection of carefully bounded and irrigated gardens containing a variety of legumes, vegetables, and grains tended by local people from Kwemekame. Some of the elders who accompanied me could visualize this landscape as it appeared in the 1930s, with its overgrown pastures and derelict coffee trees. A few of them even recalled the violence Kwai's patrons inflicted upon the local community of Mbugu families who lived in the plantation's shadow. Everyone with us knew that this landscape's history had been contentious.[3]

In contrast to Kwai, Amani has remained operational as an experimental station and as a draw for outsiders interested in tropical forests. Several of its original German buildings survive intact alongside the additional construction completed under Amani's British overlords. The Tanzanian government currently houses a malaria research project at Amani, while the station's legacy of biological study is evident in the three-hundred-acre botanical garden below the station, which, albeit neglected, still contains many of the exotic plants brought there earlier in the century. Amani's activities are copiously recorded in the archival records and in colonial-era publications devoted to tropical agriculture and ecology.[4] International conservation organizations continue to use Amani and its surroundings as a center for their efforts to preserve Usambara's biologically diverse rain forests. These days, backpackers and ecotourists occasionally hike the well-slashed nature trails that cross tea plantations and islands of old-growth rain forests.

In the Usambaras, as in many other parts of Africa, nineteenth-century European scientific ideas contributed significantly to the imperial imperative of "progress," a process requiring, among other things, a radical environmental transformation. The organization of biological research at Kwai and Amani forms part of a larger process of what Alfred Crosby has referred to as "ecological imperialism," that is, the witting and unwitting transfer of exotic plants, animals, and diseases from one part of the globe to another as part of the larger processes of European expansion.[5] Indeed, the stations had a direct ecological impact, but they also served as centers for the dissemination to European audiences of scientific and pseudoscientific ideas about proper resource management in the tropics. Conflicts inevitably grew out of the complex relations among the colonial bureaucracy, state-sponsored scientific research, indigenous peoples, and the landscape itself.[6] The record of the Amani Institute, for example, reveals the state's initially firm commitment to science, which subsequently degenerated into heated debate over the benefits of pure versus applied research. The case of Kwai features strong resistance from indigenous peoples in a battle of attrition over a piece of land that held enormous cultural significance. Rather than fonts of agronomic knowledge, these places can be more readily associated with the futility of plantation agriculture in pre–World War II East Africa.

The Political and Scientific Landscape of German Colonialism in Tanzania

By most historical accounts, Germany's foray into African colonialism was, if not impulsive and reactionary, at least politically controversial. During the early 1880s in Germany, debates about whether to enter the race for African colonial empire revolved around the state's role as an imperial power in an economic climate marked increasingly by international competition over access to potential tropical markets and speculation regarding the value of Africa's natural resources. As these issues surfaced during the 1884–85 Berlin Conference, the German chancellor, Otto von Bismarck, decided on a pragmatic approach. Rather than commit wholeheartedly to a colonial empire, the state should simply protect German merchants who formed the chartered companies that already operated in Africa. Colonial enthusiasts challenged Bismarck's limited aims by seeking to acquire actual territory. One of them, Carl Peters, dashed across East Africa in late 1884 and managed to conclude twelve treaties supposedly ceding to him 140,000 square kilometers. In order to exploit these dubious claims, Peters and his supporters formed a chartered company, the Deutsch-Ostafrika Gesellschaft (German East Africa Society, hereafter DOAG), which in February 1885 received official government sanction and protection. By 1888, substantial capital investment had turned the DOAG into a serious financial venture. Therefore, when competition between the company traders and African coastal merchants led to hostilities that same year, the German government chose to send a military expedition to secure the DOAG's and its creditors' interests. The expedition quickly evolved into conquest and, after a decade of violence, the German state found itself with a colony on what is now mainland Tanzania.[7]

By 1902 the DOAG functioned under the aegis of the German East African Protectorate, whose official bureaucracy sought to foster economic development through natural resource exploitation. Colonial confidence and enthusiasm aside, no one in the colonial community knew in those early years the extent and quality of the colonies' resources. In the first decade of colonial rule, therefore, the colonial bureaucracy worked to sort out the role of peasant production, the capitalization and suitability of the small-scale settler-farmer, and the direction of development in the large-scale plantation companies. Meanwhile, private planters and plantation companies moved forward blindly, trying to exact profits from the land.

Germany was not the first imperial power to face these difficult questions. England, France, and the Netherlands, long in the business of exploiting tropical resources in Asia, had sought answers through systematic botanical research. By the late nineteenth century, England's world-famous Kew Gardens had evolved into a truly imperial institution, with alumni serving as the directors of botanical gardens, forest departments, and agricultural research stations throughout the British Empire. Gardens in the Dutch East Indies (the Buitenzorg Botanical Garden) and Calcutta extended the reach of imperial science. As early as 1822, Buitenzorg's scientists had begun to import potentially valuable economic plants and to study their propagation. British research stations acted as Kew satellites, carrying out in Asia and the Caribbean related research on plant genetics, plant pathology, entomology, and soil science.[8] The scientists associated with Germany's imperial ventures could therefore draw upon this developing body of knowledge in order to suggest the direction of African development schemes. However, scientific knowledge specific to East Africa's environment would require the kinds of investments in facilities and training that France, the Netherlands, and England had already made. Venture capitalists could not wait for such an institution and knowledge to develop. Oblivious to their basic ignorance, the representatives of colonial societies hastily surmised from the Asian example and from the rapid assessments of explorers that the forest-covered mountains of East Africa's coastal hinterland held one of the keys to successful economic development.[9]

The East and West Usambara Mountains seemed a logical place to base experiments in agricultural production. The mountains overlooked the Pangani Valley, an important nineteenth-century trade corridor that connected the mountain hinterland with the thriving coastal port towns of Pangani and Tanga. Moreover, the mountains' cool climate, seemingly abundant rainfall, and forested soils appeared, at first glance at least, as particularly appropriate for European settler farmers and their coffee plantations. DOAG-sponsored explorers continued to build expectations with their enthusiastic portrayal of the Usambara Urwald, the forest primeval, devoid of human influence. Urwälder they were not; the Usambaras, as well as the rest of East Africa's Eastern Arc Mountains, had served for centuries as settlement nodes. Yet, German colonial interests had no trouble leasing huge tracts of these forest lands because Usambara's indigenous population, weakened and displaced by a generation of violence, could not immediately challenge German interests. Oblivious to the mountains' recent history, the German colonial state asserted itself over the Usambara Mountains.

In this context of African social and economic chaos, the collaboration between the colonial state and its imperial science proved capable in one case of large-scale and long-term ecological transformation through plantation agriculture. In her study of science's role in nineteenth-century British imperial expansion, Lucille Brockway argued for direct connections between scientific research emanating from Kew Gardens and state-sponsored economic exploitation in tropical environments. Perhaps her most dramatic example comes from the German East Africa sisal industry that flourished on the plains below the Usambaras.[10] The story begins with Richard Hindorf, a DOAG-sponsored botanist, who read about Mexican sisal cultivation in a Kew publication. Guessing that sisal, a fibrous agave used in rope manufacture and suited to arid environments, would grow on the African plains, he ordered from a Florida nursery two hundred bulbs, which he sent on to German East Africa. The sixty-two that survived the 1898 journey served as a foundation for the propagation of over one million plants, most of them planted in row upon row covering the plains south and east of the Usambaras.[11] Sisal's expansion across thousands of hectares, and the supporting botanical research subsequently conducted at Amani, helped precipitate a regional environmental and economic transformation in the plains, where valuable indigenous agricultural lands became part of a growing colonial plantation economy.[12]

Sisal's success story proved to be more a convergence of fortunate circumstances than a model for collaboration between science, the state, and capital. In the mountains above the embryonic sisal industry, private interests, eager for quick returns from coffee, clashed with scientists who tried to balance these immediate demands with their understanding of the importance of long-term, systematic, and rigorous study of East African environments. To settlers desperate to cure coffee blight or stem locust invasions, long-term replicable experiments simply bred impatience.

The Kwai and Amani examples highlight the ambiguities of scientific research and its application on the landscape, processes not always appreciated in studies of imperialism. Historians of science, for example, have presented imperialism in a narrowly defined discussion of European achievements in non-Western contexts, where the metropole serves as the point of knowledge diffusion.[13] While environmental historians have also considered the expansion of European empires, their analyses often argue for a direct causal relationship between ecological stress and degradation and the intrusion of capitalism into tropical ecosystems, seeing science as coconspirator with colonialism and capitalism.[14] As the two fields have come together, a new paradigm has begun to take shape. It is circumspect with regard to the capability of Western science or capitalism to transform unilaterally local ecology, economy, and culture. This recent work examines how the interactions of indigenous and Western practice often combined to shape ideologies of land use and environmental health, as well as the land itself.[15]

Despite the complexity of the ecological outcomes, the colonial project in economic development advocated complete environmental domination through the imposition of ecological change. The German agriculture, forestry, and animal husbandry sectors therefore demanded the introduction of a new set of plants and animals not only from Europe but also from other tropical regions. In the Usambaras, these ecological transfers, although part of an already long tradition of painstaking research in other tropical environments, were exercises in trial and error. Sisal may have prospered, but coffee's dismal failure in the Usambaras proved that not all East African environments could be quickly reworked in the interest of profit. As economic failure created a sense of urgency among bureaucrats, scientists, and plantation directors, Kwai and Amani became symbols of disaffection—Amani for an ivory-tower pretentiousness removed from the realities of settler life, and Kwai for the grievance it caused the local African society. Neither institution would survive the colonial period intact.

Kwai Farm's Contested Landscape

Hearing of West Usambara's potential from earlier explorers, Eick, the DOAG's economy director, followed their lead, and in 1896 inspected the massif's central plateau pastureland, where he found a "paradise for the German farmer" at 1,608 meters elevation.[16] The pasture, forest, and gardens, "an African Switzerland," so impressed Eick that he chose the area for a company-owned experimental station.[17] Insofar as he considered the area's indigenous residents at all, Eick believed that they simply lived off the land, rather than shaping it to their needs. Mbugu history suggests otherwise. Moreover, the communities Eick found living on the central plateau in the early 1890s lived under the same social and ecological duress that had debilitated production systems across eastern Africa.[18] The most devastating ecological event to hit Kwai was the rinderpest epidemic that killed many of their cattle, leaving the surviving animals to become targets of raids by similarly impoverished pastoralists. For safety's sake, the Wambugu closed the ranks of their dispersed communities on rolling hills they referred to as Kwai.[19] When the DOAG created the Kwai Experimental Farm in 1896, it removed from Mbugu use over 800 hectares of these carefully conditioned grazing lands.

Kwai is an important place in Mbugu stories. The tales recall a battle that drove raiding Maasai warriors out of the mountains once and for all.

> A boma was built at Malibwi and animals from the area brought there. Women, children, and old folks took refuge in the forest, while boys hid inside and shot arrows through holes in the boma walls. This was the last war between the Wambugu and Maasai. Many Maasai were killed. One of the surviving Maasai decided to go to an Mbugu house and ask for milk. He was killed by the women who gave him the milk.[20]

More than a single example of the intensity of the Mbugu-Maasai conflict, the story represents in Mbugu oral tradition the culmination of generations of conflict between Mbugu herders and the Maasai, beginning centuries earlier on the Laikipia Plateau north of Mt. Kenya. The descendants of those Wambugu who escaped found a final refuge for their families and their stock on the central plateaus of the West Usambaras. The late-nineteenth-century conflicts between the pastoralist groups conjured up a painful past, and for the Wambugu of central West Usambara, the Kwai battle represented a heroic defense in desperate times.[21]

Kwai's symbolic importance was lost on Eick, who at times must have felt isolated at his exotic outpost. His farm lay a day's journey both from the plains' caravan routes to the coast and from the nearest colonial government station at Wilhelmstal. In building the estate, Eick looked homeward and recreated a familiar world that one visitor described as a "good German farm compound." He laid out the buildings so that they faced southward toward an open valley and planted around the farmhouse a profusion of flowering plants. As he added the outbuildings, Eick created a landscape architecture that spoke to his sense of bucolic Europe.[22]

In addition to its isolation, the Kwai site had other drawbacks. What the DOAG authorities considered economic plantation crops—rubber, cinchona, sisal, and, most importantly, coffee—required a warmer, wetter climate. Instead of these "economic crops," Kwai's experimental gardens produced in profusion crops from the temperate latitudes such as grapes, potatoes, lettuce, artichokes, cucumbers, melons, cabbages, carrots, peas, and beans. What worked at Kwai—European grains and market vegetables—appealed to small-scale German settler-farmers, but these latter formed an undercapitalized and unpredictable sector of the colonial economy. The DOAG quickly recognized its problem and in the late 1890s erected lowland experimental stations just below the West Usambaras, at Mombo (450 m elevation) and Lwengera (500 m elevation). As African farmers had known for centuries, the Germans belatedly realized that they needed to utilize more of the elevation-temperature-rainfall gradient.

Kwai's successes nonetheless proved that European vegetables and horticultural products could be produced in great variety in the West Usambaras.[23] Although Eick directed his horticultural experiments at the needs of European highland settlers, African farmers in the West Usambaras noted the successes with potatoes and cabbages and quickly incorporated them into their existing farming systems.[24] Potato cultivation conferred special advantages because it allowed farmers to expand agricultural production into higher country, which could not support the staple banana production, as well as into the farmlands abandoned during the recent crises.[25] Meanwhile, European settler production languished in the face of coffee's ecological failures, poor capitalization, and high transportation costs. The DOAG had begun in 1891 to build a railway in the Pangani Valley, only to abandon the project to the government in 1899.[26] By 1902, the railhead had reached the town of Korogwe, located in the plains at the southern end of the West Usambaras, but the porterage fees required to get produce down from the mountains cut sharply into profits. Transport hurdles thus reduced to mere subsistence agriculture the very settlers Kwai's experiments should have been supporting.[27] In light of the deteriorating situation, one DOAG official felt that settlers should abandon the West Usambaras altogether.[28]

Undeterred, Eick continued to try to serve West Usambara's settlers through his efforts to build a cattle herd that reflected his faith in European racial superiority. Eick's ladder of racial hierarchy extended to his Mbugu neighbors, who he mistakenly called a "mixed race" of "Bantus and Hamites." He argued that, in addition to this detrimental miscegenation, their isolation and "continued inbreeding" had reduced them to "idiocy."[29] His attitudes applied as well to the Wambugu's zebu cattle. Eick therefore imported his livestock, but cattle diseases severely limited their survival, causing an embarrassing situation in which he initially failed to build a cattle herd in what was, ironically, Usambara's pastoral heartland. Eick therefore began a heavy-handed local "cattle improvement program," which precipitated a violent incident sometime during 1900. The experiments with crossbreeding required Mbugu herders to bring their animals to Kwai for insemination. Not only did Eick lead the Wambugu to believe they had been ordered to make their animals available, he charged a fee, payable in milk, for the insemination "service." A contingent of disgruntled Wambugu traveled all the way to the coastal port of Tanga to inquire as to the legality of the situation. Administrators there informed the herders that they were under no such obligations. This all led to a vaguely reported but clearly rancorous incident in which Keudel, the German district officer from the government station at Wilhelmstal, tried to mediate the dispute but ended up shooting and killing several Wambugu. Eick blamed the incident on Mbugu drunkenness and "insubordination," but Keudel disagrees in a pointed marginal note written on Eick's official report on the situation.[30] Very soon after this incident, the DOAG decided to end its official ties to Kwai and leased it to a private citizen named Ludwig Illich.

Kwai's new lessee likewise tried to build a herd of European-zebu crossbreeds, but continuing resentment of the German presence at Kwai undermined any Mbugu willingness to sell animals to the station. Illich therefore decided to purchase stock from the Maasai pastoralists who grazed their animals in the plains below Usambara. Unfortunately, this stock carried into the mountains East Coast Fever (ECF), a tick-borne disease, along with an unidentified but highly contagious lung disease. ECF-carrying ticks continued to infest Kwai's pastures well into Illich's administration and his zebu crosses suffered extremely high mortality rates as a result.[31] Illich nonetheless proceeded with his futile effort to create a stronger crossbreed by importing European bulls and Indian water buffalo.

German experiments at Kwai not only threatened indigenous herds, Illich and his fellow settlers along the Mkussu River also played havoc with indigenous patterns of work and residence. Usambara's settlers desperately needed farm laborers, but could not easily procure them locally as Usambara's African population dispersed in order to recolonize the depopulated countryside. At Kwai, like many other parts of the Usambaras, the local evasion of German labor and tax requirements induced Illich to bring in outside help from other regions of German East Africa.[32] Mbugu informants remember the Nyamwezi, in particular, as immigrant farm workers who reduced settlers' need to find local labor, which, in turn, provided Illich and his German neighbors with the confidence to forcibly evict Mbugu families from the settler estates by confiscating their cattle and destroying their homes. These evictions spurred a larger Mbugu migration from Kwai and the Mkussu Valley to the plains at Mombo and Mazinde, to neighboring highland agricultural areas away from German settlement, and to remote high-mountain areas like Kinko and Mgwashi.[33]

One informant remembers Illich's treatment of his father:

> One of the manumba [aforementioned laborers from outside the Usambaras] at Illich's farm happened to marry a sister of my father. This guy was a shopkeeper on Illich's farm. By the end of the month when Illich checked on the shop he found it empty because the Nyamwezi manumba had used all the profits as payment to my father on the dowry. Dr. Illich was furious and then he decided to look for a suitable punishment, which was to imprison my father for 2 months. For further compensation 12 of my father's heifers were taken for the shopkeeper's crime. After the 2 months imprisonment, Dr. Illich said that if he saw my father again he would shoot him. My father and his family left immediately for Mgwashi [northeastern section of the West Usambara massif]. Some family members returned, but my father stayed in Mgwashi with one of his wives. Dr. Illich stayed at Kwai until he left the Usambaras. Even then, my father did not return although the family and property was here. They became refugees—did not come back. This threat of Illich really had an effect on my father.[34]

Further German violence and forced evictions in Mbugu territories occurred at nearby Magamba, which informants also associate with the influx of the manumba.[35]

The Kwai estate's hostile relations with the Wambugu and its environmental unsuitability for growing tropical plantation crops like cinchona, rubber, and sisal doomed it as an experimental station. Even before Illich leased the farm, some of the DOAG's scientists began to push for one large, centralized station with labs, experimental gardens, and meteorological and cartographic research facilities outside of the West Usambaras. Although the DOAG ultimately declared total failure at Kwai, Illich remained to continue experiments with numerous exotic vegetables, grains, and horticultural crops. He also continued to import European cattle, swine, and poultry, and he further diversified his activities when, in 1905, he acquired canning equipment and a butcher. Shortly thereafter, sausage, bacon, and canned pork began to appear in Tanga and Dar es Salaam, much to the pleasure of wurst-starved Germans.[36]

After World War I, when Britain received German East Africa as a League of Nations Mandate, Kwai came under the jurisdiction of the custodian of enemy property. Like many other former German estates during the war, Kwai had been abandoned and its pastures reclaimed for African use. The custodian, citing the German government's investment of a "considerable amount of money for its upkeep," decided that the farm, now listed as 537 hectares, was too valuable to lose. In 1921, the government therefore sold the estate to a Mr. Whiting while leasing to him an additional 306 hectares.[37] In 1923, Whiting sold his entire interest in the farm at a considerable profit to a J. T. Woodcock, an ex-navy cook.[38] For more than thirty years afterward, Woodcock chided and insulted district and provincial officers in a set of correspondence that reveals one lonely man's progression toward mental breakdown. Woodcock's paranoia manifested itself in his continual efforts to define and defend what he considered to be the boundaries of his farm.

Woodcock's troubles began in 1924 when he requested that the government surveyor determine according to the original German survey the boundaries of his newly acquired property, a seemingly simple job that the Lands Office badly mishandled. First, it sent out an incompetent surveyor who never finished the task. His partially completed work, moreover, exhibited large errors that required correction by a second surveyor.[39] Next, the Lands Office delayed until 1928 a decision on the accuracy of the original German survey.[40] This episode sparked ten years of complaints from Woodcock, who claimed among other things that the surveyors had accused him of bribing the flag boys, that the "natives" had destroyed boundary trees and moved markers, that herders had grazed their animals on his land without permission, and that the Wambugu had diverted a stream from which Kwai Farm's main furrow ran.[41]

In 1931, Woodcock worriedly wrote that the "Natives are taking possession of Kwai lands. I now find that there are ten natives with their families and cattle and all declare that the government have advised them and gave them permission to occupy this land, the local Jumbe also tells me the government have given permission through Jumbe Daffa [Native Authority chief for Lushoto] and then it came to him [through the D.O., Lushoto]."[42] Woodcock's claims of illegal occupation prompted a number of visits to Kwai from various local British and "Native Authorities."

However, in early 1931, the Lushoto district officer, Hartnoll, found that Woodcock had claimed land beyond his survey boundary by setting up his own boundary markers. He had then accused African herders of trespass and blamed the Lushoto District Office for allowing unauthorized use of what he claimed as his land.[43]

Enraged by the D.O.'s findings, Woodcock took the law into his own hands and imitated his German predecessors' penchant for direct action against Kwai's neighbors. Two months after the D.O.'s official visit, Woodcock confiscated 118 cattle and 46 sheep grazing on his land, even though the livestock owners had a legal contract with him for grazing rights in return for payment in ghee (butter), cash, and labor. Woodcock apparently held the animals for over a month before Hartnoll ordered the superintendent of police to return the animals to their owners and to institute criminal proceedings against Woodcock for theft.[44] Woodcock's attorney managed to get the case transferred out of Lushoto and the correspondence indicates that Woodcock eventually won the case. He then sued the government for his legal expenses and received £120 in compensation.[45]

Perhaps chastened by the District's embarrassing loss in court, or ignorant of Woodcock's past, a new Lushoto district officer, Callaghan, sided with the ex-navy cook as he sought in 1934 to convert to freehold the leased sections of the Kwai property. The lease required property boundaries to be fenced with wire, hedges, walls, or ditches, provided that they kept cattle in or out. Cognizant of these conditions, Woodcock had made minimal attempts to fence 35 percent of the property's five-mile border by planting it up with sisal, but most of the cuttings had failed to take root and cattle trampled the rest. The lease also obliged the renter to make improvements to the property. Woodcock could claim that about 56 hectares had been conditioned for grazing, though presumably by local Mbugu herders who rented from Woodcock. In addition, he had planted between 20 and 25 hectares of coffee and then left it completely unattended.[46] In his February 1934 report to the Lands Office, Callaghan described in detail the mess on Woodcock's land. He concluded, however, that Woodcock's improvements sufficed and he recommend that the Lands Office grant the request for freehold rights.[47]

The African population objected: "Generally speaking the Washambaa [D.O. incorrectly substitutes the Washambaa for the Wambugu] have every objection to the alienation of land and their dislike of this particular alienation dates from the prewar days and is still active." In spite of this, the D.O. found no legal grounds for the objection.[48] To the Wambugu, who had lost tens of thousands of grazing acres when the Forest Department alienated the nearby Magamba forest, Woodcock's continued occupation of grazing land he did not use must have struck a sour note, especially in the wake of 1933's drought.

Woodcock kept up his complaints and accusations until the Lushoto district authorities felt it necessary to hold a *baraza* to hear the African side of the story. When asked about labor conditions on Kwai Farm, "[s]ome hundred natives at the baraza stated that they did not like Mr. Woodcock and had no wish to work for him. Woodcock was generally disliked and not wanted. Woodcock was disliked because some yrs ago before his farm was properly surveyed and demarcated he turned them off a large area of land which was outside his farm and tried to take this land away. When they refused to move he burnt their huts."[49] Woodcock's complaints continued into 1936 with accusations of petty theft, diversion of irrigation water, and property destruction, prompting yet another visit in September of that year by the police, who found Woodcock's complaints "frivolous."[50]

In June 1937, when yet another district official visited Woodcock to investigate his worries over labor, Woodcock's mental condition seemed serious enough for the officer to comment, "Mr Woodcock appeared to be in slightly better health than he was on my previous visit on the 19th February but he is far from well and exceedingly nervy, there is no doubt in my mind that he should go to Europe for a holiday as in his present nervy condition I doubt if he is capable of handling any labor which may offer itself for employment."[51]

The official record then contains a gap of sixteen years. A final letter from September of 1953 displays Woodcock's very strong sense of paranoia:

> You will surely find in your office files that I previously made complaint by letter and verbally to the DC that Mgeni [worker who filed a complaint against Woodcock] was sent and willingly came here and begged to be employed, and worked his confidence tricks all for the special purpose of being used as a pivot in this continued isolation, and the driving out and starving out process against yours truly, and also the many distractions and other matter I have put in the police and the DC's hands.[52]

A year later, in September 1954, a workman found Woodcock's dead body near his house; his feet had been cut off. In May 1955, the *Tanganyika Standard* reported that the police had opened a murder inquest, but I have found no record of its result. The *Standard* article summarizes much of

Woodcock's local troubles, including his accusations of witchcraft against the local Wambugu and the fact that Woodcock's wife left him in 1923, citing as a reason that he was "very sick."[53]

Woodcock's death ended two generations of European occupation of lands that local herders felt had been unjustly alienated from their use. Kwai's owners had abused them, and local inhabitants continually reminded Woodcock and the District Authorities that they had not forgotten the past. What began under the DOAG as a scientific endeavor quickly degenerated into a long-term and festering attack on indigenous land rights, led over two decades by a psychologically disturbed individual. Woodcock finally bequeathed Kwai to his niece, who lived only a few miles away at Magamba. She ended the turmoil surrounding Kwai's recent history by allowing local African authorities to divide it among farmers living nearby. The local preference for cultivation trumped grazing: by the late 1950s, Mbugu pastoralism was in its death throes. The herders had lost not only Kwai, but also the vast majority of their pastures. The German and British governments had turned their sanctuary into heavily policed forest reserves, a process described in chapter 4.

Woodcock's isolation reflected that of the estate. In the end, the people living around Kwai reintegrated the place into their now changed ecological world. Kwai's failure in many ways paralleled the failures of estates across East and West Usambara. Eick's energetic beginnings gave way to Illich's frustrated experiments and finally yielded to Woodcock's inertia. Moreover, none of the managers held anything but disdain for their neighbors. The scientists at Amani, only eighty miles away, also failed to provide agriculture's silver bullet. The institute experienced its own style of isolation until its eventual demise just after World War II.

Ivory Tower Imperialism at Amani

On June 20, 1916, during Britain's First World War conquest of German East Africa, a force of about one hundred men climbed into the East Usambara Mountains to lay claim to the Amani Institute.[54] From 1902, scientific work at Amani had focused on botanical research and its application to the needs of the German coffee, sisal, and rubber plantations sprinkled throughout the colony's northern mountains and plains. However, the British force found Amani's highly trained scientists reduced to wartime camp warders for German refugees. Station conditions were such that the botanical lab served as a milk distribution center, while the experimental

Fig. 3.1. Former colonial estate at Mkuzi, only a few kilometers from Kwai. This house dates to the early 1930s.
Photo Sabine Barcatta

rice fields had degenerated into a "pestilential swamp." Science had taken a back seat to survival. The station's ramshackle condition notwithstanding, British scientists, impressed both with Amani's international reputation and the quality of research conducted there, argued for the station's rehabilitation and its continued operation as a research institute. Under the Germans, Amani had been a flash point for arguments over the value of pure versus applied research, and it would remain so as part of Britain's East African colonies.

Colonialism's success in German East Africa depended in large part upon the agricultural sector. In its support of plantation-style production of coffee, and industrial crops like rubber and sisal, the state turned to botany for solutions to the challenges posed by the tropical environment. The idea of an economic botany, a branch of science devoted to the advancement of industrial civilization through the development of useful plants, gained currency during the 1840s with the development at Kew Gardens of a museum of economic botany.[55] Botanical studies continued to gain stature during imperialism's forays into Africa, as explorer-naturalists accompanied expeditions whose express purpose was to survey a region's economic prospects. The scientists meanwhile used these opportunities to fill in the phytogeographical map in the naturalist tradition of Charles Darwin and Alexander von Humboldt. Botany's increasingly dual role, at once scientific and economic, served as the basis for the eventual foundation of the Amani institute in East Usambara.

The German scientists who would staff and run the institute and the colonial financiers who stood to profit from its research argued over both the staff's activities and the station's site. In order to assist colonial agriculture, the station had to be near settler plantations, many of which had begun as coffee operations in the rain forests of East and West Usambara.[56] The scientists wanted more than simply a coffee research station, however. While keen to satisfy the station's financial backers in the Colonial Development Committee, they saw an opportunity to build a multipurpose station where scientific pursuits garnered international prestige.

Adolf Engler, who from 1889 headed the Berlin Botanical Museum, helped to convince his colleagues that the Usambara Mountains held great promise as a research site. Like the administrators of England's Kew Gardens, Engler saw his museum's institutional role as one of stalwart support for plant collection and identification throughout the tropical world. Following his special interest in African plant life, Engler began his own survey of Usambara's botanical life in the early 1890s. Skeptical of the early geographical sketches of Usambara, which he saw as amateur, Engler enlisted the services of Carl Hölst, a gardener from the Lutheran mission station at Mlalo. With the help of several small grants from the Ministry of Culture, the Imperial Academy of Science, and the German Colonial Society, in four months Hölst collected 4,600 plant specimens throughout the East and West Usambaras. Engler praised Hölst's methodical specimen collections and his careful analyses of each plant's ecological context.[57] In this way, Hölst's work began the still ongoing project to systematically describe the mosaic of plant communities in Usambara's forests.[58]

Engler's special interest was highland plant formations, which in Usambara's case meant forests. Based on Hölst's specimens and notes, his doubt regarding Baumann's early reports of an Usambara Urwald gave way to acceptance regarding the lush forests covering some of the southeast-facing mountain slopes. However, the term Urwald meant little. Engler's work aimed to disaggregate the botanical whole into its parts and reassemble it into an ecological community. Furthermore, Engler felt Usambara forests, although seemingly isolated and relatively small in area, needed to be presented as part of the *continent's* natural history. (Engler's position as Botanical Museum curator gave him access to collections sent to him from across Africa.) Once he had determined a forest's botanical composition, he built it into a historical and geographical model that covered East, West, and southern Africa and developed a theory of plant evolution and adaptation. Engler's holistic and decidedly ecological view culminated in his massive inventory of African plants in *Die Pflanzenwelt Afrikas insbesondere seiner tropischen Gebiete: Grundzüge der Pflanzenverbreitung in Afrika und die Charakterpflanzen Afrikas,* one of the volumes in a larger work he helped edit entitled *Die Vegetation der Erde,* published in 1910.

Engler's 1894 taxonomy of Usambara's vegetation focused on plant communities.[59] He improved upon Baumann's crude ecological triad—settled regions, grazing lands, and forest—by identifying six separate forest communities. He carefully described how each interconnected association of plants varied with elevation, temperature ranges, and rainfall patterns, as well as the tendency of the forest types to overlap. Engler thus folded his view of Usambara into his intellectual world of systematic botany, which focused on plant form, function, evolution, migration, and adaptation. In a tendency that foreshadowed twentieth-century ecology, he paid attention to indigenous peoples only insofar as they influenced secondary forest growth.[60] His theoretical work likewise spoke only indirectly to the possibilities of botany's role in agricultural development. With the assistance of Hölst's extraordinary acumen and tremendous physical efforts, he initiated what has become a substantial scientific focus on the Eastern Arc Mountains, and the Usambaras in particular.

Hölst also described in painstaking detail the agricultural world that surrounded him at the Mlalo mission. His notes found their way into publication in an 1894 article by Otto Warburg, a botany professor at the University of Berlin. In his lengthy piece entitled "Die Kulturpflanzen Usambaras," Warburg described vicariously a farming system of great complexity and efficiency. Much like Engler's forests, this agricultural landscape exhibited an ecological equilibrium in which prosperous farming hamlets managed productive, irrigated gardens. That the gardens contained a number of different cultigens, as well as their individual varieties, testified to the centuries of adaptation in Usambara agriculture. Warburg's crop list included banana (numerous varieties), maize, rice, manioc, taro, sweet potatoes, sorghum, sugar cane, beans, and tobacco.[61] The horticultural sophistication extended to the set of agricultural techniques and social arrangements employed to produce those crops.[62] Although the essay implied that agricultural complexity had evolved within Usambara's diverse forest communities, its presentation lacked an historical perspective. In any event, given the biological richness and indigenous agricultural successes, the Usambaras seemed to be a place of infinite botanical potential.

By the late 1890s, the question of the station's site had become one of simply where in the Usambara Mountains to put it. Kwai, the DOAG's troubled farm in the West Usambaras, presented a possibility, but the cloud surrounding Eick's tenure and its temperate climate dampened enthusiasm. In 1901, Richard Hindorf, the DOAG's chief agronomist, proposed that instead of Kwai, the research station be built in East Usambara's tropical rain forest zone, where plantation societies already held in freehold tens of thousands of hectares of "ancient" forest stands[63] that German scientists believed clothed the colony's richest soils.[64] Amani lay close to large sections of these mature tropical rain forests and its perch atop a steep gradient at 900 meters elevation offered easy access to both highland (>1000 m) and lowland (<500 m) ecological communities with their varying temperatures and rainfall patterns. Amani's geography gave researchers the opportunity to set up experimental gardens anywhere from 400 m to 1000 m and to reach them easily on horseback.[65]

Once the site had been agreed upon, the scientists who would eventually run the station, Albrecht Zimmerman and Franz Stuhlman, began to raise funds for its construction and upkeep. Stuhlman carried with him an international reputation as a naturalist and had broad-based international experience in the tropical botanical gardens of French, British, and Dutch colonies. As director of the German East Africa Agriculture Department, he used his bureaucratic position to appeal to the station's potential donors. In March 1898, for example, he sounded anything but the academic in a lecture to the German Colonial Society as he praised the economic and social progress that colonialism had conferred upon East Africa. German administration in East Africa, he explained, had ended the slave trade, created an atmosphere of peace and security, and imposed taxes. Furthermore, the construction of a polio hospital in Dar es Salaam in the interest of African health demonstrated the state's humanitarian concerns. In the economic realm, colonialism was enlarging its program in agricultural development.[66] Although Stuhlman dutifully played his role as colonial booster, he also devoted considerable energy to botanical research. By 1901, a year before Amani opened, he had already traveled to botanical gardens in Reunion, Ceylon and Java, Bombay, Puna, Lahore, Saharanpore, Calcutta, Utakammund, Peradeniya, and Buitenzorg to collect seed for a garden that he would construct at Amani.[67]

Like Stuhlman, Zimmerman brought international academic credentials to his colonial service. He had trained in botany but left a frustrating career in German academia to work at the coffee research station on Java in the Dutch East Indies. Zimmerman's work at the Java station fit the practical side of Amani's charter because he had studied the revival of Java's ailing coffee industry.[68] These credentials helped him to convince a German government adamantly opposed to theoretical scientific research to invest two million marks in equipment, labor, and buildings in the isolated mountain forests of East Africa.[69]

Once Amani's funding was established, the station's mission focused on economic botany, and the scientific emphasis on natural history that Engler had developed for the Usambaras disappeared.[70] The dream landscape of economic botany, featured thriving coffee, rubber, and cinchona plantations, instead of Engler's complex forest communities. Amani's botanists' created that landscape in miniature the construction of the botanical garden. The scientists and staff laid out and planted experimental plots with oil and edible palm nuts, deciduous and nondeciduous fruit trees, gums, resins, gutta percha, coffee, bananas, tea, cacao, cola nut, cinchona (and other medicinal plants), cinnamon, pepper, along with heavy oil, fat, wax, and tannin-producing plants.[71] The garden successfully boosted Amani's international standing attracting hundreds of European scientists.[72] *Der Tropenpflanzer*, the station's official journal published reports of the results of station scientists' work furthering the station's international reputation. By 1907, 144 institutions purchased or subscribed to the journal.[73]

Amani's impressive state support and its garden dedicated to colonial service could not cure the sick and dying coffee trees covering the Usambara hillsides, however. In their mistaken belief in forest soil productivity, coffee planters began in 1892 to destroy large swaths of indigenous trees and to replace them with coffee. By 1902, the first year of Amani's operations, hundreds of thousands of diseased and damaged coffee trees covered cleared and burned-over old-growth forests in the East and West

Fig. 3.2. Amani post office. Photo Christopher Conte

Usambaras. The scientists debated coffee's dismal failure. Some argued for deficient soils as the cause while others contended that lack of shade, wind damage, root fungus, and coffee borers impeded coffee production.[74] What the elements had not damaged, the market had. In the years between 1890 and 1903, the price of coffee had dropped from 175 marks to 54 for two hundred kilos.[75] In 1903, Engler at last clarified the connection between poor coffee yields and Usambara's soils and advised against further coffee cultivation in rain forest clearings.[76] At the same time, cultivators revised their own optimistic prognostications for coffee, noting that the forest soils lost most of their fertility after four years.[77] Although German scientists had identified the mechanisms of soil impoverishment, the damage was done.[78] Not surprisingly, this deforestation episode caused headaches for the forestry service, which had a keen interest in conserving Usambara's watershed.[79]

With coffee's productivity in decline, Amani scientists branched out into other experiments with plantation crops. Sisal's success spurred Amani scientists to experiment with other lowland crops such as teak and rubber, tree crops that they correctly believed would prove suitable for planting in the Lwengera and Umba valleys. In fact, Zimmerman's experiments with rubber (*Manihot glaziovii*) increased the station's visibility as the international market demand for rubber boomed.[80] Although the subsequent expansion of rubber and teak in Usambara's foothills did not prove consistently profitable, they removed fertile lowlands from indigenous use. Amani's influence on these lands may have been indirect, but its experimental program nurtured an agricultural trend directly inimical to interests of indigenous husbandry, something Amani's scientists knew very little about.

As an institution committed to agricultural extension, the station failed, but Amani's very presence proved that under colonial state auspices, an experimental scientific laboratory and botanical garden could function on the ground. However, the initial confidence among private and state-sponsored colonial interests that science could quickly turn failed plantations into profitable enterprises was unrealistic, and led to a strained relationship between the Amani establishment and their demanding constituency.

The immediate social effect on East Usambara's indigenous population of Amani's presence under the Germans remains difficult to gauge. Over the longer term, however, heated disputes over land did erupt under the British Mandate. Ecologically, change on the Amani station's grounds was dramatic, as hundreds of exotic plants made their appearance in the botanical garden and experimental fields.[81] Of the exotic plants, forty-eight species have become naturalized in East Usambara, and some have become quite aggressive invaders in the mountain rain forests.[82]

In 1914, when World War I imposed Europe's conflict upon East Africa, botanists, chemists, and zoologists transformed the station into a wartime production center and refugee camp. Their services became especially necessary when a British blockade cut off German East Africa from the sea. In order to support the German and African troops in the field, essential import substitutes began to flow from Amani. The station's cinchona plantation became the colony's center of quinine production. Other wartime necessities produced at Amani included medicines, bandages, distilled alcohol, asthma and heart medicine, soap, and toothpaste. The troops also needed chocolate, and more than two dozen workers at Amani produced over thirty kilograms of chocolate each day.[83]

Germany's experiment in colonial agronomic development ended in 1916 when British troops took over the station. Impressed by the German accomplishments, Amani's new British wards argued for its continued operation as an agricultural research center. In September of 1916, A. C. MacDonald, Tanganyika's first agricultural director, called Amani "one of the most important agricultural stations in the tropics" and pleaded with the military government to maintain the stations *in situ*.⁸⁴ In the meantime, the German scientists became prisoners of war. When the British established their League of Nations Mandate in 1920, the colonial administration appointed Alleyne Leechman as Amani's director. In his correspondence with Tanganyika's director of agriculture, Leechman requested that the more expert of his German colleagues remain to help with the station's transition to British hands: "Bronnle [head gardener at Amani for 13 years] speaks excellent English and of course Swahili and possesses qualifications of so special a nature that every effort should be made to retain his services." He also recommended that Karl Braun, the former assistant director, be retained.

> He has already published a great deal of original work on the economic and medicinal plants of the colony and has been chiefly responsible for the organisation of the splendid library on which important subject his advice will be invaluable. He also has an extensive knowledge of the flora of the district. He is now engaged on a study of the Mtama (*Andropogon Sorghum*) and he should be given every facility to complete his work. He has also done excellent work as officer in charge of the Dispensary. Although he is not a qualified physician, he was originally a pharmaceutical chemist. Since Feb. 1919 treated nearly 1800 patients, and vaccinated nearly 400. His private funds are exhausted and his prospects in Germany are of the poorest.

Zimmerman had also remained at Amani after the war, but seeing over a decade of work destroyed must have been extremely discouraging. He barricaded himself in an intellectual fortress of botanical experimentation. In January 1920, Leechman reported to the Tanganyika's chief secretary:

> Professor Zimmermann [*sic*] is now relieved of all responsibility as Director of the Institute and he, very naturally, feels his loss of position acutely. He has lost interest in the place he did so much to build up ... and he has certainly allowed his inclinations as a botanist to run riot. The German Government sternly repressed the pursuit of pure science, as such, at Amani, and clearly placed before the staff the primary objects of the foundation—which were to endeavour to solve problems of practical value to the agriculture and industries of the colony. ... The professor is wrapped up in his cucumbers (so to say) and, when I wished to begin the cleaning of his chemical lab, he protested volubly that his experiments with cucumbers would be interfered with.⁸⁵

D. Prain of the Royal Botanical Gardens at Kew supported Leechman's plan to keep the station open. Prain felt Amani should continue as a scientific research station, but he also recognized the problems inherent in defining the lines of separation between theoretical and practical work. He therefore argued that Amani become a scientific institute wholly independent of Tanganyika's Department of Agriculture, devoted fully to the fundamental problems of agriculture across Britain's African domains. Prain's argument implied that the Agriculture Department's scientists, saddled with the day-to-day work on the ground, had neither the time nor the expertise to tackle such complex and long-term problems.[86]

The question of East Africa's Agricultural Departments' research capacity proved to be a sensitive one. After all, they had to pay the station's bills, and Leechman knew that he had to get the agriculture directors behind Amani's British program. In November 1920, only ten months after his original praise for German scientific accomplishment at Amani, Leechman derided it.

> The organ of the Institute 'Der Pflanzer' was, seemingly, never 'edited' in the English sense: concrete instances will be found in Dr. K. Braun's published work on Rice and Sisal. Then the planting at Amani is, I think, typical of German work as a whole in this colony: the tea cultivation is an object of derision to every practical British planter who has seen it, the coffee is but little better and this is true of all the large coffee plantations in the Amani district—while the planting of trees on the estate can be considered only as crudely experimental. These remarks are necessary to dissipate the myth of German super-excellence in scientific work, and to combat the rumour already spread by them that it will be impossible for the British to follow the Germans at Amani and for a British Director to hope to emulate Professor Dr. A. Zimmermann [sic].[87]

His strategy failed and the agriculture directors in Kenya, Tanganyika, Uganda, Zanzibar, and Nyasaland moved forcefully to place the agricultural research agenda firmly under their control. Some of them went so far as to argue for dismantling the station altogether while refusing to contribute their share of funding. Leechman battled the bureaucrats until September 1923, when Tanganyika's governor, Horace Byatt, placed the facility into cold storage.[88] Leechman quickly resigned.

Four years later, in a 180-degree about-face, the Tanganyikan government prepared in 1927 to reorganize Amani as the East African Agricultural Research Station (EAARS). The addition of the nearby Kwamkoro estate enlarged the station by 8,000 acres, 7,000 of which remained under tropical rain forest. The staff included F. J. Nutman (plant physiologist), Geoffrey Milne (soil chemist), H. H. Storey (plant pathologist), Arthur Greenway (botanist), and Reginald Moreau (librarian). W. Nowell, the new director, traveled to Germany to meet with Zimmerman and to further acquaint himself with the station's history.[89] All of these scientists would make significant contributions to their own fields, and two in particular, Milne and Moreau, would publish broadly influential studies in the *Journal of Ecology*.[90] Both remained at Amani for over a decade and developed a particular sensitivity to ecological relationships in the Usambaras.

The funding for the EAARS that had suddenly materialized in the late twenties just as quickly evaporated with the Great Depression, when East African colonial governments tightened their budget belts. Once again, Amani's sponsors argued over the relevance of research in the East Usambara Mountains to problems with export crops in Uganda and Kenya. In London, the Colonial Advisory Council for Agriculture and Animal Health (CACAAH), the station's overseer in the Colonial Office, continued to view the station's role as that of an imperial institution charged with studying "long range" problems which were beyond the purview of the local East African departments of agriculture.[91] Despite the CACAAH's assurances, some of the agricultural directors on the ground in East Africa feared that work at Amani encroached directly on their administrative turf. They picked away at the station's program, declared its isolated location unsuitable, and ridiculed what Uganda's agricultural director believed to be its irrelevant long-term research on soil conservation and agroforestry. Further complicating Amani's financial situation, Kenya's Legislative Council voted in May 1930 to stop its annual contribution of £2,000 because of Amani's isolation from the public eye.[92] In August 1930, the Colonial Office, through the CACAAH, sought to ease the tension by setting out a five-year plan for Amani research that would satisfy all of its East African sponsors. Like their German predecessors, Amani's scientists would focus on problems of immediate concern to the estate sector, which produced coffee, sisal, tea, and cinchona. In response to intensifying global concerns over soil erosion, Amani's soil specialists would also break with tradition to survey shifting African cultivation practices and suggest ways to transform indigenous production (see chapter 5). Amani's plant pathologist would likewise keep busy by studying viral diseases of maize, sugar cane, cassava, groundnuts, tobacco, coconuts, and cotton.[93] To fund this ambitious plan, the Advisory Council called for increases from each of the beneficiary governments.

In the end, Amani could not be all things to all concerned so long as its budget was borne by the East African colonial governments, and, by 1939, Tanganyika Territory's director of agriculture could argue that "[it] is quite obvious that under severe financial stress, the Amani Station could be abolished without any visible effect to the social services accorded the agricultural producers of East Africa, or to immediate development. Conversely there is every need for a far-sighted policy of development to include means for fundamental research."[94] In 1940, the other East African directors of agriculture agreed; they deemed Amani unsuitable as a center for either long- or short-term research on agricultural problems and suggested the station be moved to Uganda.[95] The station did move in 1944, but the Colonial Office transferred Amani's staff and equipment to Kabete, near Nairobi and closer to Kenya's large population of settler farmers.[96] The move to Kenya did not remove Amani from historical reckoning, however. As I will demonstrate in subsequent chapters, conservationists from international organizations have developed around the old station grounds a renewed momentum toward biological research, but one now aimed at forest conservation.

Neither Amani nor Kwai fulfilled colonial expectations. Kwai's local history speaks to colonialism's violence both to individual families and to local rights in land. The Amani Institute's history demonstrates the contradictions inherent in colonialism's attempt to use biological science in the service of colonial development. Under the British Mandate especially, the East African agricultural directors sought solutions to agronomic problems, but wanted them immediately and without financial repercussions to their individual departments. Their public complaints about the institute ranged from its location to its agenda, but they all seemed to invoke, at least implicitly, a private resentment.[97] Amani's scientists, on the other hand, showed through their published research a broad range of interests not always tied directly to colonial imperatives. Their work covered topics as diverse as plant disease, climatic history, soil science, and ornithology, to name just a few. The eclecticism of this body of scientific work may well have worked against Amani's survival as an intellectual enclave tucked away in the East Usambara Mountains. On the ecological front, plant introductions at both Amani and Kwai have had unintended consequences. Eick and Illich designed their experiments with temperate-climate crops to help German settlers in the mountains. But while settler estates languished, African farmers adopted the potatoes, cabbages, carrots, peas, and beans and spread their agricultural landscape into new environments, where forests and pasture had formerly dominated. At Amani's botanical garden, many of the exotic plants brought there from other tropical climes have adapted themselves to the surrounding forests. These processes, though less obvious in the historical record, are evident today on Usambara's mountain landscapes.

CHAPTER FOUR

Seeking the Good Forest

WALKING IN THE PATCHES OF USAMBARA'S remaining natural forests continues to evoke the sense of a landscape alive with primates, birds, butterflies, frogs, toads, and flowers, all sheltered beneath the towering canopies of light-barked trees. Some forest islands stand intact, but, around their edges, colonists carve out sections for new gardens in an ancient pattern of piecemeal forest exploitation. Lines of women walk the forest border pathways carrying massive head loads of firewood, replaying labor patterns established in the distant past. Like their ancestors, Usambara's cultivators use what the forest offers because it still serves their survival. While conservation and development organizations tend to vilify these indigenous cultivators for destroying forest, they often fail to recognize that, in addition to indigenous population growth, a century of failed forestry policy has also placed immense pressure on the mountains' natural resources. Under circumstances where indigenous peoples struggle for access to a diminishing land base, they respond ambivalently to forest conservation, regardless of the lofty ideals of the international development projects based in cities like Tanga and Lushoto.

Fig. 4.1. Forest boundary near Mkuzi in West Usambara. Photo Sabine Barcatta

The tension over land use has set up a potentially powerful conflict between local farmers and those in the scientific community who attach immense value to the biodiversity of remaining Eastern Arc Mountain forests. To conservation-minded biologists, forest ecological communities, which have behind them millions of years of natural history, face a grave threat. And, in fact, seen on the time scale of forest evolution, human history's brief instant has significantly altered mountain forest ecology. In order to save what remains, an international cadre of forest preservationists, supported by a growing body of scientific research, has taken up the cause of the Eastern Arc Mountains. Recent biological research has enhanced our knowledge of natural history and ecology in what appear to be undisturbed forest landscapes, but we know little of the human history of these places or what took place on now deforested lands where tea and small-scale agriculture currently predominate. This chapter seeks to unravel the story of how Usambara's forests have changed over the recent term, while it traces the underlying cultural and ideological processes.

African Forest History

In large part, East Africa's forest history is a story of exploitation. As chapter 2 argued, agriculture and pastoralism in the Eastern Arc Mountains evolved over millennia inside, or in close proximity to, a forest. Much of human history in these mountains, therefore, involves the transformation of exceptionally complex and productive biological landscapes into simpler forms that more readily support a human economy. Unfortunately, our understanding of the rate and character of the changes in mountain forest ecology, and of the cultural elements that accompanied them, remains sketchy. This ignorance has often coalesced into simplistic portrayals of indigenous peoples as forest destroyers or as living on the land in ecological harmony. Yet, the historical evidence argues for dynamism between human societies and the forest, where periods of exploitation, deforestation, and regeneration operated in different combinations to produce numerous and often unpredictable scenarios of landscape change.

Recent scholarship in geography and social anthropology has examined the prevailing Western orthodoxies regarding African land-use systems in and around forest landscapes. The research suggests that the dominant paradigm finds a powerful correlation among deforestation, soil erosion, overgrazing, and desertification, all of which stem from African land use. In their introduction to a collection of essays called *The Lie of the Land* (1996), editors Melissa Leach and Robin Mearns argue that the tradition of scientific investigation that created this model of ecological change spread through African colonial agencies as an unquestioned "received wisdom." They claim therefore that erroneous, or at least simplistic, ideas ultimately form the foundations of resource conservation policy. These theoretical lines are further pursued in James Fairhead and Melissa Leach's *Misreading the Landscape* (1996), a book-length investigation of agricultural practice in Guinea's ecological transition zone where forest meets savanna. Using a variety of evidence, including aerial and satellite photos, along with a careful on-the-ground assessment of local land-use practices, the authors demonstrate that, contrary to the prevailing historical interpretations of deforestation and degradation built around received wisdom, local practice had actually fostered an increase in forest cover.[1]

The study suggests some important questions for African forest history in other contexts. For example, does *Misreading the Landscape* portray a unique situation of afforestation or a broader pattern in African land-use systems? The Eastern Arc Mountains certainly show differentials in the comparative area, biological makeup, and condition of their remaining natural forest. The East Usambaras, for example, retain as a percentage of total area of remaining natural forest a larger proportion of biologically diverse forest than any of the neighboring Eastern Arc Mountains.[2] The spatial disparities alone argue against any sort of simplistic reading of the relationship between changes in forest cover and local land-use history.

Leach and Fairhead's presentation of colonial forestry science also raises questions about how investigators understand forest history. Their study questions implicitly the analytical utility of colonial depictions of human-environmental relationships. As they clearly argue, scientific explanation and policy pronouncements authored under colonial regimes fit into an ideological context that generally devalued African land-use practice. A similar generalized view emerges from the annual forestry reports for Tanganyika Territory. The local-level forestry files nonetheless reveal a great deal about the forest's changing ecology, as well as the sharp conflicts that developed among colonial foresters, indigenous land users, and the local district administration. In the Usambara cases, where foresters saw African "encroachment" and "violations" in the forest reserve, district officers tended at times to sympathize with African claims over forest landscapes. At the same time, local Forest Department officials criticized the destructive practices of timber concessions, much to the chagrin of their superiors desperate for timber royalties. The archival record, when read across these bureaucratic levels and in conjunction with the published accounts on forest ecology, reveals layers of tension that express themselves in many of the ecological changes now evident on the landscape. That said, documentary evidence for forest history explains little about the ideological and cultural transformation that accompanied landscape change. As colonial governments restricted forest access and pushed African agricultural economies in new directions, indigenous practice in forests and indigenous ideas about forest changed in response. *Misreading the Landscape* introduces copious oral evidence for the historical continuity and change in cultural understanding and use of forest resources, as do other recent studies of Africa's forest history. Similarly, in the Eastern Arc case, indigenous people have much to say on the topic. Their stories, both at the symbolic level and as testimony to specific events, enrich the record and help to unravel the story of ecological change.

New Ideologies of Forest Use and Changes in Forest Ecology: The West Usambara Mountains

As chapter 2 demonstrates, although human settlement of Eastern Arc forests looks to be relatively recent, the environmental effects have been large.[3] The shifting horticultural practice that sustained areas of dense settlement like Mlola, Mlalo, Vuga, and Bumbuli altered forests in significant ways, both in the immediate vicinity of the settlements and in the village hinterlands. In more lightly settled areas characterized by periodic migration into and out of the mountains, forest conditions must have also changed continually. The nineteenth-century forest colonization of the Lwengera Valley, which splits the East and West Usambara massifs, is just one example. Demographic change and agricultural practice thus shaped forest regeneration on a variety of scales where populations remained mobile. In more densely settled areas, intensive farming, wood gathering, and ironworking began to arrest forest regeneration.

Johannes Buchwald's 1896 descriptions of West Usambara argue for a great deal of spatial and biological difference in vegetation cover. He found, for example, a bracken of ferns covering the completely abandoned and deforested farmlands on the countryside depopulated by war, while on the massif's southeastern side at elevations from 1,100 to 1,400 meters he discovered thick forests, or Urwald, in abundance. Buchwald, and the biologists who followed him, noted the strong correlation of forest type to altitude, rainfall patterns, and location. Within the range of forest types, Buchwald reserved his most copious praise for the beauty of the mix of forest and pastureland high in the central plateau, which he claimed resembled Switzerland. He called this place the "high mountain forest and pastureland." Here, Buchwald describes the tree formations as "flower-forest": big, round groups of trees interspersed with turf. The groves resembled "flower bouquets strewn on a green carpet." Nowhere, he claims, had he seen such beauty in abundance. Above 1,700 meters elevation, the small forest patches gave way to much larger stands, dominated in turn by Usambara camphor (*Ocotea usambarensis*) of 40 meters height and with trunk diameters of 1 to 2 meters and by the evergreen of Podocarpus and cedar (*Podocarpus spp.* and *Juniperus procera*), both at heights reaching 30 to 40 meters.[4] The parklands and the high-elevation natural forests he described formed the environmental context for the incursion of European-style forestry and the bitter contest over forest resources in West Usambara.

Chapter 3 describes part of the German forest conquest linked to coffee cultivation in the lush forests of East and West Usambara. By 1899, estate owners had planted 6.5 million coffee trees in the Usambaras.[5] The estates were huge, some containing tens of thousands of hectares, but the coffee fields had to be carved out of heavy forest, so that by 1906 the cleared area on East Usambara amounted to only 2,035 hectares. On the West Usambara estates, German landlords and plantation companies had likewise employed imported labor to clear and plant coffee on 100- to 200-hectare pieces of land.[6] Coffee thus claimed, piecemeal, thousands of hectares of forestlands. Unlike the ecologically diverse plant and animal communities they replaced, the coffee stands proved vulnerable and quickly succumbed to wind, root fungus, and coffee borers.

The disaster proved so complete that the Berlin Botanical Museum chief, Adolf Engler, advised against further coffee cultivation in rain forest clearings.[7] The wasted effort may have angered colonial settlers, but it absolutely alarmed the forestry service, which saw forest protection as an important part of its mission to set up its own brand of plantation commodity production.[8] Felling and burning relatively large acreages of closed canopy forest, a dramatic ecological event in itself, ultimately destroyed the land's agricultural potential. Where indigenous agricultural practice allowed for the quick reestablishment of biomass on their clearings, coffee plantations, through tillage, kept the soils clear of any plant growth. As a result, a greatly impoverished biological mosaic replaced the old.[9]

Colonial Forestry in West Usambara:
Changing Forests and Forest People

German forestry brought a new ideology of forest value to the Usambaras. It differed from the crass hit-and-miss exploitation of the colonial plantation companies in that forestry incorporated a long-term vision of land use that served a variety of purposes, including resource conservation. In the end, their environmental purpose was the same: the German and, subsequently, British forest departments sought to exercise absolute power over forest trees, soils, and anybody who used these resources. In its determination of resource value, colonial forestry's ideology placed no value on forests' natural biological diversity. Rather, it sought consciously to impose a biological order that would result in efficient, sustainable timber production. The ideology, furthermore, left no room for indigenous knowledge of forest resources or the biological study of the forest for the historical knowledge it could provide about evolution and ecological change.

At the same time, biologists oriented toward theoretical research began to recognize Usambara's forests' importance to the study of ecology and evolution as soon as they set foot in them during the last decade of the nineteenth century. That vision, largely separate from the interests of the colonial forestry industry, is today exceptionally powerful. At the time, however, the more powerful paradigm belonged to the strongly utilitarian forestry science, which recognized the forest's biological riot as an obstacle to the goal of order.

> In the mountain forests there is a hodgepodge of tree types. These are usually found in single stands; only a few are found in groups or in a larger area: the African cedar (*Juniperus procera*) as well as the two other conifers *Podocarpus milanjanus* and *usambarensis*. Of the deciduous trees there are Mkulo, the wild camphor (*Ocotea usambarensis*), as well as Mnyassa (*Piptadenia buchananii*), Takula (*Ochna holstii*), and many others. Also, the age of the trees and tree groups varies constantly: here you'll see smaller bushes in a smaller area, overgrown with vines; there you'll see singular, medium-sized poles and weaker trunks that have just barely emerged; and there you'll see strong trunks useful for wood production.
>
> If one considers the difficulty of terrain . . . in which man's force cannot always be replaced by draught animals, its large distance from the presently existing railway, the mess of arm-thick, wooded vines . . . the practically impenetrable underbrush through which one would have to cut a path to every single trunk, then one will understand that the demands of our wood importers—to send stem cuttings of certain minimal measurements of the best quality, and of the largest volume—cannot presently be met.[10]

To German foresters, this vexing and chaotic forest, created by the partnership of natural and human history, simply could not lend itself to efficient and profitable exploitation without a massive makeover.

The German colonial government dutifully legitimated the forestry service's philosophy by legalizing its suzerainty over all unused or unoccupied lands deemed suitable for use.[11] With large estates in control of much of East Usambara's forest wealth, as well as many of the well-watered and forested sections of southeastern West Usambara, German East Africa's Forest Department settled for 54,371 hectares of the West Usambara plateau. The forest reserves ostensibly alienated the Shume and Magamba grazing areas of Mbuguland that had been abandoned during the last decade of the nineteenth century.[12] Wambugu returning to reclaim this rangeland met the colonial government surveyors' delineation of Usambara's forest boundary. They found, moreover, that under German colonial law their settlement patterns and economy did not constitute a legal use. The new forest ordinances eliminated their carefully negotiated usufruct rights and they faced eviction from most of Shume and Magamba.[13] The Wambugu retained land rights only in what the forest survey designated as lands that showed continual use over time by settled populations. The Forest Department referred to these as "free settlements." Although German *de jure* restrictions theoretically constrained Mbugu grazing practices, effective control of the forest settlements and those on the forest borders proved difficult. All the same, the German colonial government established a legal superstructure that would extend largely intact into the British colonial period, and ultimately kill the Mbugu pastoral economy and the forested landscape they had created.

With its rights over forest land established on paper, forestry had now to serve German colonial interests by efficiently exploiting the holdings. Policy and silvicultural science aimed therefore to improve timber production by carefully regularizing it. By the turn of the twentieth century, forestry science had been developing in Germany for over a century. Its scientific tradition was grounded in quantitative methods that aimed to create a forest filled with standard trees that yielded a sustained and predictable amount of timber. The process transformed a forest into an economic entity.[14] In West Usambara, German forestry therefore set out to introduce suitable exotics as silvicultural experimentation determined the most profitable botanical composition of the new forest. As early as 1900, foresters began to "improve" the forest through the introduction of Japanese camphor, a tree they hoped would replace what they saw as a defective indigenous hardwood (*Ocotea usambarensis*).[15]

The successful application of silviculture required that timber concessions completely harvest the forest adapted through evolution because it blocked efficient timber production. The transformation began when the forest service granted 3,000 acres to Wilkins and Wiese Co., which constructed a sawmill at Shume. While close to the trees, the Shume concession lay perched along the isolated western edge of the central plateau, thousands of feet above the railhead below in the Pangani Valley. The colonial government proved its confidence in forestry science and its commitment to timber profits when it subsidized the concession by building a cableway that ran between the western escarpment edge and the plains 1,400 meters below.

Despite the big plans for forest exploitation and regeneration under a scientific rationale, German efforts lasted just over a decade, hardly enough time for a landscape makeover. The colonial power vacuum during the war years allowed Mbugu herders a respite from harassment, but the German colonial state had erected new types of legal boundaries around settler farms and forest reserves that would persist under their British successors. Moreover, German silviculture and logging had begun a process of biological change that under British control would almost completely undermine forest health in West Usambara.

After World War I, when the British Colonial Office reorganized German East Africa as the Tanganyika Territory, it created a Forest Department that mirrored its German predecessor in policy and in action. British foresters advocated the same sort of ecological transformation in the forest and chanted the German mantra of sustained yield as they tried to construct a colonial timber industry. Policy also dictated that the Forest Department protect forested watersheds in order to conserve the permanent flow of rivers and streams. In their conservation function on steep terrain, indigenous forests found a limited place in the new landscape configuration. Indigenous people also fit into the Forest Department's plans as a labor force whose sole purpose was to serve timber concessions. In keeping with its plans, Tanganyika's Forest Department evicted African herders and farmers, who both resisted this imposition and struggled to create new and workable ecological relationships around the forest edges.

The Tanganyika Territory Forest Department saw the West Usambaras as so integral to its future operations that it built the headquarters for the entire territory at Lushoto. Anxious to evaluate the estate, rangers began a lengthy survey of the old German boundary line. As the foresters carried out their survey, they found a number of newly established settlements inside the forest reserve and on some former German estates abandoned during the war. In 1921 and 1922, A. S. Adamson, the Shume Station forester, found that most of the boundary markers had either been destroyed or rotted away, and he immediately set about recutting the boundary lines and giving notice to indigenous cultivators and herders to clear out.[16] Indeed, Adamson noted that the Wambugu around Mshangai, Ndabwa, Longoi, Rangwi, and Shume had successfully cleared large tracts for cultivation.[17] Adamson could not have recognized that the Wambugu had begun a transition to a mixed economy on what had been almost exclusively grazing territories. Their new emphasis on cultivation signaled Mbugu

Fig. 4.2. Eucalyptus. Foresters introduced this fast-growing species, which was used to mark forest boundaries and to produce fuelwood. Photo Sabine Barcatta

recognition that clearing, bounding, and planting crops on land implied secure usufruct rights. Although the strategy clearly reflected the spirit of colonial land law, it did not meet the 1921 Forest Ordinance requirement that claimants prove seven years' permanent residence.

In his classic handbook, *Colonial Forest Administration,* R. S. Troup, the head of Oxford's Imperial Forestry Institute, who had long experience in colonial forest administration, explained the government race for resources with indigenous peoples.

> Forest reservation is usually unpopular with the local inhabitants as it imposes restrictions which are seldom understood. The process of reservation is considerably easier where the land belongs to Government than where

> it belongs to native communities. . . . The difficulty of carrying it out varies directly with the density of the population and the demand for land. In sparsely populated tracts there is usually little difficulty in reserving forest to the extent considered necessary. Here timely reservation, before pressure on the land becomes acute, can be carried out with the minimum of hardship and friction, and at a much lower cost than after rights of user have been established. Where possible, therefore, reservation should proceed in advance of any immediate pressure on the land.[18]

His explanation shows a disturbing ignorance of the ways pastoralists and farmers apportion and use land in tropical forest zones. Usambara's pastoralists had negotiated and allocated grazing rights in Usambara's high country based on social alliances, ecological conditions, and climatic change. Their strategies relieved potential pressure on resources in the forest. In this sense, they had established rights not through dividing and populating the forest, but by using it to reproduce their pastoral economy and culture. In this light, "friction" became the inevitable result of forest policy, even in a "sparsely populated tract." In addition to directly violating the established rights of Mbugu herders, colonial forest policy intended to convert them into a reliable pool of landless laborers whose toil served a forest industry that purposefully destroyed the mountain grazing ecology.

Largely ignorant of the potential for future conflict along the forest boundary, the Forest Department, armed with the power of its ordinance, began in 1923 to issue leases to concessionary companies for commercial exploitation.[19] D. K. S. Grant, Tanganyika's first conservator of forests, sounded very much like his German predecessors when he argued in 1921 that "[i]t is a matter of urgency to commence exploitation of the Territories' [sic] forests, which as in the case of all virgin forests, contain excessive quantities of mature and over mature trees. These not only represent idle capital but are a deteriorating effect and are preventing by their presence establishment of new vigorous crops."[20] The forests needed to be cleared and replanted to meet the growing needs of Tanganyika's railways and the expanding colonial edifice.[21]

In 1924, the Tanganyika Forests and Lumber Company (hereafter TFLC), which held a government-subsidized timber concession of 27,945 hectares, reopened the old German mill at Shume. The concession's very generous terms allowed the TFLC to operate for one hundred years, instead of the usual twenty. In spite of favorable long-term contractual arrangements, labor shortages immediately threatened the concession's viability. The Forest Department accordingly introduced a "squatter system," based on the labor arrangements developed in colonial India, whereby the Forest Department kept laborers in the forest without bestowing upon them any rights in land ownership.[22] In the system's East African incarnation, forest labor, or "squatters," could cultivate crops temporarily on clearcuts where tree farms would ultimately grow. The laborers tended the tree seedlings that grew among their crops for three or four years, at which point they moved on to other newly felled areas. In return for their labor, "squatters" received rights to a modest wage and the right to grow their own food in the driest and coldest area of West Usambara, an area historically shunned by agriculturalists. Moreover, the incentives carried no tax exemptions.[23] Not surprisingly, the Forest Department continually failed to capture a sufficient labor force.[24]

Forestry's labor arrangement attracted only the most impoverished, that is, those who lacked disposable wealth in either livestock or land. For those unlucky enough to serve the timber industry, life was difficult. Shume's relatively dry and cold rain-shadow climate precipitated a series of crop failures, driving squatter families to depend primarily on wages to meet subsistence needs.[25] Pastoralism still presented a viable alternative to squatter agriculture, but the forest administration placed severe restrictions on the number of animals laborers could keep in the forest reserve. Policy inextricably tied squatters' subsistence to their work for the concession and the Forest Department, and the Wambugu who still resided in the neighborhood tried to maintain their autonomy. They generally preferred to live on Public Land near the reserve boundary, bribe forest guards, and illegally send their animals into the government forest.[26]

While labor shortages plagued TFLC throughout the 1920s and 1930s, the Wambugu continued to establish pastures and gardens surreptitiously inside the forest reserve, battling the Forest Department for access to the forest's wealth.[27] Foresters attempted to crack down regarding the growing number of livestock in the forest, but continued grazing violations led the Forest Department in 1935 to issue Government Notice 103, which prohibited all grazing in forest reserves.[28]

With their legal relegation to Public Land on the forest margins, the Wambugu accelerated the shift in their means of subsistence, out of pastoralism and into arable agriculture, that had begun during the dire years of the late nineteenth century. The diminution of grazing area required that they convert into gardens the pastures and forest remaining on Public Land. Throughout this economic and ecological transformation, the forest reserve boundaries became points of sharp conflict. One well-known dispute at Nzerengembe (in the central plateau region) highlights both the shift in Mbugu land use and the ideological and philosophical gulf between Mbugu and colonial notions of forest value.[29]

In an August 1935 memo, a forest guard noted a festering four-year dispute over sixty acres claimed by both Wambugu residents and the colonial forest service.[30] Forestry officials claimed that land use on the patchwork of pasture and both primary and secondary forest found at the site was inimical to the interests of forest protection.[31] Further, they argued that the Wambugu, as "excellent exponents of shifting cultivation," could be accommodated on adjacent Public Lands, in this way eliminating the pressure on the forest boundary zone.[32] The local district officer disagreed with compulsory evacuation, arguing that shifting cultivators would *naturally* leave the reserve when the long-fallow system required.[33] The assistant conservator of forests in West Usambara rejected the suggestion that indigenous peoples, no matter what their business, belonged within the forest boundaries.

> To condone continued residence until present houses and shambas shall become untenable would, in my opinion, incur unwarrantable delay, whilst it might later be taken as strengthening the native claims by virtue of their still longer establishment.... The forester has reported ample ground available on nearby Public Lands for the absorption of these families and I would therefore ask if you can please allow my proposals to be adopted, unopposed.[34]

The assistant conservator undiplomatically resolved the dispute with an eviction notice and the Nzeragembe residents quit the reserve after harvesting their crops (by the end of March 1936).

The Wambugu of Nzeragembe, and of other regions around the forest reserve, had specifically sought rights in land by abandoning their peripatetic pastoralism for a more sedentary life as farmers. The decision against their claims set a disturbing precedent since, under colonial law, Public Lands had to be permanently settled and cultivated. An agricultural landscape featuring a mix of pastures, forest, and fields simply invited further reservation by the Forest Department. According to the Forest Department's logic, the Wambugu simply had not gone far enough in clearing the land. In their zeal to police the forest reserve, forestry officials crushed any indigenous impetus toward forest conservation outside the reserve itself.

Ironically, West Usambara's forestry officials, so concerned with protecting the integrity of the reserve, failed to recognize the Mbugu predilection toward forest conservation inherent in their understanding of the forest as a sanctuary. "Also when I asked one man who had been the most forward in cutting into the Reserve why the huge stretch [of forest] toward Majiwa was left he told me that it was the chief's portion and was left untouched so that the people could have refuge during the Maasai invasion! It is a far cry to the Maasai invasion and I relate these stories to show with what facts they back up their claims to this part of the Reserve."[35]

That the Wambugu still feared a Maasai invasion seems highly unlikely given the fact that since the mid-1920s they had peacefully sold livestock and honey to them at the nearby Kwekanga livestock market.[36] However, the fact that the subchief, who controlled access to Public Land, refused to allocate a particular forested area for cultivation suggests that forest cover retained importance as a place where rituals and honey collection could continue. The Nzeragembe case demonstrates nonetheless that Mbugu land-use practices had changed dramatically since the turn of the century. In the same region where German explorers and colonial officials had found only pastoralists in the 1890s, the government forester saw in 1935 a patchwork of primary and secondary growth forests containing pastures and cultivated fields—not a herding landscape of forest and pasture, but an agricultural area, which, in his opinion, was largely underutilized.[37]

The transition to cultivation accelerated during the famine years of the late 1940s, when many Wambugu sold off their remaining animals in order to procure cash for food purposes.[38] Informants also note that mortality caused by an outbreak of East Coast Fever and rinderpest further reduced livestock numbers in 1952.[39] By 1960, most of the public lands on the central plateau, except for a few small pockets, had been deforested. Interestingly, one subchief at Mshangai, Kadala Mlimahadala, continued to conserve at least some pockets of forest.[40] "Zumbe Kadala Mlimahadala refused completely to allow the forest to be cut, especially on the mountains [around Mshangai, Kinko, Kireti, and Kwedege]. When he heard that TANU did not really care about the forest, he said better he die before independence, he would not like the new government, and sure enough he died in 1959, before *uhuru*."[41] Mlimahadala, like the elders a generation earlier at Nzeragembe, still attached importance to the forest, but his vision had become an anachronism.

In addition to Mbugu pastoralists, government foresters had to reckon with others keen to exploit the West Usambara forest reserve. The Forest Department fought an ongoing battle with farmers traveling into the reserve to collect firewood. Some communities did maintain plantations of black wattle, a species the Germans had introduced in Lushoto, but wattle never completely met fuel demands. Women from the Mlalo Basin, for example, regularly made the two- to three-hour climb onto the plateau lands at Lukozi and Mtumbi Mountain to cut firewood. Forest products also stimulated local business ventures. By the late 1940s, people from the Mlalo Basin were importing and selling illegally cut cedar from the forest reserve, which was highly prized for construction purposes.[42] While their quest for forest resources pulled people from farming regions into the forest, increasing land scarcities pushed them as well, sometimes with the support of the local colonial administration. In 1949, the Agriculture Department representative asked for and received permission to encourage people from the drought-stricken and ecologically damaged Mlalo Basin to cultivate the bottomland of the Lukozi Valley. By the 1950s, these now permanently settled and deforested nodes of expansion within the forest reserve were clearly visible from aerial surveys.[43]

While British foresters became increasingly frustrated with the indigenous invasion into the reserve, their African employees, the forest guards, helped deflect legal sanctions against encroachers. In a case involving the Mandara cedar forests in the Shume Reserve, the forester listed a number of men whom he intended to bring to the District Court, charged with cutting large areas of cedar in order to build homes and cultivate gardens of tobacco and maize. In order to undermine the forester's case, the forest guard simply took the men to the nearby Native Authority court, where the violators paid a few shillings "fine," then returned to their work. This action prevented the Shume forester from bringing the same charges against them in his own jurisdiction, where they would likely have received prison sentences.[44] Despite the fact that forestry officials had surveyed and marked a boundary around the forest reserve, indigenous people living near its borders continued their now long-standing and increasingly successful attack on boundary integrity.

Another continuing headache for the Forest Department involved its own creation, the "squatter" labor force. Rather than forming a pliant workforce, the "squatter" population had gained a measure of autonomy from timber concessions. The workers divided their time between legal forest labor and smuggling livestock into and out of the reserve.[45] Agricultural market conditions also helped secure a measure of independence during the early 1950s when a number of forest laborers began to grow tobacco in response to favorable prices. Their earnings freed them, at least temporarily, from the dangerous work in the sawmills.[46] As he saw his workforce rapidly diminish between August and December 1950, the Shagai sawmill's manager mistook labor's stab at financial independence for laziness: "No reasonable person will begrudge them their temporary affluence but it becomes a real tragedy when such permits so high a proportion of able bodied males to live a life of indolence for several months. Again, it is pathetic that the raising of such crops [tobacco] should be permitted at the expense of food crops in a district where the cry of hunger is so frequently heard."[47] To the sawmill manager, trees constituted the forest's only legitimate cash crop.

In the early 1950s, the "squatters" began to seek permission to build permanent villages where they could cultivate without hindrance.[48] In 1954, their petitioning paid off when the forest administration excised 1,160.5 acres of the forest reserve and redesignated it Public Lands, and then purchased another 977.5 acres from the defunct TFLC's now abandoned freehold land, in order to build "ideal settlements" specifically for forest squatters.[49] These concessions tacitly recognized the Forest Department's failed labor policy while validating "squatter" strategy designed to gain permanent access to the forest.[50] In fact, "squatters" and their allies in reserve continued to move survey beacons, to clear garden plots in the Shume-Magamba Reserve, and to cultivate them as if they were on Public Land, sparking even more boundary disputes throughout the 1950s and early 1960s.[51]

While the Forest Department tried to fend off the assault on its legal rights to control its estate, it sanctioned an attack from within on forest ecology. The biological devastation came from concessions like TFLC, whose failure caused the Forest Department to revoke its agreement, and Grewal and Co., a South Africa–based firm that from 1944 held a timber concession for the Shume-Magamba and Shagai forest reserves.[52] When Lushoto's district forester inspected parts of the Grewal concession in 1950, he found the forest "completely devastated in places."[53] The Forest Department suspected that Grewal and Co., nearing the end of its lease, simply cut as much marketable timber as possible. In response to Grewal's wanton degradation, the chief conservator placed maximum milling quotas on the concession (100,000 cubic feet over six months). "I think we should impose a ceiling on the cut. We intend to apply sustained yield working to this forest and the sooner we do so the better; a maximum cut is a step towards this and it also brings home to millers that the old days of laissez faire are numbered. We also do not want another 'Kagera' in the shape of a very heavy cut just at the end of the life of a concession and masses of felled logs all over the forest."[54]

Grewal agreed, then immediately broke the contract by cutting over the maximum.[55] Overcutting throughout the reserve continued until March 1955, when the provincial forestry officer ordered Grewal to cease all felling operations in their concession at Viti.[56] Even in the face of restrictions, and with full knowledge of the Forest Department's prerogatives to restrict overexploitation of indigenous forest, Grewal requested permission to strip its concession areas of *Podocarpus spp.*, as they had with other species of indigenous hardwoods.[57] Grewal reasoned that Podocarpus's elimination from the forest would drive up the price of the remaining camphor. Even better, in the concessionaire's eyes, the road infrastructure built to exploit Podocarpus would facilitate their felling of the remaining and relatively valuable camphor. The Lushoto forester resisted on the grounds that the removal of Podocarpus, which grew in association with camphor (*Ocotea usambarensis*), would seriously hinder the latter's natural regeneration and therefore any future exploitation of West Usambara's most valuable timber.[58]

While the Forest Department tried to rein in Grewal and Co., it issued permits for timber exploitation on private land. Reports of felling practices at Sakarre and Balangai estates in West Usambara reveal more officially sanctioned damage. At Sakarre:

> [The] mill is in a disgusting state and without doubt the worst I have yet seen. Logging in hands of an African, who is working along one valley. Many of the trees that have been felled cannot be moved, the devastation of the understorey is considerable. The area of untouched forest is in first class condition, but is due to be devastated next year. Logging carried out by a Caterpillar D.7 that is being handled extremely badly and making a terrible mess of the forest floor. If the mill was in forest reserve it would be closed down without further notice.[59]

The forester found similarly destructive felling operations at the nearby Balangai estate.[60] These operations, furthermore, fueled a black market in

Fig. 4.3. Pit-sawing platform at Magamba in West Usambara. Photo Christopher Conte

timber, as many of the logs taken from private lands found their way illegally to Tanga for resale across East Africa.

Dramatic increases in timber demands across East Africa during the late 1950s undermined ecological concerns in favor of market dictates. In addition to Grewal, whose poor logging practices do not seem to have hindered its ability to receive licenses to log Usambara's indigenous timbers, and the questionable practices on private estates, the Forest Department issued more felling licenses to groups of African loggers from Kenya, known locally as the "Kisii" pit sawers.[61] Pit sawing had gone on in the forests of West Usambara and Upare for years, because Native Authority chiefs had the power to issue felling licenses to carpenters to fell one tree at a time. In 1950, the chief forester for the Tanga Forest Division remarked sarcastically, "It's amazing how many carpenters there are." He also had reason to believe that most of the timber was smuggled to Tanga for resale. He found the practice objectionable first because the Forest Department could not control it and second because of the waste left behind in the forest.[62]

Despite the objections, the Forest Department sanctioned pit sawing in West Usambara's camphor forests at Baga, Mkusu, Bumbuli, Shagai, and Magamba. The Kenyans, many merely teenagers, were highly mobile and expert at their craft. Their logging technique required no infrastructure or milling facilities. Carrying their equipment, they simply walked into selected areas, felled the best specimens, and, using platforms built into a hillside, sawed them into rough boards in the felling coupe. They then carried the boards as head loads to the main roads for transport to the large towns. By the early 1960s, they were producing over twenty thousand cubic feet of cut timber per month, which is comparable to what Grewal produced a few years earlier.[63] At the same time that the Agriculture Department officers excoriated Usambara's farmers for destructive land-use practices, their counterparts in forestry facilitated the overexploitation of indigenous forest resources on the central plateau and on estate lands. Although the Forest Department's plan called for "sustained yield," the state sanctioned and supervised timber concessions that showed no inclination toward sustainability.[64] Rather, they devoured the forest wherever possible.

In 1951, Tanganyika's conservator of forests recognized the Forest Department's role in the rapacity, but absolved it, explaining:

> There is no doubt in my mind that Tanganyika is overcutting her forest resources. I have no doubt either why this position has arisen. Past Conservators, unable to claim the ear of the Government because the Department was small and insignificant, and because it was not producing revenue at a time when the production of revenue was vitally necessary to the Territory, took the only possible line. They concentrated on exploitation, to the exclusion of much else that was vital and basic, knowing that until they were producing money, they would get no money, and arguing that, if harm was being caused to the forests by such action, this harm could probably be remedied once Government had become forest conscious.[65]

The pressures on West Usambara's Forest Reserve had reached the breaking point by the end of the colonial era. In consistently hardheaded fashion, the Forest Department pushed even harder during the 1950s to increase the size of its estate, a move that only further fueled indigenous resentment.[66] Colonial forest policy in the West Usambaras continued simply to ignore indigenous interests. Perhaps more telling was the fact that the Forest Department had failed utterly to shape a landscape that fit its own view of the good forest, that is, one managed by the state to exist in perpetuity and at the same time to provide for the colony and empire's timber needs. This forest pleased no one.

Forest History in the East Usambaras: Moribund Estates and Healthy Forests

Like their counterparts in the west, East Usambara's forests played a key role in the historical development of African husbandry systems. However, in the near term, East Usambara's forest history also diverged, and historical circumstance helped to preserve the forests that today have garnered international scientific attention.

With the ecological damage of the German experiment in coffee production evident in pockets of the huge estates, land owners under the British administration backed away from any bold initiatives in extensive agriculture while Amani scientists worked to find a solution to the fertility problems posed by forest soils. The Forest Department obviously recognized the protective value of East Usambara's woodland to the rivers that rose in the mountains, but until the late 1950s they did little to bring these forests under their administrative purview. Their inaction can be explained in part by their limited jurisdiction over forest on private lands. On the Public Lands, the Forest Department could and did grant timber concessions for the valuable mahogany in East Usambara's foothills, areas used by African cultivators. Had East Usambara's mountain forests contained the marketable timbers of camphor, cedar, and Podocarpus that occurred in West Usambara, they might well have been logged just as heavily.[67]

The forest-based farming and industrial complex that had evolved among African cultivators in East Africa's highlands had certainly influenced East Usambara's forests. However, mountain land use followed particular spatial patterns peculiar to each massif, favoring some environments to the exclusion of others, a fact reflected in the Eastern Arc Mountains' biogeography. A fire regime was clearly integral to African farming, a fact reflected in the historical geography of settlement. Nineteenth-century farmers in East Usambara favored the foothills and the relatively dry western edges of the mountains overlooking the Lwengera Valley. J. P. Farler, an Anglican missionary, described East Usambara villages and their environs in ways comparable to those of the West Usambaras, a landscape mosaic of grasslands, forest groves, and banana plantations.[68] It comes as no surprise, then, that Mbugu pastoralists formed part of East Usambara's nineteenth-century population. Their skills in fashioning pasture in dry forest likely helped form the broad band of grassland, interspersed with forest remnants, that still lined the top of East Usambara's western escarpments in the 1950s.[69] In spite of the similarities in husbandry systems, East

Usambara's close proximity to the coast and its consequently heavier annual rainfall limited the extent to which farmers and herders could create this type of derived landscape, so reminiscent of Taita, Upare, and West Usambara. The Humid Closed Evergreen forest communities facing south and southeast, where cooler temperatures and higher rainfall limited fire's usefulness, appear therefore to have been more readily avoided than exploited.[70]

The nineteenth-century geography, however, represented only the most recent in a series of land-use patterns. The more distant past emerges from archaeological excavations of four Early Iron Age (EIA) sites at the base of the hills to the west of the Mtai Forest Reserve, and in botanical investigations at other industrial sites at higher altitudes in what today is a forest reserve. The preliminary data place pottery and charcoal remains in heavy forest across the elevation gradient. Clearly, then, a farming and industrial complex functioned in and ultimately abandoned what nineteenth-century European observers described as Urwald.[71]

How did the African farmers influence the forests' structure? The modern forest's botany provides at least a clue in the anomalous distribution of Usambara camphor (*Ocotea usambarensis*) in the lower elevations of submontane forest. This same species occurs in abundance in the West Usambaras, where it thrives in high elevation and regenerates naturally in forest openings caused by tree falls. In the generally lower East Usambaras, camphor is rare, occurring only in isolated stands on the highest outcrops and in groves on the *upper* slopes of the submontane forest. Unlike these higher stands, the submontane camphor is not regenerating out in the heavily shaded forest stands. One theory suggests that these dying camphor communities cover former garden sites, where cultivation could have created the requisite open conditions that allow the camphor to sprout.[72] The camphor anomaly and the archaeological remains of Iron Age forest life in the closed high evergreen forests suggest a much more complex and dynamic history of human-induced ecological change than is apparent from the current land use and settlement geography.

Farming activity also had shaped the lowland forest communities in ways that ultimately favored their exploitation under British colonial rule. In the late nineteenth and early twentieth centuries, forest groves dotted a largely agricultural landscape surrounding the Eastern Arcs. The groves contained what the Forest Department subsequently recognized as valuable stands of East African mahogany (*Chlorophora excelsa;* Swahili, *Mvule*). The swidden farming system fostered this forest pattern because, as they cleared land for cultivation, farmers simply avoided the larger and harder-to-remove mahogany trees, which then regenerated from root suckers in abandoned gardens.[73] As early as the 1920s, mills in the Sigi Valley cut mahogany for sale across East Africa. Once the timber's market value increased in 1938, the Forest Department negotiated a concession to harvest the trees, while it moved to limit the access of African farmers whose practices had created the stands in the first place.[74] When criticisms arose over the Forest Department's subsidy of lowland forest removal on Public Land, the conservator turned, in his defense, to the 1921 Forest Ordinance, which clearly stated that Africans who occupied Public Lands had no rights over the trees on them.[75] "[On Public Land] the right is one of user only and property in the land remains vested in the Governor. As regards forest produce, the native's right is limited to the amount which he requires for domestic purposes and the state is entitled to protect valuable timber against destruction even though the timber stands on lands in lawful occupation of natives."[76] The conservator continued with a quote from Governor Cameron: "The natives have no more inherent property in the forest than they have in the land, and, besides, must always be protected against themselves."[77] Under these circumstances, African farmers who had mahogany on their lands had little incentive to do anything other than cut and sell it before the concession moved in.

Higher in the mountains, the economic malaise that had begun under German colonialism continued into the British administration and granted to the forests a respite from exploitation that lasted into the 1950s. In contrast to the West Usambaras, where the Forest Department actively promoted the forests' ecological transformation through logging and silviculture, officials regularly expressed concern over East Usambara's forest conservation in regard to maintaining an efficient watershed. Water issues notwithstanding, the main impediment to exploitation lay in East Usambara's land ownership structure, where private interests restricted the colonial government and African farmers from claiming tenure rights over forest tracts.

After claiming most of East Usambara's mountain forests, the German state had conferred upon East Usambara's African population very limited usufruct rights by providing four hectares per family on "reserves" bordering the estates.[78] The British state decided to honor this arrangement, even though German coffee producers had exploited only a very small percentage of their holdings and had failed miserably in their efforts at profitable farming. During the colonial power vacuum between 1916 and the early 1920s, some African cultivators left their "reserves" for abandoned estate land in a scenario reminiscent of the West Usambaras. However, once estate ownership was reestablished under the British Mandate, African communities found themselves once again subject to removal from the forest.

Between the wars, estate owners continued a decades-long trend and failed to establish any sort of profitable agriculture, although not for lack of state support. The scientists from the East African Agricultural Research Station at Amani conducted a number of experiments at Kwamkoro, an estate of 3,059 hectares purchased by the state in 1931 for the express purpose of supporting East Usambara's estate agriculture.[79] Researchers experimented with cinchona (for quinine production), tung, robusta coffee, and derris. Of these, cinchona showed some promise, but quinine's replacement with synthetic chemical drugs eventually doomed its prospects.[80] As the slump in estate agriculture wore on, East Usambara's forests thrived.[81]

Tea altered the status quo. As early as 1898, Otto Warburg had suggested that tea might supplement fungus-ridden coffee crops in East Usambara.[82] However, tea never achieved popularity during German times, and only a few Usambara estates continued to experiment with it during the 1920s and 1930s.[83] Despite the shrub's inauspicious beginnings, the Tanganyikan government felt that tea held possibilities, and it sought expert advice from Harold Mann, who submitted in 1933 his "Report on Tea Cultivation in the Tanganyika Territory and Its Development." Mann believed East Usambara's acidic soils to be eminently suitable for tea, but only under certain ecological conditions. First, because the old coffee clearings were moribund, tea, according to Mann, would have to be planted on "virgin forest soils." Second, he believed that tea in the Usambaras required sloped land, which would require erosion mitigation measures such as contour drains and hedged contour embankments. Third, tea planters would need at their service a large labor pool.[84] Mann's report confirmed what estate owners already knew, that successful tea production meant large capital outlays to clear and terrace heavily forested land and the importation of large numbers of immigrant workers into the East Usambara Mountains. The Great Depression stifled such a capital-intensive endeavor.

Tea held promise for better economic times, but in the interim, the government continued to look for other ways to exploit the highlands. In 1939, members of the Agriculture and Forest Departments undertook a survey of the East Usambaras in order to study the feasibility of purchasing part of the 25,949 hectares that the estates held in order to make them available to Jewish immigrants.[85] The survey report argued that under no circumstances would such an endeavor succeed. The authors first pointed out that coffee's failure proved the infeasibility of extensive agriculture. Second, intensive agriculture on the proposed two-hundred-acre farms would not be viable without annual manure applications of three to four tons per acre, which would require fifty stall-fed animals to produce it. They questioned the viability of the available cash crops, explaining that experiments at the Kwamkoro plantation demonstrated that only tung and cinchona grew well and that both exposed the soil to erosion, a grave concern in British Africa during the 1930s. The survey also argued strenuously that smallholder farming would damage the forests' protective function.

> [T]he likelihood must be recognized that destruction of dense, several storied forest maintaining an upper canopy some 130–150 feet above the ground and replacement by quinine and tung oil will affect adversely the conservation of rainfall efficiency on which stream flow depends. Clearing of forest may be expected to induce early diminution of soil fertility through exposure of the surface layers and also, if on a sufficient scale, to cause an increase in temperature with resultant decrease in rainfall and increase in evaporation.[86]

In sum, the survey shows a decided bent among the district authorities and the Agriculture and Forest Departments' local officers toward conserving East Usambara's forests, at least until an ecologically viable economic solution presented itself.

Although the forests' ecological value is absent from these official discussions, the colonial scientific community began to see forest conservation as something intrinsically important.[87] For example, Clement Gillman, the Mandate's chief engineer, argued for forest protection in particularly strident terms. Gillman, a resident of Tanganyika since German times, had traveled extensively in both East and West Usambara. He repeatedly lamented the loss of tropical forest on both massifs, especially that caused by African swidden farming systems.[88] At the same time, he had little use for colonial progress. Development, to Gillman, was "waste by Raubwirtschaft [robbery economy]."[89] In 1935, he wrote with regret about Usambara's fading beauty:

> How impressive these great features stand out from all the infinity of detail. But man, in this landscape of raised plateau blocks, of gaping rifts, of wild erosion, has altered much; Redbrown villages wherever a flatter ridge affords a patch of even ground; the corn fields of the black sinners against forest and soil in great expanses on the steep slopes, with their furrows invariably against the contours; and finally the landmarks left by the White sinners, not only against forest and soil, but also against the word economics; down in the flats the derelict chess-boards of thousands of acres of rubber, the light green of the still expanding sisal estates; and up here the huge red scars, in the velvety green of the tea experimenter who, with his criminal and senseless deep drains right against the contours will wash the rich forest soil from several thousand acres down into the plains within a few years. And he is one of those who maintains that by their good example and contact they will improve Bantu standards of agriculture![90]

Gillman formalized his views in his 1940 "Water Consultant's Report, Number 6," in which he argued strongly for "the ruthless protection of our all too small remnants of mountain forests, both evergreen and deciduous."[91]

Geoffrey Milne, Amani's resident soil scientist and another of the early voices for forest conservation in the East Usambaras, made a very influential argument against any sort of cultivation in East Usambara. His oft-cited 1937 article, "Essays in Applied Pedology: 1. Soil Type and Soil Management in Relation to Plantation Agriculture in East Usambara," which appeared in the *East African Agricultural Journal*, treats the soils on twenty-five- to forty-five-year-old coffee clearings in East Usambara. To Milne, forest conservation was at once a practical matter and one borne of an almost mystical reverence for forest equilibrium. On a very pragmatic level, the soils simply could not support cultivation because of the processes that occurred once the forest had been cleared. His article explains, in its chemical complexity, laterization, one of the principal chemical features of Eastern Arc soils.[92] In lay terms, "we have an old soil whose mineral skeleton has long been undergoing the chemical decompositions that are known as laterization, and which is therefore greatly impoverished in plant nutrients. It possesses poor powers of retention of the chemical bases against the washing out action of percolating rainwater, and is acid at all depths."[93]

Milne's almost mundane description points out the wonderful paradox found in the efficient chemical function of the luxuriant forests found on these ancient and impoverished soils. "The trees depend for their maintenance on a nearly self contained circulation of plant nutrient elements via fallen leaves and branches and trunks, through the micro organic intermediaries of decomposition, the leaching waters, the feeding roots and the stems, and so to the leaves and branches again. Bases are held in the living substance of the forest which holds its own against the leaching process."[94] Milne felt that further cutting of East Usambara's forest was out of the question and that even crops established in the abandoned coffee clearings would require large inputs of fertilizer.

R. E. Moreau, Amani's secretary and librarian, published one of the most complete ecological descriptions of Usambara's forests in "A Synecological Study of Usambara," which appeared in the 1935 issue of the *Journal of Ecology*. Moreau's chief scientific interest lay with ornithology and the ecology of bird habitats. Far from amateurish, Moreau's ambitious work integrated the dynamism of physical geography and ecology as he attempted to explain long-term responses of forest communities to climatic and human-induced change. His descriptions bore the strong influence of Adolf Engler, who, like Moreau, marveled at Usambara's forest ecology. Moreau called the evergreen forests "magnificent" and, like Gillman, worried over the forests' decline in the face of the stated imperatives of colonial development. He described the lowland evergreen forest as having been swept away permanently under pressure from sisal and rubber plantations and African agricultural practices, while many highland forests, he felt, had been destroyed by coffee.[95]

Gillman, Milne, and Moreau may have failed to completely appreciate the antiquity and complexity of Usambara's forest history. Yet their work argued for the forest's place on East African highlands and, in particular, for its continued existence in the East Usambaras in its indigenous form. These men came from outside the Tanganyikan Agriculture and Forest Departments and their work very clearly questions the overarching bureaucratic ideology of land development driven by economic concerns. Their outsider status may also explain why their opinions held little power in the state's consideration of the questions raised by agricultural production in the East Usambaras after World War II.

The stalemate between conservation and development was broken as rising commodity prices helped tip the economic scales toward profitability on East Usambara's estates.[96] The new possibilities led several estate owners to begin large-scale exploitation of the timber on their land.[97] The resulting rapid clearing clearly worried the Forest Department, whose jurisdiction covered any deforestation by estate owners that threatened the Sigi catchment zone. The Muheza district administration also considered the rising number of African immigrants to be a threat. In 1953, the Muheza D.O. found living on the Ngambo estate a number of "alien natives" who provided labor for timber milling operations. These laborers had been given land on forested slopes of the estate, where they felled trees, cut them into boards on pit-sawing platforms, and then opened the land to maize cultivation. The D.O. also described extensive clear felling on the Ngua estate, near Amani.[98] The increasingly confrontational position of indigenous cultivators who sought rights to use Private Land also worried the administration, which determined to resolve African claims on the estates before they got out of hand and discouraged "certain reputable interests with capital to invest for development."[99]

In response to the rising competition for East Usambara's forest resources, the provincial commissioner met in May 1954 with a number of his officers to discuss the East Usambara Mountains and to set up the "Land Utilization Survey."[100] Although the survey team contained no one independent of the Tanganyikan government, the authors (F. D. Dowsett, D.C., Tanga; B. Gilchrist, provincial forest officer; and D. H. Drennan, provincial agricultural officer), to their credit, carried out a thorough investigation based upon the documentation they had. They drew heavily upon Milne, Mann, and Moreau in building a detailed description of East Usambara's geography. However, they argued against the essential conservationist positions of their predecessors and advocated the expansion of tea into still intact forest blocks. In the end, 35 percent of the tea estates were to remain forested, instead of the 50–60 percent advocated by Mann in 1933, or the 80 percent recommended by the 1939 smallholder reconnaissance.[101] The survey envisioned a checkerboard landscape with tea and forest groves interspersed, an arrangement that would theoretically maintain the humid climate that tea required, while protecting the Sigi catchments. As far as the African claims went, Dowsett et al. relied upon German records, themselves based on Baumann's cursory explorations, to examine indigenous settlement and land claims. In the end, they called for a buyout from estate owners of land blocks that could be used to settle African cultivators at ten acres per family, identical to the four hectares the Germans had promised.[102] The report could not suggest how the government would carry out or enforce forest reservation, because, under the new Forest Ordinance proposed for 1956, forest protection on private estates would end. Owners could then do as they pleased, a fact that concerned the Forest Department, which felt the estates would exercise little restraint in clearing all of their land when the opportunity arose.[103] East Usambara thus emerged from the colonial backwaters.

By the end of Tanganyika's colonial era, Usambara's forests faced threats on a number of fronts. Lumbering, both by timber concessions and by individuals who fed the black market, threatened the biological diversity that had evolved over the long term of natural history and under precolonial African uses. On the West Usambara plateau, large cypress and pine plantations eventually replaced the cutover sections in a process of dramatic ecological simplification. Some old-growth forest remained, both inside the Forest Reserve on the central plateau and on the old estates, but by the 1950s they were rapidly converting forest land to tea plantations. The East Usambaras, through serendipity, had retained a great deal of natural closed-canopy forest rich in biological diversity, but pressures for development that had appeared after World War II continued apace under Tanzania's independence government.

As the forest landscape changed, so, too, did indigenous ideas about its use. The Wambugu, who once valued the sacred groves that dotted their pastureland, abandoned forest conservation as the alienation of their range forced them to shift almost exclusively into agriculture for their subsistence. Moreover, forest and estate reservation had removed from farming communities a potential area of expansion. This created a powerful resentment of both colonial policy and what forested landscapes represented. If the forest could not provide land, one could nonetheless profit from its timber.

CHAPTER FIVE

Transforming the Agricultural Landscape

THE DELINEATION OF THE FOREST ESTATE demonstrated how colonialism divided the Usambaras according to a formula of economic potential. Colonial law placed the bulk of Government Land under the stewardship of the Forest Department while it created estates on Private Land, like Kwai, which it leased or sold outright to expatriates. On Public Land, the third land-type designation, indigenous communities maintained land management initiatives, although as this and subsequent chapters point out, the state often tried to dictate aspects of land use. Those who lived on the Public Lands chafed under the larger colonial schema of land division, which dislocated them from places they and their ancestors knew well. While farmers and herders fought their relegation to the Public Lands, colonial law and the bureaucracy came to identify these places as the *only* proper realm of smallholder agriculture.

Britain's Tanganyikan government created a legal framework that theoretically allowed it to determine human-environmental relations on Public Land by placing its ownership exclusively with the state. The 1923 Lands

Ordinance codified African disenfranchisement when it vested all Public Lands and interest over them in the governor, who held them for the use and common benefit of the "natives."[1] The 1928 amended Land Ordinance seemed to back away from exclusive state control in its clarification of indigenous land rights. It stated that "a native lawfully using or occupying land in accordance with native law and custom shall in law be regarded as having indefeasible title to it, that is, he cannot be removed by the Government against his will in order that the land may be alienated to a third party."[2] However, the Tanganyikan governor, as ultimate patron, could still determine how colonial peoples used the land and what resources, such as timber or minerals, they took from it. Indirect rule, designed to confer certain rights upon colonial subjects, actually restricted tenure arrangements because British administrators appointed the African authorities who, under "native law and custom," controlled the disposition of Public Lands. This conceptualization of political authority seriously distorted the history of land occupation and use and allowed colonial authorities to determine customary rights. Colonialism's web of questionable legality limited, but did not eliminate, Africans' ability to negotiate their relationship with the land and with the colonial government's local representatives. However, threats to local control intensified during the 1930s as the state became increasingly preoccupied with what it regarded as poor husbandry techniques and environmental degradation.

This chapter examines how these processes sowed the seeds of ecological vulnerability and social insecurity among Usambara's farming populations. It concludes with a discussion of how the combination of agriculture's transformation, irregular rainfall, political upheaval, and colonial environmental concerns all coalesced during the 1940s on the northern side of the West Usambaras, where a series of food shortages struck the mountain communities around the Mlalo Basin. The crisis carried great symbolic meaning to all who lived through it and sent colonial administrators and farmers scrambling, on very different trajectories, to alleviate the danger. To the British colonial government, Mlalo's breakdown was simply a precursor of the disaster that had been brewing across colonial Africa since the early 1930s. When postwar funds became available, the Tanganyikan government instituted a land-use reform package across the territory, with Mlalo and the West Usambaras serving as a showcase (see chapter 6). As Steven Feierman has pointed out in his masterful work *Peasant Intellectuals,* the institution of soil erosion control in the West Usambaras was as much a struggle of political wills as it was an effort at ecological change. The politics surrounding land reform certainly played into the immediate context of anticolonial struggles in Tanganyika, but in terms of environmental control they initiated a much longer-term process of state intervention that continued into the independence era.

Transforming the Plains Agricultural Landscape: Disaster, Recovery, and Commercialization

Between 1897 and 1899, much of Usambara suffered yet another in a series of killing famines that struck during the late nineteenth century.[3] In Mlalo, people remember the time as *njaa ya mchele,* the famine (*njaa*) when rice (*mchele*) from the plains saved lives.[4] Drought had increased local vulnerability, but it was not the only factor contributing to famine. The depopulation described in chapter 2 undermined the maintenance and use of irrigated fields in the mountains, whose produce would have normally played a role in famine relief. Other food supplements available from local pastoralists disappeared when rinderpest struck Mbugu herds in 1897.[5] When human disease and locusts also invaded the mountains, people in the Usambaras starved.[6]

The famine's name, njaa ya mchele, demonstrates the important link between the mountains that surround Mlalo and the plains immediately below. Rice production required large labor inputs that the Mlalo region could still supply. Amani scientist Karl Braun's 1907 study of rice production below Mlalo described an intensive production regime. Entire families had moved down from the mountains and camped among the fields. In addition to planting, tending, and harvesting the rice, farmers had to build and maintain irrigation works and set up a complex of scarecrows and cowrie-shell alarms in order to protect their investment from marauding animals.[7] Rice's value for famine relief and subsistence, as well as for trade, justified farmers' commitment. The sophistication of the plains agroecology also suggested the important historical role of a specific land form, the kitivo, a place where mountain streams in flood flowed over their banks, depositing their load of eroded mountain topsoil.

German colonialism's commodity-based economy began to chip away at the ancient ties between mountain and plain. Rubber, for example, proved immensely profitable at the turn of the twentieth century.[8] In Central and East Africa, latex collected from forest vines met much of the early demand in European markets. When supplies from naturally occurring forest vines diminished, entrepreneurs planted Ceara rubber tree plantations,

Fig. 5.1. Rice farming at Kitivo, on the plains below Mlalo. Photo Sabine Barcatta

several of which sprang up in the riverine lowlands below the Usambaras. Rubber eventually rivaled cotton as German East Africa's most lucrative export. Land alienation for rubber plantations removed about 17,000 acres (6,882 hectares) of kitivo lands from African hands. Despite the optimistic prognostications, in 1913 rubber prices collapsed and by 1920 these private estates lay unused and covered in weeds.[9] Rubber's legacy remained evident on the lowland landscape in the rows of neglected plantings of Ceara trees in the Lwengera Valley, in the lowlands between the base of East Usambara and Muheza, and on the Umba riverbanks on Mlalo's kitivo.[10] Although the expansion of plains acreage devoted to German colonial commodities did not eliminate kitivo cultivation, the rubber plantations formed more islands of private land on areas normally used intensively in the indigenous agricultural system.

On the Pangani Valley plains, the German experiment with sisal had shown enough potential that, instead of returning those estates to indigenous possession, the British government's custodian of enemy (changed after the Treaty of Versailles to "ex-enemy") property assumed ownership, then auctioned them off after the war. His decision paid dividends; within ten years, the Pangani Valley's slightly acidic soils, semi-arid climate, and gentle topography contained the largest sisal-growing region in Tanganyika, and production continued to expand significantly until 1940.[11]

Fig. 5.2. Sisal fields below the Usambaras. Photo Sabine Barcatta

Sisal's commercial success induced thousands of Tanganyika's itinerant laborers to seek a living around the Usambaras.[12] The plantation work was hot, difficult, and dangerous, but plains wages for cutting sisal (24/– per month) were at least double those for casual labor in the mountains (12/– to 15/– per month).[13] Usambara's resident mountain population avoided sisal plantations, preferring to sell foodstuffs to the workers rather than risk the infectious diseases and work-related accidents that caused scores of deaths each year.[14]

Sisal profits helped to convert the Pangani Valley into the privately owned space of European commercial capitalism, and the industrialized landscape became alien territory to mountain people. The lines of sisal plants, and what mountain farmers saw as the miserable lot of the migrants, reinforced the local prejudice that, if possible, these plains should be avoided, as they had been during the troubled years of the slave trade. Usambara's mountain farmers reinforced the impersonal nature of this space by calling its African inhabitants the *manumba* (the numbers).

This dramatic landscape transformation did not occur on West Usambara's northern *vitivo*, which during the 1920s and 1930s remained largely within the domain of indigenous cultivation and outside the global nexus of colonialism's commodities trade.[15] In 1937, Geoffrey Milne, soil scientist of the East African Agricultural Research Station at Amani, revisited Braun's study area and described the system in more detail. Milne found that the kitivo cultivation system matched a number of crops to soil types and the water and flood regime. Farmers recognized soil potential from the vegetation along the slight inclines that indicated both arable soils and points of prior cultivation. Nearest the massif base, farmers had intercropped maize and bananas. A few hundred meters downslope, where the kitivo flattened out and floods periodically inundated the soils, farmers planted combinations of rice and maize. Depending on rainfall and stream flow conditions, farmers would harvest at least one of the crops, even in marginal years.[16] Milne's description highlights the complexity.

> [The] peripheral zone [outside regularly flooded areas] carried a great deal of standing maize, nearly mature at time of visit, with cotton fields along outer margin. Here was some maize on land that had already borne rice in central parts of kitivo. Some of this was so immature that it will only be harvested if normal November floods do not occur. There was even fresh maize seed being planted [September 29]. Late planting form of insurance. If river rises normally maize will be lost, but ground will be fitted by floods to carry rice. If the river does not rise, or not till later, rice will fail or will be late, but in the meantime there will be maize. Premium paid is value of seed and labor and is a light one. There is water at about 1 meter so that growth is assured throughout the dry season if germination can be effected.[17]

Kitivo agriculture had changed with the times. Where Baumann had seen millet and sorghum in 1892, Milne found maize and rice in 1937. Shifting demographic trends were also evident at this northern kitivo. Despite the presence of malaria and the heat, land shortages around Mlalo and neighboring Mbaramo pressed people to move down to the northern plains more or less permanently during the 1920s and 1930s.[18] Milne also claimed that the vitivo below Mlalo and Mbaramo were "fully occupied," meaning that all the cultivable lands had already been totally allotted and cultivated when conditions allowed. Furthermore, even though migrations had occurred, vitivo land rights remained largely in the hands of mountain residents, who continued to climb down to the plains when the agricultural calendar dictated.[19]

The Usambara massifs separated two distinct lowland agricultural landscapes and equally distinct philosophies of exploitation. Drought-tolerant agaves in their millions covered the southern plains, while grain crops formed the agricultural foundation on the northern plains. At Mlalo, crop surpluses helped support the region's densest population.[20] A significant part of Mlalo's success stemmed from the farming system's continuity with precolonial land-use patterns linking mountains and plain. In spite of its sophistication, Mlalo's farming landscape came to be cited as one of the worst examples of environmental abuse in Tanganyika Territory.

The Differentials of Recovery in Mountain Agriculture

Mlalo's history shows how important dense populations had become to the nineteenth-century agricultural economy. Where Mlalo appears to have quickly recovered from the spate of nineteenth-century famines, other farming communities in the West Usambaras slowly restored their gardens on a less tightly organized landscape, but one with more space for maneuver. Colonial land ordinances complicated the process, however, and as the agricultural landscape filled over the course of the 1920s and 1930s, farmers, herders, missionaries, colonial administrators, and scientists all participated in an increasingly contentious discourse over the land's proper use.

As the Kwai case demonstrates, the mountain estates became a point of dispute in the early years of the British administration. Where the central administration in Dar es Salaam sought to retain the estates under the rubric of Private Land, local officers often backed African claims to estates alienated under German rule. During the 1920s, the Lushoto district administration requested that the government purchase several former German properties in the mountains and restore them to cultivators and herders displaced by arbitrary colonial land alienation.[21]

In cases where African farmers had already reclaimed acreage on the overgrown and abandoned coffee plantations, the District Office decided to tacitly recognize indigenous claims.[22] The custodian of ex-enemy property, however, held the ultimate power of estate disposal, and he often decided for their continued classification as Private Land. The discontinuity between central and local administration led to eviction notices for Africans who believed they had been living legally on former estate property.

With the estates placed off-limits, the "squatters" often opted to move onto the Public Lands that had been abandoned during the famines. However, the choice presented the difficulties of tax liabilities and often unscrupulous collection practices by African chiefs. In these cases, those who could escaped the exactions by simply moving beyond the range of effective administration.[23] By 1924, the Lushoto D.O. observed that the *akida*s, political functionaries whose powers had been established under German administration, experienced "considerable difficulties" in their administrative duties, "owing to the complete indifference of the native population generally to orders emanating from them," a state of affairs attributable in part to increasingly diffuse settlement patterns. "There is a steady and growing tendency among the people to scatter and live an isolated existence in huts dotted on the crests of hills.... Akidas continually urge the desirability of Government action to reconstruct the old village communities that existed before the occupation of the country by Europeans, and which were insisted upon by the late German government in order to facilitate administration."[24]

As farming communities scattered, the British colonial administration attempted to control the situation by reorganizing and broadening colonial political power. For the "men on the spot," effective administration required that people be counted and taxed and their disputes adjudicated. The akidas had apparently used their judicial and fiscal powers to enrich themselves, and, under the weight of these exactions and people's ability to simply move beyond colonial control, the legitimacy of local political authority had broken down. In 1925, colonial officers in Usambara therefore scrapped the akida system in favor of the restoration of the former ruling clan, the Kilindi, who would have to transform themselves into British functionaries. After their training period, the Kilindi initiates supposedly espoused British ideals and could perform their bureaucratic duties.[25] The Shambaa, Mbugu, and Pare people who had lived under the previous Kilindi rule had little reason to accept its putative legitimacy. Kilindi civil wars had devastated the mountain economy and, with Kilindi acquiescence, the German colonial state had managed to alienate all of the East Usambaras and huge swaths of West Usambara. Some Kilindi had served the German state as akidas and helped run a reviled forced-labor system that served the estates. Rather than a return of "traditional paramounts," British colonial government restored a discredited political arrangement.

Indigenous understandings of political legitimacy, and the associated right to tribute in labor and livestock, depended largely on the control of the charms and rituals associated with maintaining the land's fecundity.[26] The new chiefly powers apportioned by the state far exceeded those limits. Chiefs could now control daily life regardless of their standing as ritual experts. Chiefs could confiscate cattle and therefore a person's disposable wealth. They also had authorization to confiscate home-brewed beer and attendant equipment and in this way interfere with community labor patterns where home brew constituted payment. They could prosecute their constituents for cutting trees, coerce them to labor, and control their movements into or out of a location.[27] Colonialism's new apportionment of power could now impinge on one's ability to gain access to and clear land for cultivation. By sanctioning chiefly interference in daily life, indirect rule gave the Kilindi the opportunity to reconstruct and expand their political power beyond its precolonial ideological boundaries.

The Kilindi restoration culminated in 1929 with the appointment as paramount chief of Shebuge Magogo, a descendant from the line of Semboja, one of the warlords responsible for Usambara's nineteenth-century miseries. Magogo had not inherited the major rain charms, and he had a deformity that under normal conditions would have prohibited him from entering the royal enclosure or even from coming into contact with the most important royal regalia.[28] As the new king began to remove local sub-chiefs and install his own men, he met with resistance, especially if the deposed chiefs were popular rainmakers. When in 1932 and 1933 locusts and then drought destroyed harvests, some blamed Magogo's rule for growing political unrest and hunger.

A letter signed "All Citizens of Usambara" and attached to administrative correspondence of 1933 links tax burdens, political discord, and hunger.

> [W]e should only get rain and obtain a good crop. Because if the rain fell we should obtain sufficient food and enable us to get out tax at once. But now there is a great famine that is why we are spending all our money in purchasing foodstuff[s] and it is impossible for us to get tax. The source of all this trouble is the *Wakilindi*. They are quarreling amongst themselves on account of the country. Everyone says the country belongs to my father, everyone tells the same story, and therefore all the *Wakilindi* are not on good terms. . . . Honestly speaking and according to God's arrangements this country does not belong to them. The rightful owners are the *Wakinatuli*. The *Wakilindi* are only aliens, their home is Nguu. . . . Just remember, Sir, that [the] *Wakilindi* wish that all people would die of hunger.[29]

The letter challenges Kilindi legitimacy on the grounds of their alien status, infighting, and inability, or refusal, to bring rain. By 1934, the Usambara district administration had recognized the famine, but nowhere in the available public record do officers discuss the complex indigenous understanding of its cause. Lushoto's district officer simply instructed Kilindi officers to construct maize granaries and to urge their constituents to plant cassava.[30] Although this was practical advice, it ignored the burdens that the colonial political economy had placed on cultural life.

While "All Citizens of Usambara" may have believed that rain would alleviate the hunger of 1933, colonialism had forced changes to the farming system that created new vulnerabilities to famine, even in adequate rainfall years. The necessity to procure cash required farmers to participate in the growing regional market by planting maize in the historical centers of subsistence, the banana zone at 1,400 meters elevation.[31] Subsistence strategies also changed in the higher, colder, more marginal agricultural regions, where a recent import, the "European" potato, largely replaced the sweet potato, a more ancient introduction, because it offered higher yields and required less labor.[32] Across the mountains, competition over land and water increased along the borderlines where the mission stations and estates ran up against the expanding garden complex of a growing African population.

Maize's antiquity in Usambara agriculture is unknown, but it seems to have long been grown around Mlalo, where *kishee,* the main maize variety grown in Usambara, derives its name from the area's founding lineage group. Over time, at Mlalo and Kitivo, the maize cultivars developed some resistance to the relatively dry conditions. Then, between the end of the nineteenth century, when Hölst noted the dominance of bananas on the agricultural landscape, and the 1920s, maize production took off across the Usambaras.[33] Given the fact that it required more labor input than bananas, yet yielded fewer calories per acre (11–14 million for bananas, 5–7 million for maize), the rise of maize signaled a direct response to the growing cash economy in and around the mountains. Much of the demand for maize flour came from the sisal workers who had emigrated from other parts of Tanganyika and East Africa. Most of them hailed from regions where maize, millet, and sorghum, rather than bananas, constituted the staple grains, and their overwhelming preference for maize created a profitable incentive for farmers in the hills. Maize sales to the plains during the 1920s solidified the mountain cash economy and allowed Usambara's farmers to continue to avoid wage labor.[34] While maize production favored the banana-growing zone and therefore the traditional population centers at about 1,400 meters elevation, the adoption of potatoes helped to spur population diffusion into higher and colder regions. The dispersal provided opportunities for poor farmers to move into a new ecological niche and to avoid the precarious situation of having to borrow land. However, this demographic and agricultural expansion could only succeed so long as suitably fertile and irrigable land remained available.

Although cropping repertoires had changed from the precolonial days, continuities with the past remained in force. As farmers repopulated the Usambaras in the first decades of the twentieth century, they turned again to irrigation technologies. However, where missions and the sisal industry competed with farmers for water, new types of inherently colonial conflicts developed. In 1925, Usambara's district officer reported that the year, "owing to irregular rains, was a bad one for native agriculture," with 40 percent of crops lost.[35] The rainfall deficits forced mountain farmers to rebuild their irrigation furrows on the lower Mkuzi River, 1,000 meters upslope from the Mombo sisal estate.[36] Since sisal fiber processing required large amounts of water for decorticating (removing fibers from leaves) and washing, the sisal estates below the escarpment depended on continual and adequate mountain stream flows, which farmers on the Mkuzi had cut off.[37] When the estate's managers complained to the D.O., he in turn informed the chiefs of Mombo and Vuga that people without hereditary rights to the water on the Mkuzi furrow must not interfere with water going to sisal plantations.[38]

This solution suggests that the D.O. believed that rights to irrigation water were bound up in tradition, and that they belonged to particular people. Yet, in Usambara's agricultural history, one's rights to furrow use depended on continual *use* of a plot along a furrow and participation in communal maintenance. Moreover, irrigation operated when need dictated rather than continually. Problems arose when farmers tapped the Mkuzi furrow, which their ancestors had built generations earlier in response to their own fluctuating needs rather than those of an industrial-age sisal industry that required constant water supplies.[39] Three years later, in 1928, when the Mombo estate owners once again complained about depleted water supplies from the Mkuzi irrigation furrow, the chief at Vuga explained that heavy rains had destroyed the furrow. Whatever the case at Vuga, African farmers clearly showed their determination to use irrigation waters based on claims staked long before colonial rule.[40]

Another dispute over water arose as claimants to the lands bordering the Vuga Lutheran mission reopened an agricultural area that had been abandoned during the late-nineteenth-century crises. The missionaries worried over what they held to be their own water rights over the Mkuzi stream's tributaries. The pastor claimed ownership of two furrows that fed the mission complex, arguing that his predecessors had built them and that the German colonial government, in granting leasehold, had also made specific mention that the furrows were mission property.[41] Farmers claimed, on the other hand, that no rights could have been ceded because the area's inhabitants were absent when the mission received its lease.[42] This rather innocuous entry in the administrative record masks the complexity of the conflicts at Vuga, the former capital of the mountain kingdom. In 1895, the Germans executed the Kilindi king and installed a succession of puppets. The third, Kinyassi, leased out to the mission and coffee planters huge tracts near Vuga. In the meantime, njaa ya mchele decimated the area, scattering refugees.[43] The returning families moved to exploit what had been theirs in the first place. Indeed, in 1932, the A.D.O. found, along the mission furrow, seventy-one irrigated gardens, which served about two hundred people. In 1936, yet another dispute surfaced between Shambaa farmers and the Vuga mission, this time over two acres of land that the Shambaa believed had been mistakenly included in the mission property.[44] Similar land and water disputes broke out at the nearby European estates of Mponde and Sakulla, where farmers complained about estate boundaries and asked the government for another survey.[45]

These cases, and the others that crossed the Lushoto district officer's desk during the droughts of the mid-1930s, reveal the importance of land and irrigation to smallholder farming systems.[46] While the adjudication of land claims on private estates lay with the Lands Office, local administrators could try to manipulate technological arrangements on Public Land. One case on Mlalo's kitivo highlights the administration's ignorance regarding irrigation's role and local character. In August 1935, the district officer summoned King Magogo to accompany him to the plains below Mlalo to observe as scores of tax defaulters attempted to construct an exceptionally large furrow, six feet deep and four feet across, to open new areas of the kitivo to agriculture.[47] The government project's unsuitable scale and its dependence on forced labor led to its quick abandonment, but the sheer scale of the failed irrigation project in the northern plains suggests that, in the D.O.'s inexpert opinion, bigger would prove to be better.

The land disputes at times split the administration. An argument between the district officer for Lushoto and his immediate boss, the Tanga provincial commissioner, over land use at Kauzeni, the alluvial kitivo lands below Mlola, reveals the developing philosophical rift over how to direct the agricultural economy. In October 1933, an entrepreneur who sought to develop a rice plantation of 631 hectares on either side of a four-mile stretch of the Mdando River approached the administration for leasehold rights on what the German government had designated as a rubber estate. The provincial commissioner balked, citing the future needs of the Shambaa in the mountains to use the kitivo.[48] Riverine rice cultivation, he argued further, would immediately jeopardize water access for the thirty to thirty-five African farmers downstream from the estate.[49] In a terse response, the local district officer argued that a little private enterprise would offer employment to natives and increase the availability of cash in an area he believed to be economically backward.[50]

In a decision that notes African interests, the provincial commissioner offered the entrepreneur an exceptionally short five-year renewable lease for only 101 hectares along the river.[51] The provincial commissioner justified his decision on the grounds that Usambara's population was about to explode out of the mountains onto the plains. The P.C.'s tentativeness shows he at least understood that vitivo agriculture served mountain needs and would be important in the future. Similar official concerns about the future of mountain farming surfaced again in 1937, when the Tanga provincial commissioner authorized the East African Agricultural Research Station's soil scientist, Geoffrey Milne, to conduct a soil survey of Usambara. They hoped to ascertain both the damage to mountain soils due to accelerated erosion and the suitability of the soils below the escarpment for future settlement.[52] Apparently, the provincial administration had judged that food shortages, coupled with the land and water conflicts across the Usambaras during the 1930s, required an assessment of agroecology from an Amani scientist, rather than the Agriculture Department.[53]

Milne entered the Usambaras at the height of a worldwide debate in British colonial territories over the diminution of natural resources, especially through the mechanism of accelerated soil erosion. The fact that the discussion took place during the Great Depression and treated regions as geographically diverse as India, North America, and eastern and southern Africa encouraged in colonial circles both a general crisis mentality and a correspondingly diffuse reading of the problem.[54] In East Africa, colonial administrations worried that African-induced resource degradation ultimately threatened European interests. Because they held dense populations, mountain areas in particular attracted the worry of officials, and, in this context of fear, they identified the Mlalo Basin as one of the most blatant examples of a degraded mountain landscape.[55]

In their incipient struggle to understand exactly how ameliorative efforts should be carried out, colonial administrators and extension agents tended to depend on the crude and generalized paradigms inherent in the debate, rather than on close personal knowledge of the affected regions. An illustrative example of the formation of "received wisdom" occurred at an early 1930s meeting of the Royal Geographic Society, where a panel on soil erosion in eastern and central Africa characterized the core problem as one of a primitive society confronting the modern world.[56] Even scientists with decades of experience in southern, central, and eastern Africa argued that, until the *pax Britannica,* wandering tribesmen and women, who "never gave a thought to preserving the productivity of the soil, had carved a path of destruction across Africa's landscape."[57] It followed that only so long as these intrinsically migratory African farmers remained few in number could nature, over centuries, repair the damage of "primitive" and "destructive" methods.[58] However, the colonial era had witnessed, according to this view, an unfortunate surge of population growth that had devoured and destroyed once productive lands.[59]

By 1931, the Tanganyikan administration had formed, along similar lines of thinking, a Standing Committee on Soil Erosion. Taking its cues directly from the Ceylon Soil Erosion Committee, Tanganyika's newly formed counterpart formulated soil and water conservation recommendations designed to help agricultural officers in the field.[60] In the absence of funds and the support of public opinion, the committee decided that its initial efforts should be to educate rather than to coerce.[61] As its recommendations filtered down to the agricultural officers and foresters, they began to preach the evils of soil erosion and to demonstrate "proper" land use on small experimental plots.

The government's highland focus drew upon Clement Gillman's influential work on East African resource conservation.[62] Of Gillman's several influential analyses of Tanganyika's ecological imbalances, perhaps the most important was his 1936 article, "A Population Map for Tanganyika Territory."[63] He found that over two-thirds of Tanganyika's population had consolidated itself on and around granitic upthrust mountains and volcanoes that constituted only 10 percent of the total quantity of land. Gillman explained this phenomenon by maintaining that the relationship between high rainfall and elevation had determined a particular population distribution and allowed for intensive and sedentary agriculture, a cultural advancement over more mobile arrangements in the plains. "[F]avorable defensive topography and ample water supplies have also led to the gradual evolution of a higher cultural standard than that of shifting cultivation as practiced in the surrounding savannas and steppes, including permanent crops such as bananas and coffee, irrigation, stabling of cattle, manuring and the beginnings of individual tenure."[64] Given Gillman's demographic analysis, conservation of the highland forest watersheds was essential to Tanganyika's future.

> They [the mountains] are the country's most valuable asset but have, unfortunately, attractions for agriculturists, both white and black, who seriously endanger their continuance; not only have settlements intruded into these forests, but even where no actual encroachment has taken place, the difficulties of protection against fires from the surrounding steppe or savannah lands are so great that the annual loss of forest areas along their margins is very appreciable.[65]

Gillman argued further that the rest of the land, or 82 percent, could not be looked upon as a reserve "to accommodate the dense masses if and when they have been driven from their heritage."[66] Mountain environments in East Africa, therefore, performed a crucial double duty: they supported dense agricultural populations while carrying the forest cover essential to local and regional water needs.

Gillman's work anticipated much of current conservation thinking in elucidating the dynamic relationship between population and East African mountain environments. He saw three related problems stemming from dense mountain populations: forest depletion, soil erosion, and a diminishing water supply. Taken together, these ongoing processes made for a very dangerous situation in which preservation was "infinitely more important than so-called development."[67] But African land use figured into the degradation equation as only one element. Large European settler mountain farms and plantations in the highlands, although few in number, also exercised potentially dangerous environmental impacts all out of proportion to their small numbers. Gillman's opinions drew upon Geoffrey Milne's soil studies, which had examined how Usambara's settler coffee plantations had precipitated heavy soil-fertility losses in large forest clearings.[68] Ultimately, he realized the general and preliminary nature of his argument and called for further research.[69]

Although Gillman recognized that African land-use systems had evolved, he failed to understand the dynamic adaptations that indigenous people had made to environmental change. The Tanganyikan highlands, he felt, required scientifically based reform directed by the state.[70] Only the application to farmers' fields of a number of "enlightened" husbandry techniques, coupled with the movement of some peoples out of the congested mountains, could save the highlands.[71] Significantly, Gillman often cited the West Usambaras generally, and the Mlalo Basin in particular, as one of the potential ecological disaster areas in need of immediate action.[72]

In response to the growing international crisis mentality, the colonial administration in 1937 implemented across the Tanganyika Territory a set of anti-erosion rules that conferred upon district agricultural officers the power to direct land-use practice. The rules and their implementation represented the governor's ultimate prerogative to impose his will upon the Public Lands. The district officer could, for example, order African farmers, under penalty of fine and imprisonment, to ridge or terrace their fields, prohibit cultivation along stream banks, and order communal labor on lands "in danger of erosion."[73] The rules, however, applied only to African land-use practices and did not extend to the Private Lands, where European tea and coffee planters committed what Gillman had described as their own "ecological sins."

A Closer Look at Erosion at Mlalo: Milne's 1937 Reconnaissance

Just after the new conservation rules went into effect in 1937, the Tanga provincial commissioner asked Amani's (by 1937 known officially as the East African Agricultural Research Station) soil scientist Geoffrey Milne to travel to West Usambara to reconnoiter its soils, especially the kitivo soils below Mlalo. In the report's introduction, Milne explains that his purpose is to learn if the plains' soils could support the relocation of some of Mlalo Basin's population, thus relieving the population pressure inherent in Gillman's model.[74] Milne carried impeccable scientific credentials and had nine years' experience in the Usambaras, serving as Amani's soil scientist from 1928. Furthermore, he had recently finished pulling together years of research into a provisional soil map of Tanganyika Territory.[75] His focus on intricate ecological relationships at scales ranging from soil molecules to their deposits across a few hundred meters steered him toward very local analyses of ecological problems. Milne's report on Usambara represents the careful thoughts of a respected scholar who had traveled at length in the Territory, observing land use and soils. However, Milne's official affiliation with Amani would prove problematic.

Milne's report clearly describes the region's topography, climate, and soils, as well as the possibilities for agricultural expansion. Just as Carl Hölst had discovered forty years earlier, Milne found the best kitivo land under cultivation. Moving people onto what remained, Milne realized, posed an unacceptable famine risk to anyone forced to live there. His observations thus confirmed the wisdom of centuries of upland adaptation patterns.

> Under existing conditions, as judged by the dry aspect of the natural vegetation, agricultural success could not be looked for oftener than once in every other or every third year. If these terms were accepted, and the land were planted with full knowledge of risk, by a people based on the kitivo lands for their main subsistence, it could carry cotton in rotation with millets, ground nuts, pulses and pumpkins. It could never fully support a resident population; it would always rank as supplementary marginal land.[76]

In his explanation of soil erosion in the mountains, Milne looked systematically at soils and cultivation along slopes. He noted that, generally, Usambara's heavily bisected topography determined that farmers had little choice but to cultivate slopes, since only a few upland valleys held arable alluvial bottoms broad enough for cultivation. Given slope and soil type, Milne assumed "that the greater part of cultivated Usambara has suffered loss of soil in some degree, and that losses [were] continuing."[77] He noted further that, as cultivation spread, it tended to creep upslope until a hillside and ridge had been completely denuded of trees. This phenomenon occurred particularly around the Umba headwaters above the Mlalo Basin, a situation he clearly believed dangerous to river flow. However, rather than a general prescription, Milne suggested soil erosion control methods appropriate to each soil type he encountered along the hill slope. For the valley bottoms, he argued against the Agriculture Department's prohibition on streamside cultivation, pointing out that stream banks in the Usambaras often carry naturally stabilized and fertile colluvial soils eroded from hillsides above.

Milne also noted the arbitrary application of the government's antierosion rules.

> At Mlalo I saw Mission land being ploughed to the brink of the main stream at the very time that the native-owned stream-side land was being flagged by the instructor for preservation from the hoe under the N[ative]

A[uthority] rule. Mission ploughing was crude and no precautions against soil loss were evident, so this particular case would cause bewilderment to the native riparian owners and might well alienate goodwill from soil conservation measures generally. Whatever decision is taken about a given stretch of riverside land, it ought to be enforceable equally on European and on native owners."[78]

In contrast to the Agriculture Department's blanket treatment of soil erosion in East Africa, to Milne, soil erosion control was a complex endeavor: "The tactics of defense on each hillside require to be thought out in regard to the particular set of circumstances found there. No simple universal set of soil protection rules is possible, for however well adapted certain measures may be to a given case, they may be ill advised, or even directly mischievous, if applied without discrimination to another."[79] Milne's report chided the Agriculture Department for not having assigned a permanently resident agricultural officer to Usambara. He contended that before the government could attempt to address the problem, agriculture assistants and instructors should actually live for a time in the densely populated areas where ecological problems appeared to be most severe.[80] Milne concluded that Usambara's residents could successfully farm the highlands and that Mlalo's farmers could not be expected to move to the plains, but must be provided with land in the mountains. "But the most immediately profitable field of work towards the desired end, namely towards putting the Sambaa tribe in permanent possession of enough productive land for their needs, lies on the highland plateau rather than on the arid lowlands."[81]

By implying that the problem, although pressing, was more complex than his colleagues had suggested, the report prompted a flurry of correspondence up and down Tanganyika's bureaucratic hierarchy. In a letter to the chief secretary, the provincial commissioner backed Milne's conclusions that further research should be carried out in this regard and requested a permanent agricultural assistant for Usambara.[82] However, Harold Gillman, the agricultural officer responsible for West Usambara, wrote to the district officer to dispute Milne's conclusions regarding the efficacy of the Native Authority rules. Milne's report also struck a nerve with Tanganyika's director of agriculture, who, when asked to send a permanent agricultural assistant to Usambara, complained with vitriol to the chief secretary. The tenor of the letter suggests that the director resented both the fact that the district officer and the provincial commissioner, rather than he, had commissioned a soil survey and the choice of an Amani scientist rather than one of his own men.[83] In light of this controversy, the chief secretary buried the report and decided not to approve an agricultural assistant for Usambara.[84] The correspondence and Milne's personal observations regarding official reaction to his report explain how turf battles between the Agriculture Department and Amani proved more important than careful study.[85]

Milne's and Gillman's writings highlight the contrasts inherent in the degradation narrative coalescing during the 1930s and early 1940s in eastern and southern Africa. Gillman's highly influential studies point out the very important phenomenon of the relationship between highland environments and population densities in places like Mlalo, but his historical reading of that situation fit into what was then an uninformed view of the transformations in African agricultural practice. Clearly, his scholarship helped solidify the colonial government's thinking regarding ameliorative action. At the same time, Gillman despised the direction in which the capitalist colonial economy drove land-use practice, an element of his broader view seemingly lost on the postwar development-scheme planners. In the end, his allegiances lay with the resources he believed to be dwindling before his eyes. Milne's work, more careful and tightly focused on the soils he knew so well, represented a highly professional and thus unusually valuable contribution to the small corpus of material on African land use. His work formed an important foundation, which policy makers should have built upon.

Milne's brief investigation suggests that at certain places, accelerated erosion did pose a threat to the Umba watersheds and to productive agriculture on particular hillsides. Moreover, his report shows the importance of interpreting ecological change and degradation over differing time scales. However, neither Milne nor Gillman quantified soil erosion or conducted the type of systematic description of the history of agricultural practice required for sound policy. Even if they had, the fact that neither was directly associated with the Forest or Agriculture Departments lent to their critique an edge unappreciated by the very services they were striving to help understand ecological problems.

Once cleansed of dissenting viewpoints, the central thrust of the bureaucratic readings of the Mlalo situation continued to argue for a generalized agroecological decline driven by overpopulation and a destructive and rigidly conservative farming system. Examined in depth, however, the agrarian history of Mlalo showed the flexibility of a combination of adjustments in cropping and tenure, along with responses to twentieth-century economic opportunities. While population growth, site-specific accelerated erosion, and land shortage were arguably problems facing farmers, the answer to their alleviation lay in an understanding of the longer-term history of ecological change, in which innovative farmers adjusted to demographic, ecological, and economic change instead of succumbing to it.

The evidence for demographic change does suggest that nineteenth-century immigration swelled Mlalo's population. However, the record also shows that the indigenous authorities realized this and, by the mid-1930s, had significantly adjusted tenure arrangements to accommodate the land-poor.[86] Before the twentieth century, the local land tenure system's design assured everyone, including newcomers, enough land to procure subsistence. Under normal circumstances, each Mlalo Basin community would hold certain lands in reserve (Shambaa, *dezu*) for allocation by a village official, expert in such matters.[87] Upon allocation, recipients held the land in temporary usufruct for two generations, at which time the land reverted to dezu and was again liable for reallocation. The system seemed to allow enough time for immigrant families to establish themselves as landholders in the local community, through either marriage or purchase or the clearing of forest. However, during the 1920s and 1930s, when the colonial Forest Department restricted expansion onto forest reserves immediately surrounding the basin, uncultivated land became a precious commodity.[88]

With dezu lands restricted, communities adjusted the tenure system by incorporating a mechanism of land borrowing.

> A man who has no land of his own borrows fields for cultivation from neighbours, relatives or friends, who have more than they are using. There are a considerable number of land owners who have more than enough land for their own needs. They are usually descendants of the original settlers or sons of men who acquired land by purchase. By custom an owner cannot refuse to loan his land on the score that it is under fallow.[89]

Field borrowing shortened fallow periods and likely contributed to the kinds of soil degradation that Milne noted during the late 1930s.

While smaller holdings and a changing twentieth-century political economy placed additional stress on the soil, farmers' initiatives with exotic cultigens like potatoes, maize, and rice helped them respond successfully to market opportunities. Neither Milne nor Gillman commented on the tenure arrangements or cultigen shifts, even though they would have been discernible from a close reading of available German materials or a discussion with farmers. However appropriate they were to economic circumstances, the new crops proved both vulnerable and ecologically dangerous. For example, during the early 1940s, blight attacked the "European" potato crop, wiping it out completely. Maize, with its shallow root system exposing soils to damaging effects of wind and rain, diminished the farming system's ability to slow soil erosion as it had under the deflective influence of wide banana leaves. In the plains kitivo, the sorghum and millets that precolonial farmers had depended on survived periodic drought far better than maize did. The growing popularity of another exotic, cassava, signaled the trend toward vulnerability to drought and declining soil fertility. Cassava tubers are considered a quintessential drought crop because they can remain dormant in dry soils until moisture again becomes available, and they flourish in soils depleted of nitrogen.[90]

Changes to agricultural and social practice in the Mlalo Basin between 1890 and 1940 corresponded with an historical conjuncture where demographic, ecological, economic, and political forces coalesced into a crisis. The antiquity of settlement at Mlalo spoke to a long-standing pull on regional migration. However, the basin's late-nineteenth-century popularity placed pressure on resources just as colonial forest policy restricted access to uncultivated forest lands. Communities adjusted tenure arrangements accordingly, but the changes necessarily reduced fallow periods. Farmers also incorporated new crops, a common strategy in the history of East African mountain farming systems, but maize adoption led, in the first half of the twentieth century, to erosion as land-poor farmers moved to cultivate the basin's slopes. When two generations of complex agrarian change met with seasonal rainfall deficits in the early 1940s, the resulting subsistence crisis legitimated the simplistic colonial degradation narratives in which the Mlalo Basin figured so prominently.

Njaa ya Chankola: Politics, Crisis Mitigation, and Adaptation

Mlaloans named the 1941–46 crisis *njaa ya Chankola,* after a former tax clerk who colonial officials appointed to replace Hassani Kinyassi, a very popular and well-known chief and rainmaker. The district administration appointed Chankola in the name of effective administration. However, the choice proved unfortunate; the coincidence of his appointment with several years of drought, insect infestation, and hunger doomed his administration to infamy.⁹¹ Meanwhile, njaa ya Chankola fulfilled the colonial prophesies of impending crisis and ecological breakdown and justified the state's implementation of the Mlalo Basin Rehabilitation Scheme, a project designed to destroy the vestiges of the Mwitu tradition.

Njaa ya Chankola began as a political dispute between Mlalo's Native Authority chief, Kinyassi, and the Lushoto district administration. The district officers wanted to exert more control over Mlalo's perennial shortfall in tax receipts. Beginning in 1940, J. L. Fairclough, Lushoto's district officer, blamed the problem on the incompetence of the local Native Authority, headed by Hassani Kinyassi.

> Complaints have been regular and loud since Zumbe Hassani took over in 1935. He is idle and supine generally and that in particular his collection of tax is not all that it should be, that he fails to answer correspondence, that fees for muzzle loading guns are not collected regularly, and that judgments given in his court are not sound. I may add that the Shebuge [i.e., the Kilindi paramount king] is also of the opinion that Hassani is not pulling his weight.⁹²

Fairclough's replacement, K. B. A. Dobson, continued to stress Kinyassi's fiscal irresponsibility, but also linked it to potential political troubles. He worried that Kinyassi's lax attitude toward tax collection and Mlaloans' predilection toward tax dodging "may be converted into . . . passive resistance."⁹³ Dobson therefore recommended that Kinyassi be replaced, or, at least, that a substantial portion of the Mlalo subchiefdom be hived off and placed under the suzerainty of a new subchief at the hamlet of Mbaramo. According to Dobson, the move would ease Kinyassi's tax collection burden, allowing him to concentrate his efforts on Mlalo's immediate vicinity. Dobson must have known that the loss of Mbaramo would significantly weaken Kinyassi by undermining his right to distribute valuable agricultural lands, which, by 1940, were in short supply.⁹⁴ In November 1940, the district administration received permission to separate the two subchiefdoms.⁹⁵

In January 1942, Dobson again called for the removal of Hassani Kinyassi, citing his poor record of tax collection and his inability to round up and prosecute tax defaulters.⁹⁶ Kinyassi's reluctance to punish his constituents becomes clear in the light of wartime conditions in which wages were low and money scarce. Dobson's persistent protests moved the provincial commissioner to seek political cover in a commission of inquiry, which he appointed to investigate all of Mlalo's Native Authorities. The commission consisted of a member of the paramount chief's executive committee and Dobson's choice of "six of the most intelligent elders of Mlalo."⁹⁷ With the elders presumably in his pocket, the commission would provide Dobson with the official cover he needed to fire Kinyassi.

By early May 1942, this "Commission on the Jumbes of Mlalo" had finished its work. It recommended that eight of the sixteen Mlalo headmen be replaced, although Hassani Kinyassi did not appear on the list. Dobson reported that, immediately after the commission submitted its evaluation, the Mlalo elders asked to meet him in private, away from the executive committee appointee, that is, the Shebuge's observer from Vuga. Dobson stated that during this interview the Mlalo elders expressed concern over the political situation in Mlalo, but refused to implicate Kinyassi directly. Dobson then claimed that they disavowed their own report. Whatever transpired in the private meeting, the elders likely found themselves caught between the desires of the D.O., those of the paramount chief, and Hassani Kinyassi's local popularity. Dobson decided to make further inquiries "in private." His final report to the district commissioner, based on these "inquiries," states simply that the commission had *intended* to tell him that Hassani's misadministration was at the root of all of their troubles.⁹⁸

On July 29, 1942, at the height of the dry season following a poor agricultural year, the D.O. informed Hassani Kinyassi, renowned rainmaker, that his services as subchief were no longer required. "The natives of Mlalo are in such a chaotic state, all squabbling amongst themselves, that the time has arisen for a native with a strong personality to take charge and endeavor to make them realize that their lazy and indolent habits of the past have been the cause of the present disastrous state of the Zumbeate."⁹⁹

Dobson nominated for the position Ali Mashina (a.k.a. Chankola), the head tax clerk for Lushoto division. Chankola's appointment fits with the then prevailing view in the British administration that educated clerks best served the official conceptualization of effective administration.¹⁰⁰ Dobson thus drew the political battle lines in Mlalo along an oft-cited colonial dichotomy—tradition and modernity, Kinyassi and Chankola. No stranger to Mlalo politics, Chankola was a Kilindi from Dule, a small hamlet about a half hour's walk from the Mlalo chief's compound. He was not a rainmaker, nor did he hold legitimate authority in the eyes of his con-

Fig. 5.3. Maliki Kinyassi, Hassani's grandson, stands in front of the ceremonial hut where the rain shrines are kept at the chief's compound at Mlalo. Photo Christopher Conte

stituency. Informants recall that when Chankola moved into the Mlalo chief's quarters, the worst drought in living memory began.[101]

Informants refer to the years from 1942 through 1946 as njaa ya Chankola, a crisis with clear causes and an equally clear resolution. Almost without exception, the stories recall that the drought-induced famine occurred because of Chankola's disrespect for his constituents and Kinyassi's enmity toward his successor. According to one informant, Kinyassi offered prayers to God, whereupon "the sun increased in intensity and hunger came into the country."[102] Another characterized the episode as "a story of bitterness between Kinyassi and Chankola."[103] In the prevailing narrative, not only did Chankola lack the powers of a rainmaker, he also supposedly went so far as to extinguish the perpetual fire kept in the small hut used for the rainmaking ceremony.[104]

In Shambaa cultural discourse, drought and food deficits grew out of such political turmoil, and it logically followed that once the situation had reached crisis proportions, the people of Mlalo moved to remedy food shortages by solving the political problem, Chankola's illegitimate rule.[105] The district administration had placed Chankola in an extremely difficult position. Wartime conditions required him to conscript for the army and for labor on the plains' sisal and rubber plantations. In order to feed the war machine, his position also required him to confiscate cattle. These exactions, along with a dramatic increase in his prosecution of tax evasion cases heard in his court, clearly fueled the fires of resistance to his tenure in office.[106]

Women played a key role in the opposition. They demonstrated against Chankola in substantial numbers and in a militant fashion.[107]

> Women led the struggle against Chankola because they were very close to the hunger because they stayed with the children. Also they were used to working and meeting together, like when they gathered firewood, or at the market. In fact attendance at markets was mostly by women.[108]

> That was a very rough time. There was hunger and hoards of locusts. Once the hunger became evident, Mashina was to be removed by the strength of the women. The women of Dule, Mwangoi, Mlalo joined hands and drove the protest forward. The women climbed [to] the Kitala, and entered singing.[109]

The women's protest, moreover, suggests that the ancient ties forged among the Mwitu mountain regions had maintained themselves and helped to spur anticolonial protest. Informants claim that Mlalo's Shambaa women joined recent immigrants from neighboring Upare who were emboldened by a successful 1945 tax revolt centered there.[110]

Colonial correspondence also mentions another growing political force in the Mlalo Basin called the *chama,* or simply, "the party," which actively sought Chankola's ouster.[111] C. C. de Rosemund, Dobson's replacement, noted that the chama was "capable of influencing and expressing public opinion."[112] Clearly, both groups played a role in the revolt.[113] Their grievances grew out of their increasingly difficult task of managing Mlalo's agriculture in a milieu of deteriorating ecological circumstances that forced men into working for cash remittances in the cities of Tanga, Mombasa, and Nairobi, while women increasingly bore the brunt of producing subsistence at home.[114]

> Early in April [1946] the people at Mlalo expressed, at a mass meeting of about 6000 people, their dislike of this Zumbe and asked that he should be removed. They were led by a group of men which gained the name of

the 'Chama.' Women also demonstrated and nearly ransacked the house of the Zumbe and set it on fire. The disturbance subsided by the end of the day but there ensued a policy of passive resistance to the Zumbe which eventually led to his resignation in June.... After careful inquiry this request was finally granted and Hassani bin Kinyassi was installed as Zumbe in August to the general satisfaction of the population of Mlalo.[115]

According to the narrative, the end of the drought coincided with Chankola's removal and Kinyassi's return to Mlalo, whereupon "the rains fell all the way to Europe."[116] Despite what the story says, the difficult times did not end with the return of the rainmaker. The short rains fell in late 1946 after Kinyassi's return, but difficult agroecological conditions continued in northwestern Usambara through 1949. The story of survival and adaptation to the decade-long drought, though not as deeply embedded in the community's collective memory as the metaphors of conflict between Kinyassi and Chankola, show a food production system and a landscape stretched, at times, beyond the absolute limits of its capability to meet the needs of the population.

Moreover, the traditional ruler's triumphant return after four years of exile capped a period in which, in terms of mountain political ecology, everything had changed. World War II had ended, and, as of 1946, the colonial government was prepared to make the financial commitment necessary to go beyond the forest reserves and to control Tanganyika's Public Land, beginning with the Mlalo Basin. At the same time, new indigenous political forces had begun to coalesce in opposition to the Native Authorities and their mentors in the district administration.

The official correspondence never mentions njaa ya Chankola, but it does indicate that an alarming situation began to develop after rainfall deficits in 1941. The drought led district authorities to impose the Native Foodstuffs Ordinance, which restricted removal of food from the district without the permission of the D.C. The ordinance also required permission for the purchase or barter of food from Africans for resale in the district. Given the growing importance of regional markets in and around Usambara, this act, if enforced, would have hindered the movement of food from areas of abundance to those of shortage. Oral evidence suggests that marketers disregarded the ordinance, but its imposition nevertheless shows how little the administration at district headquarters understood about the important role of regional exchange in famine relief.

Table 5.1 Census data for Mlalo Basin

	Mwangoi	Mlalo	Handei	Shita	Dule	Zaizo
1931	2,366	3,115	2,819	285	1,135	446
1945	3,805	4,518	4,348	338	1,799	701
Increase	37.8%	31%	34.9%	15.6%	36.9%	36.3%
Subtotals for 1945						
Men	968	1,275	1,098	81	435	175
Women	1,099	1,317	1,282	105	518	206
Boys	872	1,010	944	93	375	186
Girls	866	916	1,024	59	471	134
Total basin pop.						
1931	10,733					
1945	15,509					

Based on TNA 72/3/25, "Comparison of Population Figures for Mlalo Basin 1931 and 1945," Mlalo Basin Rehabilitation Scheme, 24e.

By December 1943, the provincial commissioner informed Tanganyika's chief secretary that food supplies were "dangerously scarce" across much of West Usambara, particularly on the northern tier around Mlalo, Mbaramo, Mtae, and Mlola, where blight had devastated the potato crop and dry weather had limited maize harvests.[117] The provincial commissioner estimated that 39,000 people had been affected and requested 430 tons of food aid. Three months later, in March 1944, the provincial commissioner again requested food aid owing to poor short rains and locust depredations. In his annual report for 1944, the district commissioner noted "severe drought" at Mlola, Mlalo, and Mtae, which, along with poor harvests and more locust depredations, continued into 1945 and 1946.[118] During these difficult years, a committee of provincial and district officials (simply, the Provincial Committee) met periodically, in large part to formulate a plan to "rehabilitate" the Mlalo Basin once the financial pressures of World War II had receded.[119] The reports they commissioned to guide policy seem to have been but *pro forma* exercises in that regard, but they can now be read to uncover how communities reacted in the immediate term to this episode of njaa. Food imports helped ease the regional hunger, but Mlalo's residents also took a number of ameliorative steps.

Table 5.2 Acreage devoted to major crops on average holding, Mlalo

Crop	Acreage
Bananas	0.90
Cassava	1.23
Sugar cane	0.56
Maize	1.01
Beans	1.27
Sweet potatoes	0.73
	3.43

TNA 4/269/5, vol. 1, J. B. Clegg, "Report," *Mlalo Basin Rehabilitation Scheme,* 150.

Intercropping techniques similar to those observed by Baumann and Hölst half a century earlier helped farmers endure the crisis, but population increases and the resulting limited land supplies required poor farmers to make the most of their meager holdings by stretching each field's productive capacity to the absolute limit. Figure 5.2 shows an estimate of the acreage devoted to each crop on 3.43 acres. (The fact that the total acreage adds up to over 5 acres is accounted for by seasonal crop rotations.)

While 3.43 acres represents an average-sized holding, most of the basin's farmers held two acres or less, divided into several fields, each in a slightly different environmental situation. An intensively cultivated field's productivity depended on the individual farmer's acumen, edaphic (soil) and climatic circumstances, and labor inputs. On Usambara's acidic and easily leached soils this type of intensification could only be sustained through fallow, a concept the Provincial Committee felt beyond the understanding of local farmers.[120] In another intensification strategy, Mlalo's farmers employed the irrigation technologies that had so impressed nineteenth-century observers cited above, and in August 1946, the same month Kinyassi returned to his seat, Mlalo's irrigation systems were operating at full capacity.[121]

Intensification could not meet all the challenges placed on the system by njaa ya Chankola and so farmers moved to incorporate lands formerly considered marginal, or difficult to manage. For example, highland marshes (Shambaa, sing. *dau*), historically important as water catchments and for their reeds and grasses, which provided occasional grazing and roofing material, became an essential feature in arable agriculture during njaa ya Chankola.[122] In fact, farming in daus came to be known as *kija mshare*

(Shambaa, delivery from hunger).[123] The first written reference to the technique turns up in F. J. Nutman's 1944 report to the Provincial Committee of his reconnaissance of the Mlalo Basin.[124] Dau draining helped ease the regional hunger, but the long-term environmental effects on the Umba watershed became evident with increasingly severe flash floods thereafter.

Farmers also sought to extend cultivation below the massif at Kitivo. Unfortunately, as Milne had explained during the 1930s, productive plains lands below Mlalo were limited. Moreover, the presence of malarial mosquitoes threatened the health of new residents who were previously unexposed to the disease. In spite of these conditions, hunger drove people into the vitivo in 1944.[125] As Milne had predicted, the migrant cultivators, inexperienced in plains farming, disrupted the finely tuned plains system by indiscriminately opening fields along the Umba, interrupting the river's regular flow and flood patterns, and ultimately decreasing yields of more experienced farmers downstream.[126]

In another strategy to meet subsistence needs, women from the Mlalo Basin walked for several hours a day to and from the villages of Tewe and Mbaramo to perform day labor in return for payment in cassava. As Cory reported in 1946, "The procedure at Mbaramo is that women from the villages of shortage go to work there as day laborers and are paid in kind. In May and June I saw many women laborers returning daily with their loads of muhogo [cassava] after work at Mbaramo.....It is difficult for the people so long as their supplies are assured, to recognize loss of fertility in any particular area."[127] Informants substantiate Cory's read on the food situation: "Tewe and Mbaramo still had trees so that mists brought some water to the area. Also folks at Mbaramo and Tewe planted cassava in great quantities even though they didn't know that the drought was coming. This in particular helped the people of Mlalo."[128] The testimony also points out the importance of social relations between neighboring mountain communities in stemming the hunger.

In yet another strategy to cheat famine in an increasingly degraded environment, young men moved temporarily to coastal towns to work in the wage economy, following a pattern established during the nineteenth century. Cory estimated that at any one time during the year, 25 percent of young men were abroad working for cash.[129] In cases like njaa ya Chankola, where food aid had to be purchased, cash remittances from relatives working in urban centers could mean the difference between eating and going hungry. In another report commissioned by the Provincial Committee, the writer went so far as to conclude that labor was the area's main export.[130] The strategy had drawbacks. In their absence, Cory reported, the men's fields suffered neglect while their huts fell into disrepair.[131] Labor for irrigation works may also have become dear, and out-migration would have placed additional burdens on the remaining men, women, and young children.[132]

Farmers in the Mlalo Basin, like their counterparts across East Africa, had a long history of adjusting their agricultural system to meet challenges to their food security. By developing and maintaining an irrigation system, they had invested in the land's capability over the long term. By adopting exotic cultigens, they had shown a willingness to experiment and to innovate on the fly in response to the multitude of changing ecological, demographic, and economic conditions. None of the European observers demonstrate an understanding that the changes over the two generations of contact with Europeans showed both continuities and breaks with past practice. Adaptation, however, had brought with it a risk. Population increases, soil erosion, and crop diseases heightened the chance of a breakdown in both subsistence and market-oriented production, even in good years, and, without the grain imported by the colonial government, the rainfall deficits of the 1940s would likely have killed people.[133] Mlalo's farming system had overreached, in its twentieth-century context, the limits of its resiliency.

CHAPTER SIX

Agriculture and the State

Imposing a Landscape Makeover in Insecure Times, 1946–1961

NJAA YA CHANKOLA USHERED IN a period of rapid changes in local politics and land use. Although Hassani Kinyassi's reappointment in August 1946 as Mlalo's subchief temporarily calmed the political unrest, the colonial state almost simultaneously imposed the Mlalo Basin Rehabilitation Scheme (MBRS) as a pilot for a far more ambitious conservation scheme across the Usambaras. The MBRS signaled the state's determination to control where and how people lived on Usambara's Public Lands. The Agriculture Department's decision to carry out the projects without consulting the people whose labor they required created a sense of extreme insecurity among a population who saw colonial reform as an attack on their ideal of a mountain sanctuary.

The MBRS and its successor, the Usambara Scheme, formed part of a larger post–World War II push across Britain's African colonies for agrarian reform, which historians often refer to as the "second colonial occupation."[1] Employing funds allocated from the Colonial Development and Welfare Act, the Tanganyikan government financed several large regional development projects, most of which ended in agroecological disarray and political turmoil. The money paid for an increase in the number of agricultural staff assigned to what had been semiautonomous farming regions. Smallholders bristled against the increasing interference and substantially enlarged the scale of anticolonial political action. While Tanganyika's historians have carefully examined how the political unrest helped to mobilize rural people under the umbrella of Julius Nyerere's Tanganyika African National Union, key questions remain about the era's ecological legacy on the agricultural landscape.

In his seminal history of Tanganyika, John Iliffe hinted at an ecological aspect of the resistance to rural development when he argued that the projects succeeded in areas where they "coincided with African drives toward capitalism" and sparked resistance in zones of "agricultural involution."[2] Clifford Geertz developed the concept in his analysis of the declining productivity of hyper-intensive Javanese rice farming systems.[3] In Geertz's analysis, the Javanese rice farming system, which smallholders sustained for over a thousand years through technological innovations, ultimately broke down under the weight of its continual intensification. The result was widespread rural poverty. Although not exactly parallel to the Javanese case, njaa ya Chankola demonstrated that at Mlalo the continual fine-tuning of the farming system in response to demographic and economic change had altered the mountain ecology, diminishing the land's long-term productivity. Adding to the pressure were the constraints that colonialism placed on farmers through land alienation that deprived farmers at Mlalo of the mobility so important to East African agriculture. Under circumstances often beyond their control, they had manipulated the system as best they could in order to survive where they were.

Although, in 1937, Milne had pointed out that Mlalo's problems were not representative of the whole of the Usambaras, the conservation projects of the 1940s and 1950s reduced a complex regional situation into a simple ecological equation solvable by known technologies. Most of the schemes failed, but in places like Usambara their legacy is still apparent in local responses to state-sponsored and internationally based conservation initiatives.

The Mlalo Basin Rehabilitation Scheme

With Milne's report purged from official consciousness, district and provincial officers responsible for Usambara continued to impress upon Tanganyika's central government the immediacy of Usambara's ecological problems, particularly at Mlalo. In 1942, R. R. Staples, the government's chief biologist, assessed Mlalo's agroecological difficulties; two years later, the provincial government assembled a team to draw up a five-year plan for environmental rehabilitation.

Beginning in 1945 and continuing through 1946, a succession of "experts" traversed the Mlalo Basin, formulating reports on husbandry and society, complete with suggestions for their reform. F. J. Nutman penned the most interesting although most poorly received of the reports. Nutman had some experience in the Usambaras, as a plant pathologist at Amani and later as the head of the Fibre Board Plant at Shume in West Usambara's forest reserve. Nutman offered the standard argument about the imbalance between population and resources.[4] However, he felt that Mlalo's farmers understood that degradation was occurring, but low producer prices and the wartime dictates to "grow more crops" had trapped them economically. Nutman proposed a long-term plan for economic diversification that included a manufacturing sector to absorb excess labor and allow itinerant workers to remain at home.[5] The Provincial Committee largely dismissed his report as superficial and inaccurate.[6]

In early October, about a month after Nutman submitted his report, H. J. Van Rensberg, the territory's pasture research officer, arrived at Mlalo to assess the ecological situation. He stayed two days.[7] In Van Rensberg's expert opinion, environmental degradation at Mlalo constituted an "emergency situation" whose cause could be found in "unlimited, uncontrolled and wasteful methods of cultivation; and lack of effort to build up a system of balanced mixed farming where the animal can play its proper role."[8] He advocated environmental controls such as ridges and grass leys placed along steep slopes.[9]

The Provincial Committee met twice during December 1945 to consider all the plans and subsequently agreed on the following:

- 80 percent of arable land in Mlalo was under cultivation; population density exceeded 500/mi^2; the basin was "grossly overcrowded" with an average holding of 4.48 acres.

- Crowding resulted in cultivation of steep slopes, reduction of communally owned grazing lands, and accelerated erosion.

- Mlalo's soils were not then, nor had they ever been, very fertile.

- Food imports proved that the population could not produce its own subsistence.

- In order to procure cash, much of Mlalo's population performed wage labor outside the basin.

- Mlalo's population did not enjoy a higher standard of living than other regions in the Usambaras, as Nutman had contended.

- The population did not understand the seriousness of the erosion problem.

- Current scientific knowledge could solve the erosion problem.

- Erosion control was the first priority and any scheme must be enforced with maximum diligence.[10]

Based on these assumptions, Mlalo faced environmental problems whose solution lay in "scientific knowledge." Significantly, the report did not examine Mlalo's agricultural history or the variety of indigenous farming practices, nor had any of the experts actually measured the rate of soil erosion on even one of Mlalo's slopes. To the Provincial Committee, overpopulation had simply overtaxed a farming system without the flexibility or technological capacity to adapt. Nutman continued to press for economic diversification, but the Provincial Committee ignored him and adopted the "Staples Plan," which advocated a mixed system of animal and crop husbandry operating under strict erosion control measures on ten- to fifteen-acre farms. Given that Mlalo's farmers seldom held more than four acres of widely scattered gardens, the Staples Plan clearly would drive substantial numbers of people out of the Mlalo Basin.[11] Who would leave? Where would the migrants go? In these preliminary meetings, the committee never directly addressed the issues of displaced families except in the following vague reference: "Any scheme which will tend to relieve the population pressure in the Mlalo Basin is to be commended and despite the danger of malaria the Kitivo and Lwengera suggestions mentioned in the Report of the Tanga Province Sub-Committee on land for post war development should be considered from this point of view."[12]

In Dar es Salaam, the colonial administration accepted the committee's findings, but expressed concern about the implications of the government actively displacing people, a move central government correctly believed would be resisted. The central government preferred to let economic pressures reduce the numbers living in Mlalo. In the end, central government and the Provincial Committee decided to ignore the issue of population control and the ongoing famine conditions under njaa ya Chankola. The director of agriculture approved a five-year, £15,000 budget and gave Hans Cory, the government's sociologist, permission to proceed with a demographic and sociological survey. Soil erosion control would begin in July, once the Native Authorities, through the "compulsory exchange of land," had identified and laid out a thousand acres of suitable land for the project in a place where no such contiguous acreage existed.[13] The pilot project would create an agricultural landscape heretofore unknown in the Usambaras, and therefore challenge the cultural history of local agriculture by directly attacking land-tenure arrangements and gardening techniques.

Of the numerous reports and correspondence for 1946 regarding the Mlalo Basin's rehabilitation, only one referred to the four continuous years of chronic drought, insect and disease infestations of crops, and hunger.[14] In early June 1946, just as local dissatisfaction with Chankola reached its peak, Cory arrived to survey Mlalo's social conditions, to take a census of human and livestock population, and to determine each household's land holdings. A provincial tax team had also been slated to accompany Cory's survey team. Under the circumstances, the surveys proved impossible, and by June 19, Cory wanted to leave Mlalo altogether.[15] In light of Cory's difficulties, the P.C. asked the central government in Dar es Salaam to postpone the anti-erosion measures for fear that they "might lead to further agitations which would be embarrassing [to the Provincial Administration]."[16]

In keeping with the MBRS's inauspicious beginnings, J. B. Clegg, the newly appointed agricultural officer in charge of the project, arrived at Mlalo in July 1946, at the height of the yearly dry season and one month before Hassani Kinyassi would be reinstated as the location's chief. Making perhaps the most intelligent choice of his tenure at Mlalo, Clegg decided to live in Malindi, a market town located on a mountain ridge on the edge of the basin and removed from the vortex of hunger and unrest. Informants remember Clegg as severe, militaristic, and righteous about his mission.[17] Clearly, the old men of Mwangoi did not like him. Clegg reported that "some *Wazee* [elders] from Mwangoi came up early on Thursday 7/25/46 and put a curse on the camp site. I have warned the Jumbe Ndodo of Mwangoi that unless he takes adequate action against them, I will run him up before the D.O. for permitting the practice of witchcraft in his village and also permitting his *Wazee* to hinder my work. He seemed to be very worried."[18]

On this note of intimidation, Clegg began the Mlalo Basin Rehabilitation Scheme. Although Cory had found it impossible, Clegg believed he could direct a detailed sociological survey of all villages and hamlets in the Mlalo Basin. At the same time, Clegg proposed to lay out a demonstration area on about one thousand acres at Shita, a hamlet a few kilometers from Mlalo. On this experimental farm, labor gangs recruited by local headmen would rehabilitate eroded slopes through hedge plantings along hill contours. The workers would also demonstrate livestock husbandry techniques by planting fodder grasses, which they would harvest and feed to cattle confined to stalls.

Clegg immediately encountered resistance.[19] Early in October, the district officer, trying to assuage fears of land alienation, organized a baraza where he and Clegg tried to explain the aims of the scheme to a suspicious crowd of eight hundred men.[20] Uninterested in technological discussions, the throng wanted information about long-term plans, particularly if the government intended to evict them once the land had been "rehabilitated." If not, why, the men wanted to know, was precious fallow being planted up with fodder grasses? Furthermore, why was Clegg measuring homes and gardens at Shita? The D.O. reassured the skittish crowd that he would evict no one.[21]

Despite the D.O.'s promise, Clegg quickly discovered that cultivable land was in such short supply that the demonstration project's planned thousand acres would have to be reduced to 650 acres, and he could only obtain that through the coerced alienation of communal grazing fields and subsistence gardens.[22] By the end of 1946, Clegg's African staff had encountered stiff opposition to the village survey, especially around the demonstration areas at Shita and Mwangoi, where resistance to Chankola had been especially strong.[23] Continuing famine conditions only heightened the tension, because those most affected ended up working on the demonstration farm. In effect, they worked for food. Meanwhile, hundreds of men traveled to the coastal urban centers to find work. Clegg estimated that, of males thirteen years old and upward, 20 percent were out of the basin working for cash in Tanga and Mombasa.[24] Even if one had cash, food prices had reached exorbitant levels at the local markets.[25]

During the second half of 1947, the food shortages eased after adequate fall rains in 1946 and again in 1947. Nonetheless, resistance to the scheme continued. Many still refused to cooperate with the survey, and when Clegg ordered farmers across the basin to adopt his anti-erosion rules, they dragged their feet.[26] The resistance appears to have again coalesced around the chama, which the provincial administration believed to be a coalition of former headmen and business-minded farmers who had helped to foment some of the agitation against Chankola. Chama members had reportedly turned their opposition toward the Mlalo Scheme by spreading a rumor that the D.O. had purchased the Shita demonstration area and that it would be taken over by Europeans. They had also allegedly threatened the agricultural instructors at Shita.[27]

In response, the district commissioner sent to Mlalo F. H. Jackson, an assistant district officer from Korogwe. His mission was simple: secure the people's cooperation. In order to apprise Jackson of the local political context, Clegg organized a baraza at Mlalo, which about two thousand "taxpayers" attended. When the crowd once again assailed the officers over the demonstration project at Shita, Jackson decided to visit practically every village and hamlet in the Mlalo subchiefdom in order to undermine the chama's opposition and to secure cooperation for the scheme. In less than a month, he believed he had succeeded. "[I]t is difficult to accurately gauge the shift of native opinion in this backward and intrigue ridden area of Mlalo; but I think I may fairly say that I have got the cooperation of the people ... and have undertaken a propaganda offensive against the chama which is bearing fruit."[28] Despite Jackson's confidence, the rehabilitation scheme continued to operate under a cloud, and Clegg decided to ease the enforcement of the soil conservation rules.

In January 1948, Clegg appointed to Kinyassi's office a new assistant chief, who "forced the various divisional headmen to produce labor for the scheme." Labor turnout at the demonstration farm increased fourfold while all those voicing opposition were cited for heavy fines.[29] While his enthusiastic assistant rounded up scheme labor and fined protesters, Kinyassi, as a local judge, slowed progress by delaying his rulings on violations that came before him.[30] At the hamlets of Mwangoi and Handei, the headmen openly allowed livestock to graze on crop stubble, a contravention of scheme rules.[31] Even agricultural instructors began to oppose the scheme surreptitiously.[32]

Still, Clegg kept pressing. In April 1948, he directed laborers to build Hehe-style tie ridges to replace what had become a useless system of contour hedges. The so-called Hehe system, originally suggested by Van Rensberg and adopted from ridge cultivation practiced in southern Tanganyika, required yearly building up and breaking down of raised mounds of soil and organic matter. When the women of Mwangoi visited the demonstration area and saw the ridges, they immediately objected to the hard work involved. Soon after, the women of Handei arrived at Shita to protest the ridges, and Clegg handed out citations.[33]

By March 1949, drought had ruined the fall-season plantings of 1948 and some areas of the basin were again experiencing severe food shortages. Weevils attacked the banana gardens left untended by farmers away working at the coastal towns. By May, the food shortages had become general and only the quintessential famine crop, cassava, staved off starvation.[34] By June 1949, most of the cassava crop had been harvested and eaten, so that during October and November preparations for the all-important short-rains plantings slackened as the able-bodied population searched for food. Some went so far as to feed on the plantings formerly used to establish the contour hedges. Those living adjacent to the demonstration areas broke down tie ridges, then dug up and destroyed elephant-grass plantings to make room for cultivation. Relief arrived in the form of the fall rains of 1949, and by May 1950 farmers once again harvested their crops.

With full knowledge of these circumstances, Clegg's final report claimed that the Mlalo Scheme was an unqualified success.[35] His "before" picture painted the usual negative view of an overcrowded, eroded, and deforested landscape, complete with a farming system teetering on the edge of collapse. His demonstration farm (650 acres) introduced a radically new

Table 6.1 Acreages devoted to major crops, old system and new system, Mlalo Basin

Type	Acres old system	Acres new system
Forest	5	130
Bananas	50	130
Cultivated land	295	330
Pasture	285	10
Fodder crops	0	30
Roads	0	5
Villages	15	15
Total	650	650

TNA 72/69/9j, "Report of Mlalo Rehabilitation Scheme 29/10/49," by J. B. Clegg, Agricultural Officer, Lushoto, to Executive Officer, Development Division, Dar es Salaam, 6.

landscape organization. Under this arrangement, Clegg argued, milk yields had increased fourfold, streams around Shita ran clear and neither flooded nor dried up during 1949, and yields on ridges had increased.

Although, according to Clegg, the demonstration project had succeeded, in general he lamented the fact that land use in the Mlalo Basin had continued to degrade the environment. He warned that fertility must be raised and maintained through the addition of organic matter to the soil and the application of "Hehe ridging." Moreover, Clegg believed that successful agriculture in Mlalo depended on the permanent expansion of annual cropping to swamps, which had only been used during times of dearth. He also recommended that the irrigation system be limited to terraced, ridged, or flat land. He argued that under the new system the area available for food would increase by 36 percent (1.25 acres per family). However, Clegg also maintained that "when . . . the annual increase of population of 2.54% is taken into consideration the conclusion is inescapable . . . a portion of the population should be moved." He also believed that only coercion through heavy fines, imprisonment, or exile would secure cooperation. Finally, in Clegg's view the state, rather than the Native Authorities, would have to step in to oversee conservation.

The approaches to Mlalo's problems reflect what Piers Blaikie has identified as the "classic approach to soil erosion and conservation."[36] That is, the government identified soil erosion as primarily an environmental problem with environmental solutions. Thus, in the Mlalo case, conservation meant physical and biological soil erosion control, and, ultimately, forced depopulation. The provincial team saw a picture of too many people destructively mining too little land, rather than a group of knowledgeable farmers adapting an agricultural system to changing environmental, demographic, and economic realities. In an extremely complex situation, governmental action remained simplistic and inflexible.

Beyond Mlalo: West Usambara's Agricultural Economy and Ecology

While the drama of the MBRS and the njaa ya Chankola dominate the historical record, the rest of West Usambara experienced an agricultural transformation as well. The economic and agroecological trends that had been in place from early in the twentieth century intensified as the agricultural economy expanded. The periodic markets that linked mountain regions had helped to distribute what food was available, but their proliferation during the 1940s and 1950s also signaled both an increasing importance of commodity flows and farmers' need for cash. The markets also served as local nodes in the wider regional web of exchange that included the growing urban populations of Tanga and Dar es Salaam, where demand grew for the cabbages, tomatoes, onions, carrots, and other horticultural crops grown in Tanganyika's highlands.

By the early 1950s, market gardening in the West Usambaras had become potentially lucrative. In 1953 alone, 700 tons of vegetables left West Usambara's mountain markets bound for coastal cities. Unlike the agricultural expansion of the 1920s and 1930s, where farmers reopened abandoned lands, market gardening of the 1950s involved cultivation of the dau, a swampy valley bottom in the mountains where the presence of abundant ground water and fertile alluvial soils suited the moisture needs of the vegetables. Until njaa ya Chankola, daus had served occasionally as pastures, but clearing and draining their swampy soils required large labor inputs.[37] Famine increased their food production value dramatically, while the growing market for vegetables during the late 1940s and 1950s provided strong incentives to farmers to keep them open to production permanently.[38] Once Clegg's work crews opened the swamps, the local subchiefs distributed them, although not always equitably. At Nyassa dau near Mlalo, informants claim that the subchief simply ignored long-held tenure strictures and sold dau plots to the highest bidders.[39]

The less affluent also gained access to profitable markets because increasing demand for grains had raised the value of maize and rice. The maize trade benefited poorer farmers because they could grow it on the hillside plots to which they had access. However, maize export involved a calculated risk because, in response to the food shortages, the Lushoto district administration permanently forbade the export from the mountains of maize and beans during the 1940s. Farmers generally ignored the rule and secretly channeled commerce in these commodities into a thriving unofficial market.[40]

The prosperity in mountain commodity production had another spatial component in that it usually occurred where lines of efficient transportation intersected alluvial soils. In the Mlalo Basin, for example, those who had participated in the 1949 land grab at Nyassa dau, or had riverine plots along the Umba, or had kitivo plots, could cheaply send their produce to market via the bus line operated by Tanganyika Railways and, later, by private entrepreneurs. Similarly, the profitable dau lands around Lushoto, Soni, and Ubiri lay near the main mountain road, which wound down to the railway depot at Mombo. Between 1949 and 1953, road construction

Fig. 6.1. Market ladies at Kwemakame's Friday market on West Usambara plateau.
Photo Sabine Barcatta

in the plains spurred farmers there to expand the area devoted to rice to four thousand acres, a 200 percent increase.[41] By the late 1950s, tens of thousands of kilos of rice left the Usambaras through official and unofficial channels.[42]

Table 6.2, which represents official exports over about two years, shows both the volatility of the trade in agricultural commodities and the dominance of vegetables. The market structure marginalized farmers short in land, lacking access to dau plots, or living away from the main roads. Even in the favored zones, population growth in Usambara between 1931 and 1957 reached 3 percent and undercut the viability of peasant farming for the land-poor. Poorer peasant families, already squeezed onto hillside

Table 6.2 Extract of monthly exports from Native Authority markets, W. Usambara Mountains, 1955–57 (in kilograms)

Month/Year	Vegetables	Potatoes	Beans	Onions	Tobacco
5/55	43,067	93		669	
11/55	124,830	3,292		3,411	6,091
12/55	49,248	9,737	500	4,816	
2/56	55,080	8,374	10,100	3,252	2,864
5/56	40,203	5,366	100	4,821	1,053
6/56	38,716	23,613	6,700	332	1,150
7/56	24,034	7,392	21,315	1,357	
9/56	30,371	8,467	4,430	943	686
11/56	39,435	15,438		16,219	570
12/56	77,130	8,617	100	10,077	1,132
2/57	51,165	13,514	18,740	9,403	1,583
3/57	84,151	23,936	43,186	6,278	1,270
4/57	164,767	17,109	5,670	1,610	1,117
6/57	37,933	14,340	4,944	46	645

Figures derived from monthly reports of the Usambara Scheme, TNA 72/US/30, volumes 2 and 3 entitled respectively, Usambara Scheme: Safari and Monthly Reports and Usambara Scheme: Monthly Reports.

lands of marginal fertility, had to make tough choices regarding the amount of labor and acreage they devoted to production for subsistence (increasingly, cassava) versus the market (maize and vegetables).[43] Land shortages in Mlalo had limited access to the point where even the time-honored tenure arrangement under which the land-poor could borrow fallow fields as a hedge against hunger became increasingly difficult.[44] Census data shows, furthermore, that women increasingly bore the brunt of agricultural production as men moved out of the mountains to find wage labor.

In some areas, poverty cycles became entrenched. For example, in the Mlola Basin, where the German explorer Baumann had been so inhospitably received, three years of rainfall deficits and insect infestations destroyed maize harvests in the late 1940s, and by 1951 the area had run out of cassava reserves. When adequate rains did fall, hungry peasant farmers could not wait for their crops to mature. They ate their immature crops and supplemented their diet with white ants. Those with cash could purchase

Table 6.3 West Usambara, population by ethnicity, gender, and age, 1931

Group	Male adult	Female adult	Total adult	Male child	Female child	Total child	Total
Shambaa	16,264	16,472	32,736	11,579	10,947	22,526	55,262
Kilindi	3,056	2,400	5,456	2,592	2.508	5,100	10,556
Zigua	1,190	1,039	2,229	802	724	1,526	3,755
Pare	2,441	2,363	4,804	1,544	1,577	3,131	7,935
Mbugu	2,117	1,561	3,678	1,087	1,034	2,121	5,799
Migrant workers[1]	1,546	186	1,732	209	192	401	2,133
Taita	22	16	38	16	13	29	67
Segeju	39	64	103	30	47	77	180
Kamba	114	97	211	46	28	74	285
Digo	8	9	17	2	5	7	24
Total	26,797	24,207	51,004	7,907	17,075	34,982	85,986

[1] Includes following groups: Manyema, Sukuma, Bondei, Iramba, Ngoni, Nyassa, Wemba, Mabwe, Nyamwanga, Kinga, Nyakyusa, Yao.

TNA 4/183/2, vol. 1, "Census, 1931."

Table 6.4 West Usambara, population by gender, age, and location, 1957

Area	Adult males	Adult females	Children	Total
Lushoto	3,076	4,250	7,996	15,322
Vuga	4,772	6,203	12,224	23,199
Gare	1,430	2,067	3,676	7,173
Mlola	3,646	5,373	8,966	17,985
Mlalo	6,568	10,410	18,261	35,239
Mtae	2,472	3,775	6,922	13,169
Bumbuli	4,985	6,342	12,237	23,564
Mgwashi	2,015	2,266	4,357	8,638
Lushoto town	391	235	369	995
Total	29,355	40,921	69,008	145,284

From Tanganyika Population Census 1957, East African Statistical Bureau. See also Patrick Fleuret, "Farm and Market: A Study of Society and Agriculture in Tanzania" (Ph.D. diss., University of California at Santa Barbara, 1978), 100.

imported government food supplies, while the less fortunate walked to the Lwengera Valley that separated the eastern and western massifs, or on to the East Usambaras, in search of land or employment. Other families abandoned their farms and migrated to Upare.[45] Mlola's situation represented the worst case in a more general condition in West Usambara, where thousands of kilos of food—vegetables, maize, beans, rice, and livestock—left Lushoto District while emergency food supplies had to be imported to supplement subsistence crop losses in vulnerable farming areas.[46] Even beans, normally a subsistence crop, were black-marketed outside the district in 1951, a year when two hundred tons of food imports were required to meet shortages in January and February alone.[47] Under these difficult circumstances, more and more farmers sought opportunities outside the mountains. In addition to men working temporarily outside the mountains in order to supplement family income at home, by 1957 a substantial number of Washambaa families (33,000 men, along with their wives and children) lived permanently in districts outside the mountains.[48] As the Shambaa moved out of West Usambara, new European settlers moved in. They leased sections of former German estates around Soni and Lushoto or made outright purchases of patches of freehold land. In addition to the European newcomers, Tanganyikans from outside Usambara also entered the mountains to labor on newly formed tea estates, where "large bodies of squatters" had begun to cultivate, much to the chagrin of the local Shambaa population and the district administration.[49]

The Usambara Scheme

In this economic context of rural differentiation, the British administration extended the soil conservation principles of the Mlalo Basin Rehabilitation Scheme to the rest of the West Usambara mountains beginning in 1950. The Lushoto District Development Committee, which planned and oversaw the Usambara Scheme, aimed to reorient the region's agroecology in the name of soil and water conservation and environmental restoration. The reams of paper generated by the agricultural officers assigned to the scheme, along with the bitter testimony of those who participated under threat of fines and imprisonment, showed its implementation to be a tragic administrative miscalculation. In addition to its conservation component, the Usambara Scheme operated under the assumption that a substantial percentage of the population would eventually have to take up permanent residence on the plains below the massif. Therefore, agricultural reform in the hills depended on simultaneously expanding lowland agriculture into areas heretofore avoided by knowledgeable cultivators who had for centuries already farmed in the plains.[50] The scheme's planners anticipated some resistance:

> Although the people of W. Usambara are being forced by hunger and propaganda to [a] growing awareness of their difficulties, there is no certainty that they will move voluntarily into even the best prepared settlement areas in the plains. They love their hills; they are less hardy than the Wapare, indolent and politically minded. On the other hand there seems no alternative to movement but swiftly advancing denudation of the hills and destitution of the people. The enforcement of the Rehabilitation Scheme is bound to displace some hundreds of families and if the first resettlements [in the plains] are a patent material success and above all, not too far removed from the worst areas of overpopulation the mind of the people is very likely to change.[51]

In theory, enforcement of scheme rules and prerogatives rested with the Native Authority courts and the subchiefs' councils, the latter a brainchild of the Lushoto district administration designed to further decentralize political power. The district commissioner's insistence that the Native Authorities be thoroughly identified with the scheme and his desire to deflect local hostility away from his office fooled no one.[52] The intentions behind the Usambara Scheme became clear: the state would exert its authoritarian power in order to enforce unpopular conservation measures and push families out of the mountains altogether.

The physical environment that the scheme attempted to create bore little resemblance to what then existed on the farming landscape. Rules required that all slopes between 10° and 15° be ridged using the "Hehe system."[53] The technique involved building up an earthen ridge along the contour of a hillside and connecting the ridge to the hillside at every two paces. Cultivators would then plant sweet potatoes or legumes on the ridges. After the harvest, scheme rules did not allow the usual practice of allowing livestock to graze the crop stubble, nor could fields be burnt in preparation for the subsequent planting season. Instead, the ridges had to be broken down and rebuilt with the leftover organic matter buried inside. In this way mulch, rather than animal dung or ash, recharged soil fertility. Another anti-erosion measure on steeper slopes, between 15° and 25°, required farmers to plant lines of banana trees and fodder grasses along the hill's contour. Slopes over 25° were banned from any kind of cultivation. Instead, farmers would plant tree crops, especially wattle, a fast-growing acacia that provided firewood and building poles.[54] The regulations imposed uniformity across a region where a multitude of ecological conditions and a number of land-tenure and land-use arrangements reflected centuries of cultural evolution.

Some of the agricultural officers in the second colonial occupation saw weaknesses in the scheme. Over a decade earlier, Milne had suggested that the Agriculture Department plan for the region's geographical diversity. W. D. Gibbons, an Usambara Scheme agricultural officer, came to the same conclusion in 1951 when he discovered markedly different ecological conditions in very close proximity. He noted that the farming areas of Bumbuli and Mgwashi "were of a vastly different character and it is difficult to imagine an overall scheme fitting both." Echoing Milne's earlier proposals, Gibbons suggested that "a regional survey should be carried out to better suit the scheme to particular areas."[55] In this case, he found erosion control unnecessary at Mgwashi but urgently needed at Bumbuli, only a few miles away.

The rules undermined farmers' links to their agricultural economy. In hindsight, the impracticality of ridging and replanting hillsides covered in patchworks of hundreds of gardens of varying size and composition seems evident. As part of the ridging process, hundreds of maize gardens would have to be uprooted and replaced with bananas.[56] Bananas helped control erosion and they had made sense as a subsistence crop a century earlier, but in 1950, the maize exclusion constituted a direct assault on poor peasant households where maize sales often provided one of the main sources of income. In fact, the most vocal opposition emanated from this requirement.[57] Another scheme requirement, a moratorium on stream bank cultivation, struck at market gardening, the realm of the more financially secure peasantry. Thus, even the most economically productive land-use arrangements directly violated the rules.

When agricultural officers began to circulate throughout the mountains in order to explain the scheme rules to farmers, they met with immediate and vocal resistance, especially from women in northern Usambara. On September 18, 1950, two women interrupted the Mbaramo baraza to claim that everyone knew that Shita (center of the Mlalo Pilot Scheme) had been given to Europeans. Later that day at nearby Tewe, R. H. Gower, the scheme's local officer, decided to head off any debate by forbidding ninety village women from attending the meeting.[58] On September 26, 1950, at Mlola, where systemic agroecological impoverishment was well under way, one thousand angry protestors besieged the agricultural officer in the government rest house. Gower observed that "[t]he women here (mostly Wapare) were as ill-mannered as we have met anywhere.... Future bad behavior must be quickly and sharply punished to avoid the impression that bad manners and much noise from women is tolerated and condoned by authority."[59]

Despite the sharp tenor of the women's protests, much of the resistance took on a more subtle tone. For example, in compliance with scheme rules, farmers at Shita dutifully planted banana trees above the 15° contour, but then planted maize among them, an obvious contravention. In 1951, at Vuga, banana trees marking the 25° contour were uprooted, as were the grasses which had been planted along the stream banks. The D.C. described these and other acts of noncompliance as a "mass civil disobedience campaign."[60] Subsequent reports from Vuga, Soni, and Bumbuli document a clear pattern of passive resistance culminating in a very overt protest at Vuga in 1956, which ended with a group of women trying to mob the district officer's car.[61]

In the face of ongoing resistance, the staff pressed on with the difficult task of supervising farmers and quantifying their gains.[62] African agricultural staff carried out much of this work. In the early years they seem to have believed in the scheme. They came from all over Tanganyika to receive a six-week training course at Lwandai Middle School (Mlalo) or at the Bomo School at Malindi. The District Committee also hired, as an agricultural officer, David Mwakosya, a Tanganyikan from Unyankusa who had been trained in colonial agriculture at Makerere College in Uganda.[63] A former instructor explained that, despite the unpopularity of the scheme, the African instructors' training led them to believe very adamantly in the dangers of soil erosion and the state of degradation that threatened the Usambaras.[64] Their veracity is reflected in a dramatic rise in criminal prosecutions, from 1,349 in 1953 to 2,177 in 1954. In 1956, Native Authority courts heard over three thousand cases, most of them violations of Scheme rules.[65] Because the instructors worked closely with farmers, however, a number of them began to sympathize with their charges once the difficulties and harassment now inherent in peasant life came to light.[66] By the late 1950s, African field staff began to participate in the resistance by not enforcing ridging or non-burning requirements, by simply looking the other way, and, at times, by accepting bribes for doing so.[67] By 1956, many staff had decided to end their participation altogether and requested retirement or simply resigned.[68]

Agriculture and the State | 143

Fig. 6.2. Stall feeding cattle, one of the Usambara Scheme's initiatives that has become popular.
Photo Christopher Conte

The highland component of the Usambara Scheme subsequently disintegrated in November and December 1956, as cultivators in northern Usambara openly violated scheme rules by burning large tracts of natural forest in order to plant crops. At Soni in southern Usambara, farmers grazed their livestock on crop stubble in harvested gardens. In nearby Vuga, Gare, and Vugiri, cultivators purposefully flattened out ridges and planted crops. In spite of threatened prosecutions from the Native Authorities, on July 30, 1957, all penal sanctions on "non-compliance" were lifted.[69] A year later the D.C. referred to Hehe ridges as museum pieces.[70]

The plains component of the Usambara Scheme depended on mechanization to stimulate a mass migration from the hills in three to four years. The District Committee believed that tractors coupled to scientific expertise could create, in a difficult environment, a landscape attractive to a population whose cautious relationship with the plains stemmed from the realities of a limited water supply and cultivable soils, endemic malaria, high temperatures, and unreliable rainfall. Poverty pushed people into the plains and, given that fact, the Usambara Scheme's promises of productivity rang hollow. The scheme's administrators remained adamant that "only mass emigration of people and livestock to unoccupied territories" would alleviate the threat of ecological breakdown posed by agricultural practices in the mountains.⁷¹

By July 1953, Lushoto's district officers had identified 29,000 acres at Mkundi below Mtae on the western side of the massif, and 200,000 acres between the Pangani Valley railway and the Pangani River. These areas proved subsequently to be either already occupied or unusable.⁷² District Committee members also suggested resettling Shambaa farmers in the Lwengera Valley between East and West Usambara, and on "scores of miles" in northeast Handeni district.⁷³ Although tsetse flies infested the area and it lacked any sources of permanent water, the report characterized the regions as "excellently suited for cultivation and settlement."⁷⁴ In fact, most of the experimental areas around the base of the Usambara massif consisted of saline soils, to rehabilitate which would cost a great deal in both labor and funds.⁷⁵ Only at the kitivo below Mlalo did African families agree that an irrigation scheme would be feasible and beneficial.⁷⁶

The Usambara Scheme in Hindsight

Usambara's farmers resisted the Usambara Scheme from its imposition in 1950 until 1957, when the district authorities completely abandoned their efforts. The scheme could not have succeeded, because its designers decided to attack single-mindedly an environmental problem rather than rural poverty. Given the prevailing social and economic conditions, soil conservation, as conceived in Usambara, as well as other highland farming regions in East Africa, required an agricultural revolution. Farmers quickly recognized the scheme's ramifications, and they were not prepared to abandon what they and their ancestors had so painstakingly built.

Steven Feierman has asserted that rejection of the scheme centered on the unpopularity of ridge building. The ridges, known locally as *matuta*, clearly served as a symbol of resentment for things foreign and allowed those forced to build them to focus their anger on the chiefs responsible for enforcing the rules. Ultimately, in Feierman's interpretation, the issues boiled down to "the burdens of matuta, the problem of a king who had no rain, and the prominence of the chama in leading the resistance. The rain chiefs [like Hassani Kinyassi] follow the Shambaa way; the rainless were accused of serving foreigners. People understood that if the chief controlled rain, the scarcity of land and labor would recede as a problem."⁷⁷ He contends that the Usambara Scheme's defeat "preserved the guarantee of subsistence land for the poor and slowed down the process by which land became a commodity."⁷⁸

The record of njaa ya Chankola shows, however, that on the northern side of the massif, local agricultural conditions could no longer guarantee subsistence and that in response many left the mountains altogether. Furthermore, the poor who remained worked for wages to buy imported famine relief during the difficult years of the late 1940s and early 1950s. Land had also become a commodity.[79] Although the subchiefs could not issue official title deeds, they in fact sold large tracts of land in the daus in the 1940s during njaa ya Chankola. Feierman's analysis also points out how the politics of environmental control pitted rainmakers against bureaucratically appointed chiefs. While daily acts of resistance at particular times coalesced into disturbances directed against chiefs without rain during njaa ya Chankola, the archival record also shows subsequent acts of defiance directed specifically at European administrators and agricultural officers, as well as the African instructors associated with the Usambara Scheme. While the tensions of hunger stoked the fires of resistance, the ancient ties that bound the mountain peoples with their environment strained under the pressure of agrarian change. In the new era of maize production and market gardening, tenure arrangements had become supremely insecure for those on the margins forced to borrow land or to migrate. Mobility, another hallmark of the farming system, now often meant movement into unfamiliar realms of urban employment or illegal entrance into the forest reserves.

Under these complex circumstances of heightened insecurity, the scheme discredited the native authorities and the colonial administration because of its blanket application to a region where diverse agroecological conditions prevailed. The uniform displeasure expressed by those it touched reflects how monumentally ill-suited it was. Paradoxically, the scheme's unpopularity played directly into the nationalist movement, which promised security but, once in power, turned to its own ill-conceived authoritarian schemes aimed at national agricultural reform under the mantra of Ujamaa socialism.

Tanzania's independent government did not apply its now infamous villagization project to the Usambara Mountains. However, the colonial projects in Usambara presaged a number of more benevolent, though no less ideologically strident, postindependence development programs aimed at reforming what they perceived as a conservative and backward peasantry. Like their colonial predecessors, contemporary conservation and development projects continue to seek solutions in proscriptions on particular land-use practices within the farming system.

Environmental degradation and ecological breakdown, processes that form part of East Africa's long agricultural history, have occurred in West Usambara. The demographic, agricultural, and economic changes discussed above suggest a long-term pattern of decreases in soil productivity on the massif's *northern* side and probably in other densely populated areas in southern Usambara.[80] Marginal lands came under cultivation as shortened fallows, and an explosion of maize production occurred on soils that could not support them. Maize, with its shallow root system, exposed soil on slopes to sheet erosion. When Clegg's laborers drained mountain wetlands that formed the headwaters of streams, the dau lands quickly dried and hindered stream flows. This situation, in turn, hurt the function of hill-furrow irrigation downslope.[81] Scheme "solutions" simply added to the ecological problems. The Hehe ridges, for example, introduced as soil stabilization measures, actually accelerated erosion because they tended to wash away in heavy rains.[82]

Sudden disasters sometimes punctuated these creeping trends toward degradation. On the night of January 23–24, 1956, an exceptionally heavy rainstorm struck the extreme northernmost salient of West Usambara at Mbaramo. Between ninety and one hundred landslides on either side of the ridge carried thousands of tons of topsoil down the mountainside to the plains. The largest erosion scar measured approximately one hundred fifty yards in width and extended down the mountain for over eight hundred yards. This particular slide carried with it a hamlet, killing fifteen of its inhabitants and many of its livestock. It began in a cassava garden planted on a very steep slope.[83]

Although the Mbaramo landslides cannot be blamed solely on then-current agricultural practice, the cassava plantings at least suggest poverty of garden soils on a very steep slope, the culmination of long-term changes in cropping patterns tied to the regional economy. The rain fell "heavily," but heavy downpours occur with relative frequency in Usambara. In this case, the Mbaramo hillsides had developed into increasingly deadly points of vulnerability over the long term. Severe flood- and landslide-related disasters have become increasingly common in West Usambara. In the worst case to date, on January 24, 1993, heavy rains caused a flash flood of the Umba River that carried away much of Mlalo town. The raging waters killed scores, destroyed roads, and cut off the entire basin from its links to Lushoto and Tanga. The flood also ruined short-rains plantings, and food aid had to be transported in by air for more than six months.[84]

While ecological disaster has visited northern Usambara, other parts of the mountains have remained resilient. Rather than seeking to understand historical and geographical trends in mountain bioproductivity, colonial observers tended to portray historical ecology as riding uniformly a trajectory from baseline stability to breakdown,[85] with little regard to the scale and regional peculiarity of ecological change.[86] The trend gathered momentum when vulnerability to food shortages of the northern Usambara communities in the Mlalo and Mlola basins fulfilled the colonial prophesies of the land's steadily decreasing productive capacity. Precisely because the Usambara Scheme based its program on Mlalo, where the Malthusian logic of population-to-resource imbalance seemed to apply, colonial perception contained a very large blind spot that obscured other historical scenarios of human-induced environmental change. Without the ability to read the differential signals of degradation's severity, colonial authorities could not possibly formulate a plan to alleviate it.

CHAPTER SEVEN

Preserving the Usambaras in Independent Tanzania

THE COLONIAL PROJECT FOR EAST AFRICAN mountain conservation and development continued in new guises after independence in 1961, and it began to involve a number of international organizations. Rural communities therefore continued to bear the burden of externally driven projects for soil, water, and forest conservation, although government land grants helped to dissipate some of the contention that had marked the colonial-era schemes. Over the past three decades, resource conservation projects have successfully embedded environmental issues into the discourse of political economy at all levels of society. Farmers have learned to tout conservation while they negotiate measures of environmental control among themselves, with the state, and with development organizations. This chapter examines the historical context of the growing links between environment and development in the Usambaras.

Natural History

Environmental history joins natural and human history in a way that illuminates the paradoxes inherent in landscapes. As chapter 2 points out,

Usambara's mountain lands have for centuries harbored farming and pastoralist communities that modified forests which had evolved under nature's regime. Over many generations, they created ecological mosaics, but their long-term dependency upon forest resources linked them inexorably to mountain natural history. Over the past century, however, Western scientific perception served to isolate, ideologically, forest environments from their human history, while forest law and forestry practice introduced the physical boundaries. Forests eventually took shape in the colonial mindset as islands of biological productivity surrounded by agricultural lands of degradation, involution, and poverty. Since their removal from the forest, Africans altered their views to fit into the Western paradigm. As cash entered Usambara's farming economy, peasant interests began to coincide with the valuation of forest as a commodity that offered a relatively lucrative source of income.

This separation of forest and garden has had very different outcomes in the comparative environmental histories of the East and West Usambara Mountains. On the eastern mountains, the failure of plantation agriculture and area timber's limited marketability kept rather large swaths of forest intact, until intense mechanized timbering operations began in 1984. An international outcry from conservationists led to a moratorium on logging, and subsequent momentum for preservation has successfully lobbied the Tanzanian government to declare an 8,380-hectare nature reserve. Because much indigenous forest has been eliminated on the West Usambaras, development strategists continue to stress environmental restoration rather than forest preservation, in order to maintain the viability of small-scale agriculture in the post-forest mountain environment. Despite the successful ideological separation of forest and garden, human and natural history in both landscapes remain intimately linked by agriculture, which continues to shape the mountain economy and ecology.

Science

The imperialist states that built and staffed the Amani Institute leavened their pretensions toward colonial control with an idealism borne of a faith in science. Through biological research, the state hoped to support colonialism's agrarian project, the economy's most important sector. Chapter 3 pointed out how Amani served German colonialism as much through the prestige that the station lent Germany in the realm of international science as for its support of plantation agriculture. But the apparent divide between its practical and theoretical agendas brought the Amani Institute's scientists under heavy criticism from planters and the state, on account of the marginal relevance of wide-ranging research in light of coffee's rapid decline in the Usambaras. The trend toward hypercriticism continued into the British colonial era, as exemplified by the Agriculture Department's hostile reception of Milne's 1938 West Usambara study discussed in chapter 5. Numerous publications in German and British scientific journals reveal, however, that Amani's scientists carried out valuable work of direct relevance to economic crops such as coffee, sisal, cassava, cinchona, derris, and tea, to name a few. In any event, the rivalry between the practical men in colonial East Africa's Agriculture Departments and their more theoretically inclined colleagues at Amani led to the station's closure in 1944.

Far from disappearing into the colonial sunset, Amani's legacy as a haven for scientific study lives on in the research that began in 1892 with Carl Hölst's first inventories in the Usambaras and has continued throughout the twentieth century. Biology, as an inherently historical science, has come to recognize the environmental and evolutionary affinities of the Eastern Arc Mountains and their priority as areas for continued research and conservation. In making their case for protection, conservation biologists have ascribed botanical values to the Eastern Arc forests, a trend that reaches back into the 1955–56 East Usambara Land Survey, cited extensively in chapter 4. A decade later, Amani's former librarian, Reginald Moreau, released *The Bird Faunas of Africa and Its Islands* and helped to bring to a general audience Usambara's complex ecology.[1] That same year, R. M. Polhill began to explicitly advocate Eastern Arc conservation for the mountains' biological value. A number of impressive studies have followed Polhill, invoking the mountains' remarkable biological diversity and the threats to it.[2]

What has changed is the international scope of the conservation project and the consensus among biologists and donor organizations regarding the importance of Eastern Arc forest preservation. With the global community's increasing involvement in research and policymaking comes a concern for state sovereignty and the equitable treatment of local communities. The conservation priorities of donors do not necessarily jibe with state interests or local community needs.[3] The requirements of the Convention for Biodiversity, which Tanzania signed in 1992 and ratified in 1996, illustrate the quandary for signatory states that are required to form a system of protected areas while respecting the "traditional lifestyles" of forest-based communities. If the state sides with the imperatives of biodiversity conservation and errs on the side of forest protection, it alienates forest-based communities but safeguards its conservation dollars.

Smallholders, therefore, continue to fight for forest-land access under new pressures brought to bear by international conservation efforts, in addition to those pressures brought to bear by development.

Forests

Chapter 4 outlined the scenarios of forest enrichment that Fairhead and Leach found on savanna agricultural sites in Guinea, where land use actually fosters forest growth. In the distinctly dissimilar case of the Usambaras, indigenous interests have combined with state policy to accelerate deforestation. In fact, forest loss has been a general trend in the Eastern Arc Mountains. In West Usambara, some of the blame rests with postcolonial governmental practice, which attempted to secure peasant interests while maintaining a viable forest estate. On the one hand, they made available to peasant farmers large tracts of forest reserve, while on the other hand the government maintained the forestry bureaucracy and its failed policy of sustainable forestry. In East Usambara, the immediate aftermath of colonialism brought to the mountains rapacious timber concessions reminiscent of those operating during the 1940s and 1950s in West Usambara.

Table 7.1 Forest loss in the Eastern Arc Mountains

Eastern Arc Mountains	Original natural forest cover (km²)	Current natural forest cover (km²)	Percent loss in original forest cover
Taita Hills	318	6	98.1
North Pare	300	151	49.7
South Pare	1,245	333	73.3
West Usambara	2,005	547	72.7
East Usambara	950	413	56.5
Nguru	3,595	647	82.0
Ukaguru	1,845	184	90.0
Rubeho	788	499	36.7
Malundwe Hill	35	6	82.9
Mahenge	2,710	291	89.3
Udzungwa	8,019	2,103	75.6
Uluguru	1,505	528	64.9
Total	23,315	5,708	75.5

William Newmark, Conserving Biodiversity in East African Forests: A Study of the Eastern Arc Mountains (New York: Springer-Verlag, 2002), 10. Although Newmark's figure provides an idea of the magnitude of forest losses, the idea of a baseline "original natural forest cover" is ahistorical.

During the late 1950s and early 1960s, peasant farmers' demands for arable land became a popular nationalist rallying point in the West Usambaras. Tanganyika's new leaders made good on their promises of land for peasant farmers in 1964, when Minister of Agriculture Tewa Said Tewa authorized a number of forest-reserve excisions. The Lukozi Valley, part of the Shume-Magamba Forest Reserve, constituted the largest section, about 14,175 hectares. The original plan called for the area to be declared Public Land and divided up among the "squatter" population by newly formed Village Development Councils (VDCs). One of the former VDC leaders explained that, by order of the Department of Agriculture, each eligible applicant was to receive ten acres, with the balance remaining as a multiuse forest zone. He implied, however, that political patronage subverted the process. "The district council gave the VDC the responsibility to divide the area. The VDC was of uneducated people from the villages who had the ability to sing TANU songs and [were] elected as village executive leaders, or TANU chairmen. They had no expertise concerning the forest. They only knew to give out, to divide."[4] A former forest guard remarked:

> The region was given out to enhance the popularity of the politicians.... These folks began to say that the forest was for all, not only the squatters. It should be distributed to all raiya [citizens]. This was a violation of the parliamentary instructions for the division of the forest. The VDC received applications from anybody who wanted a shamba and they received a lot of applications. Corruption was the order of the day, the dominant system. If you don't give *chai* [a bribe], no shamba.[5]

Accordingly, the Village Development Councils tabled discussion of forest zones on Public Lands and distributed the entire parcel as agricultural land. The bribery accounts are reinforced by the testimony of those who benefited from the land grab. They state quite clearly that the extent and quality of one's grant depended directly on the amount of money one could offer the authorities in charge of distribution.[6]

While ceding to peasant demands for land, the state still sought to protect valuable supplies of remaining natural and plantation forest in the Shume-Magamba reserve. The excision therefore followed the botanical dividing line between forest communities of cedar and Podocarpus (*Juniperus procera, Podocarpus, spp.*) on one side, and camphor (*Ocotea usambarensis*) on the other, the latter containing valuable timber.[7] Also clear is the rapid character of the transformation from forest to farmland in the Lukozi Valley. Within two years, farmers had cut down most of the valley's forest cover, though few benefited financially from the sudden appearance of available timber because farmers could not obtain pit-sawing permits, nor did they posses the expertise to saw the timber into boards. Most of the trees were simply felled and burnt as firewood or charcoal.[8]

There are no census data on the number and origin of the people who moved into the Lukozi Valley in the early 1960s, but the immediate availability of land likely eased the pressures on lands in the Mlalo and Mlola farming basins. The excision nonetheless weighed heavily on the ecology of the Lukozi cedar forest. A comparison of aerial photos taken in 1947 and 1968 shows an extensive loss of tree cover. In a study of the transformation of Usambara forest vegetation and soils, Björn Lundgren describes the effects of clearing of natural forest on the soil microclimate. Once the Lukozi farmers removed the trees, physical processes common to Africa's forest latosols transformed the edaphic microenvironment. More rain reached the soil surface. Radiation increased. Maximum temperatures increased while minimum temperatures and humidity decreased. Humus decomposition sped up with the increased wetting and drying of the soil. Moreover, because the Lukozi cultivators burned everything—an act that in the short run increased soil fertility but in the end decreased the soil's nutrient retention capacity—the topsoil structure rapidly deteriorated.[9] In a discussion of pressure on the Shume-Magamba Forest Reserve, Lundgren noted severe soil erosion and rapid land deterioration, specifically in the Lukozi Valley.[10]

Testimony from informants living at Lukozi supports the Lundgrens' descriptions of the longer-term repercussions of the clearing. Lukozi residents claim that the streams in the valley and on the surrounding hills have become seasonal and subject to dramatic episodes of flash flooding. They believe that the formerly heavy mists that used to dampen the valley soils have dried up. They argue that soil fertility decreased on cleared and cultivated slopes and that sheet erosion of the hillside has deposited much topsoil in the valley.[11] Although the worst ecological deterioration occurred at Lukozi, similar, though smaller-scale, changes occurred at other forest excisions in West Usambara. For example, at the Gare Mission forest excision (mostly camphor and Podocarpus forest), farmers argue that maize yields declined in the four years after forest clearance (1964 to 1968). As with Lukozi, farmers now cultivate most intensively in the stream valley, where eroded soils have collected.[12]

Inside the forest reserves, commercial practices tended to reduce drastically the forest's biological diversity. Before the movement of large numbers of

Table 7.2 Change in land use in the West Usambara Shume Ward, 1957–76

Land use	Estimated area (ha) 1957	Estimated area 1976	Change	Percent change
Natural forest	16,700	4,200	-12,500	-74.8
Forest plantations	3,000	8,800	+5,800	+193.3
Farmlands and village settlements	400	7,000	+6,600	+1,650.0
Bare lands	100	200	+100	+100.0

From A. R. S. Kaoneka and B. Soldberg, "Forestry Related Land Use in the West Usambara Mountains, Tanzania," Agriculture, Ecosystems, and Environment 49 (1994): 207–15.

pit sawers into Lushoto District in the late 1950s, commercial firms generally clear-cut areas which the forestry service replanted with monoculture stands of exotic species of cedar, pine, and cypress. Clearing, especially with the aid of heavy machinery, and planting of exotic species decreased the capacity of the soil to maintain nutrient and moisture levels.[13] Now the plantation stands will not support any other type of forest except commercial forestry, and that condition is likely limited to two rotations, until productivity decreases to the point where commercial exploitation becomes uneconomic.[14] Indiscriminate cutting, carried out by commercial concerns before and after independence, has led to the virtual extinction of Podocarpus (locally, *Msee*) and entandrophragma (*Mbokoko*), and their replacement by invader species (*Macaranga spp.* and *Policias spp.*), changing completely the species makeup of the logged-out area. In other areas, poor logging practices have led to the disappearance of sandalwood.[15]

The Tanzanian state's forest giveaways legitimated local cries of land shortages by bestowing upon local authorities the power to distribute forest lands. The process represents the state's recognition just after independence that colonial land law and land confiscations had disregarded African needs. In these early days, the state was willing to provide land in order to solidify its popularity, an exception to its later authoritarian stances under its policy of forced villagization during the 1970s. Moreover, even though the government de-gazetted Lukozi and some other reserves in West Usambara, it did not abandon the ideology of profitable forestry that it inherited from the British Mandate. In East and West Usambara, forestry policy meant the continued and dramatic biological simplification of natural forest and the increasing exploitation of both natural and plantation forest under mechanized logging and pit sawing. Another blow to conservation began in 1972, when the central government removed from the Forest Division its jurisdiction over most of the country's forests and distributed power to the regional and district development directors, who were anxious to secure quick returns from felling licenses. State policy resulted, therefore, in a two-pronged attack on its own forest resources.[16]

Although ecological trends in forest use reminiscent of West Usambara have played themselves out in the East Usambaras, the failure of plantation agriculture allowed some large tracts of natural forest to remain relatively undisturbed until the late 1950s, when immigrants began to claim land rights through usufruct on the forested sections of the old estates. After independence, the Tanzanian government de-gazetted forest reserves in the lowlands around the base of the East Usambaras and reclassified them as Public Lands, leaving the estates intact. Rather than move onto Public Lands, many African farmers chose to continue cultivating and living in the unexploited highland estate forests.[17] These farmers remained not simply to meet subsistence needs, but to exploit growing commodity markets by introducing new crops, the most lucrative of which was and remains cardamom, a spice used throughout the Indian Ocean world. Farmers grow cardamom all over the Eastern Arc, but by far the most comes from the Usambaras, where farmers plant it in the forest understory. The spice's cultivation begins a process that results in forest loss over the course of several years. Cardamom's yields decline after five to seven years, by which time many of the forest trees that shaded it have died and toppled due to the understory desiccation. After that, cardamom farmers move their plantings to new forest areas and follow up in the previously planted plots with maize and sugar cane, which again remain viable for only a few years. In an ecological sequence that recalls the coffee debacle of the German colonial era, exotic weeds invade the former forest landscapes.[18]

Although the colonial Forest Department only became closely involved in East Usambara's mountain forest management during the 1950s, their short-run policy has had immense ecological repercussions. In 1958, logging of a naturally occurring hardwood, *Cephalosphaera,* commenced in the Kwamkoro forest reserve, followed by the cutover areas' replanting first with *Maesopsis,* a fast-growing hardwood introduced from Uganda. Once the *Maesopsis* saplings matured, silvicultural practice called for understory plantings of *Cephalosphaera,* which would theoretically thrive in the larger trees' shade. *Cephalosphaera* failed to reproduce, but the exotic spread prolifically, successfully colonizing almost any open area in the mountain forests. The *Maesopsis* invasion has been facilitated by its rapid growth relative to other natural forest trees and by hornbills who appear around the original Kwamkoro "plantation" forest in great numbers during July and August. They gorge on the abundant *Maesopsis* fruits, then spread the seeds in their droppings.[19]

While silviculture and African agricultural needs have altered the forest piecemeal, the international commerce in tropical hardwoods that boomed during the 1970s and 1980s led to a particularly rapacious assault by the state under its nationalized subsidiary, the Sikh Saw Mills. The company had been operating in the East Usambaras since the 1950s, when it purchased several tea estates. At that time, Sikh Saw Mills had extensive lumber interests in Kenya and Uganda and, rather than cultivate tea, it logged and milled the forests on their Tanganyika purchases. In the mid-1970s, the Tanzanian state nationalized the firm, and it became a monopoly interest in the East Usambaras, seemingly immune to any regulation or sanction by the Forest Divsion.[20] As tropical hardwoods increased in value, Sikh's logging standards declined significantly. The mechanized logging operation caused soil erosion and compaction, destroyed riparian habitat, and generally cut trees without regard to the forest's future. The Finnish government supported the shoddy logging with gifts of chain saws, bulldozers, skidders, heavy trucks, and a high-capacity peeling plant for plywood.[21] National and international protests against the logging forced Sikh in 1986 to cease their operations in the East Usambara Mountains, whereupon pit sawers moved quickly into the forest to fill the void.[22]

Pit sawers, in this case peripatetic loggers from Iringa in southern Tanzania and financed by local businessmen, have cut, very selectively, four tree species (*Khaya nyasica, Milicia excelsa, Newtonia buchananii,* and *Ocotea usambarensis*). They tend to exhibit some care in their timber harvesting and cutting, which damages the forest floor far less than Sikh's mechanized operation. Even so, the lucrative nature of their business, where much of their harvest finds its way into the black market, has led to a significant reduction in the abundance of these species.[23] The cumulative damage raised so many international concerns that the Tanzanian government banned all logging in East Usambara's Amani division in 1989.

Conservation and Development of the Modern Forest and Garden

Two very different development scenarios have evolved in the Usambaras. In the East, an ideology of forest preservation has prevailed. Two years before the logging ban, the East Usambara Conservation and Development (EUCD) project had begun to link biodiversity management with economic development. Its institutional structure featured an international top-down funding arrangement with its monies flowing from the European Economic Community and the International Union for the Conservation of Nature (IUCN). One of the central problems, amazingly, turned out to be the project's neglect of ecological monitoring, thus limiting its ability to evaluate and adapt its program on the fly.[24] Another, no less important failure stemmed from the basic incompatibility of forest preservation and poverty alleviation in the eyes of East Usambara's citizens. In 1990, a new project, the East Usambara Area Management Programme, filled the funding void left by EUCD. This time, support came from FINNIDA, formerly one of Sikh Saw Mill's chief backers in destroying East Usambara's submontane forest. East Usambara Conservation and Management Programme (EUCAMP) also has a decidedly forest-centered ideology, although one of the project goals is to assist villages in managing forested Public Lands. Project leaders now readily admit that unless forest management includes a dialogue with local communities, forest protection cannot succeed.[25]

EUCAMP learned from its predecessor that it must concentrate a large part of its focus on the forest itself. After the Tanzanian government declared the Amani Nature Reserve, the project has carried out extensive biological inventories in order to classify the forests' ecological richness and spatial variability. Moreover, scientists associated with EUCAMP have surveyed and classified land use and forest types in the East Usambaras and have monitored ecological change.[26] There are also plans under way to create forested corridors between forest patches in the East Usambaras in order to allow isolated faunal populations a wider range.

In West Usambara, the postcolonial impetus toward conservation development in the early years produced a set of projects very similar in purpose to the Usambara Scheme. Mostly devoted to soil and water conservation, the projects functioned for decades under a number of acronyms, the most notable of which is the Soil Erosion Control and Agroforestry Project (SECAP) in the West Usambaras. Extensive and continuing deforestation in the West Usambaras prompted a reorientation of these projects toward forest conservation along the boundaries of threatened government forest reserves. These newer, forest-based initiatives—for example, the Natural Resources Management and Buffer Zone Development Programme—

promote sustainable forest management in the mountain forests in North Pare, West Usambara, and Handeni. The project literature for the North Pare Forestry Action Plan claims:

> The North Pare Mountains used to be an area favorable to agriculture with large tracts of land covered under forest.
> However, in recent years land became scarce due to a high population pressure (150–200 inhabitants km^2), leading to an alarming degradation of natural resources, characterized by the cultivation of marginal areas and decreasing soil fertility as well as encroachment and uncontrolled exploitation of the remaining forest reserves.
> Under these conditions, the traditional environmental protection measures and farming practices could not ensure the sustainability of natural resources.[27]

This template historical reading pits a static traditional land-use system against the dynamism of demographic change. Under these Malthusian conditions, degradation appears inevitable without intervention. The answer to deforestation lies in "village-based participatory land-use planning" (VLUP) along forest reserve boundaries, where the VLUP committee, as a subcommittee of the village government, identifies environmental problems and works out solutions with its constituency. Other village-based project organs include the Neighborhood Land Management Groups, who receive training in soil and water conservation, and Village Afforestation appointees, who identify afforestation sites and who receive usufruct rights over planted trees, while their plots remain Public Land. Meanwhile GTZ (Gesellschaft für technische Zusammenarbeit) and the Tanzanian state support and train the village conservationists. Over the sixteen-year life of the project, the German government will contribute more than twelve million euros. The Tanzanian staff concentrate on community organization while the Germans focus on policy and planning. Similar projects operate across East Africa's highlands.

The projects seem on the surface to reorient development around forests toward impoverished communities, who desperately seek to increase their lives' material quality. At the same time, they aim at an equally noble and necessary goal, arresting resource degradation on an agrarian landscape. The Pare project quantifies its successes: nine VLUP committees founded in four years, twenty-three villages involved in soil and water conservation, annually forty hectares of farmland protected, two hundred farmers trained, a hundred thousand trees raised and planted on farms yearly. Yet, given the German government's investment, the scale of the successes seems small, while the project's publicity literature simplifies a complex social situation, leading to a number of questions. Who participates in the conservation project and what motivates them? Who evaluates and approves the village plans? Who will monitor ecological change? If village development goals and market realities conflict with conservation imperatives, which side prevails? What are the political relationships among the state, donors, and the local village? And finally, why should rural Africans conserve and foster forests with a lifespan of centuries over the course of their relatively short economic lives? Roderick Neuman's extensive fieldwork in Arusha suggests that buffer zone management plans actually increase the state's power, along with that of conservation-oriented nongovernment organizations (NGOs) and international development organizations, over local-level environmental control.[28] Furthermore, in Arusha, as in Upare and Usambara, the stereotypical view of local "traditionalists" continues to emerge in the development literature. The language is only slightly more benign than the colonialist tales generated by the 1940s Mlalo Basin Rehabilitation Scheme.

How far these projects go toward rehabilitating damaged farmlands or conserving forest remains to be seen. Clearly, their policy formulations and goals do not account for the diversity of mountain land-use history or even the diversity of the biological communities they seek to save from axe and hoe. How do the project and the community differentiate between cypress and pine plantations, eucalyptus woodlots, natural closed-canopy forests, open secondary forests containing indigenous trees? How do they ascribe value? Why should local communities impose sanctions on their own use of forest resources when they apparently receive, as a community, limited material benefit from conservation? Finally, what will happen when project funding runs out?

As ideas about conservation and development continue to swirl about in academic conferences and publications, World Bank meeting rooms, and local village development councils, the biophysical world they discuss continually changes in concrete ways. In the East African highlands, forested landscapes have fostered and maintained immense biological values over the long run of their natural and human history. Their transformation in the relatively recent past threatens to impoverish them ecologically and affect life far beyond the mountain boundaries. The time scales of these transformations vary greatly and often escape notice in a

Fig. 7.1. Palms below the Usambaras near Muheza. Photo Sabine Barcatta

single lifetime. African cultivators and herders have met basic economic needs in and around these forests and their history shows that a very complex and changing relationship developed between them. Development programs largely fail to recognize that historical relationship. Instead, they tend to formulate blanket approaches insensitive to history, local politics, and economic differentials in villages where people have for generations struggled with outsiders over environmental control. In its last-ditch efforts to save East Usambara's forests through the Amani Nature Reserve, the government has criminalized forest farming, which among mountain land users has been hard to accept under the tough economic circumstances that prevail in Tanzania. The growing consensus among all interested parties suggests that pressure on the forest may be reduced through dialogue, not just with village authorities, but with individual farmers—about what kind of forest they need, whether it should contain fuel wood, agroforestry products, timber, building poles, or some combination thereof. It also seems to hold that the Usambara communities who live near forests will in the near term continue to bear the burdens of their own poverty and the international imperatives of forest conservation.

Notes

Chapter 1

1. For an argument for the Eastern Arc Mountains as a distinct floristic region, see F. White, "The History of the Afromontane Archipelago and the Scientific Need for Its Conservation," *African Journal of Ecology* 19 (1981): 33–54.

2. For the book's concept of landscape, I draw upon Emily Russell's definition in *People and the Land through Time: Linking Ecology and History* (New Haven: Yale University Press, 1997), 3. Russell describes a landscape as consisting of an assemblage of ecosystems that interact, though less directly than do the components of ecosystems.

3. For an exception, see Dan Flores, "Nature's Children: Environmental History as Natural History," in *The Natural West: Environmental History in the Great Plains and Rocky Mountains* (Norman: University of Oklahoma Press, 2001).

4. See the publications of East Usambara Conservation Management Area Programme, including Ecological Surveys, Working Papers, Technical Papers, and Administrative Reports, at http://www.usambara.com/library.htm. For a series of essays stressing the importance of Eastern Arc biodiversity, see volume 19 (1–2) of the *African Journal of Ecology*, especially F. White, "The History of the Afromontane Archipelago and the Scientific Need for Its Conservation," 33–54. Another set of reports on the East Usambara forests appears in A. C. Hamilton and R. Bensted-Smith, eds., *Forest Conservation in the East Usambara Mountains, Tanzania* (Gland, Switzerland: IUCN, 1989). *Nature* magazine has declared the Eastern Arc forest to be one of the world's biodiversity hotspots and therefore in need of immediate protection; see *Nature* 405 (May 11, 2000).

5. Samuel Wasser and Jon Lovett, "Introduction," in Lovett and Wasser, eds., *Biogeography and Ecology of the Rain Forests of Eastern Africa* (Cambridge: Cambridge University Press, 1993), 3–6.

6. For a discussion of climatic and botanical history of the Eastern Arc forests, see Jon Lovett, "Climatic History and Forest Distribution in Eastern Africa," and "Eastern Arc Moist Forest Flora," chapters 3 and 4 in Lovett and Wasser, eds., *Biogeography*.

7. Lovett, "Climatic History," 23. The Intertropical Convergence Zone is associated with oceanic solar heating and oceanic currents across the equatorial seas.

8. W. A. Rodgers and K. M. Homewood, "Species Richness and Endemism in the Usambara Mountain Forests, Tanzania," *Biological Journal of the Linnean Society* 18 (1982): 205.

9. Jonathan Kingdon, *Island Africa: The Evolution of Africa's Rare Animals and Plants* (Princeton, N.J.: Princeton University Press, 1989), 135.

10. Tilman, *Nature* 405 (May 11, 2000): 208. See also *Nature* 403 (February 24, 2000): 856, which describes the character of Eastern Arc diversity, where a small surface area contains high numbers of endemics and species. Specifically, there are 1,200 endemic plants in 2,000 square kilometers, giving a ratio of 75 species to 100 square kilometers, represented as 75:1, and 121 endemic vertebrates, for a ratio of 1.6:1, both ratios topping the lists for all such hotspots. Furthermore, the mountains exhibit high species congruence, i.e., high counts for endemic plants matched by high counts for endemic vertebrates.

11. For a fascinating attempt to do this, see Craig Stanford, *Significant Others: The Ape-Human Continuum and the Quest for Human Nature* (New York: Basic Books, 2001).

12. For general discussion of ironworking and resulting deforestation in these processes, see Peter Schmidt, "Historical Ecology and Landscape Transformation in Eastern Equatorial Africa," in *Historical Ecology: Cultural Knowledge and Changing Landscapes,* ed. Carol Crumley (Santa Fe, N.M.: School of American Research Press, 1994), 112–22. For an explanation of long-term agricultural adaptation in West Usambara, see Christopher Conte, "Colonial Science and Ecological Change: Tanzania's Mlalo Basin, 1888–1946," *Environmental History* 4.2 (1999): 220–44.

13. David Schoenbrun, "We Are What We Eat: Ancient Agriculture between the Great Lakes," *Journal of African History* 34 (1993): 4. Bantu languages originated in West Africa and their spread and effects on culture and production in eastern and southern Africa are well documented. See, for example, Jan Vansina, "New Linguistic Evidence and 'The Bantu Expansion,'" *Journal of African History* 36 (1995): 173–96; Robert Soper, "Iron Age Sites in Northeastern Tanzania," *Azania* 2 (1967): 19–36; David Collett, "The Spread of Early Iron Producing Communities in Eastern and Southern Africa: Volume 1" (Ph.D. thesis, Cambridge University, 1985), 131; and Peter Schmidt, "Eastern Expressions of the 'Mwitu' Tradition: Early Iron Age Industry of the Usambara Mountains, Tanzania," *Nyame Akuma* 30 (1987): 36.

14. Schmidt, "Mwitu Tradition," 37; Collett, "Spread," 50.

15. The Cushitic language family forms one of six represented on the African continent. Very few Cushitic speakers remain in East Africa. For a linguistic history of East Africa, see Christopher Ehret, *An African Classical Age: Eastern and Southern Africa in World History, 1000 B.C. to A.D. 400* (Charlottesville: University of Virginia Press, 1998).

16. For Mbugu history, see Christopher Conte, "Nature Reorganized: Ecological History in the Plateau Forests of the West Usambara Mountains, c. 1850–1935," in *Custodians of the Land: Ecology and Culture in the History of Tanzania,* ed. Gregory Maddox, James Giblin, and Isaria N. Kimambo (London: James Currey, 1996): 96–122.

17. Usambara Interview Transcripts (hereafter UIT), Mzee Seuya and Baharia, at Magamba, 3/12/92, 5.

18. For simplicity's sake, I will refer to them subsequently as the "Wambugu," the name by which they are known today. "Mbugu" is the singular form of the noun, as well as the adjectival form.

19. See the exceptional works of Richard Waller on Maasai history, especially

"Emutai: Crisis and Response in Maasailand 1883–1902," in *The Ecology of Survival: Case Studies from Northeast African History*, ed. Douglas Johnson and David Anderson (Boulder: Westview Press, 1988), 73–114; and "Interaction and Identity on the Periphery: The Trans-Mara Maasai," *International Journal of African History Studies* 17 (1984): 243–84.

20. For evidence of burning forest to create pasture, see B. D. Copland, "A Note on the Origin of the Mbugu with a Text," *Zeitschrift für Eingeborenen-Sprachen* 24 (1933–34): 244; UIT, Paulo Mwavoa and Mlango Msasu, at Kinko, 3/3/92, 39; UIT, T. Mganga, at Kwefingo, 2/92, 14. Mzee Mganga claims that the Wambugu never cleared forest to create pasture. For pasture regulation, see UIT, Mkanda Shusha, at Mshangai, 2/92, 25. For reclusiveness, see E. C. Green, "The Wambugu of Usambara (with Notes on Kimbugu)," *Tanzania Notes and Records* 61 (1963): 175.

21. See Steven Feierman, *Peasant Intellectuals: Anthropology and History in Tanzania* (Madison: University of Wisconsin Press, 1990).

22. Conte, "Nature Reorganized," 114.

23. Johan Ludwig Krapf, *Travels, Researches, and Missionary Labours During an Eighteen Years' Residence in Eastern Africa* (London: Frank Cass and Co. Ltd, 1968; orig. ed., London: Trübner, 1860), 378. For subsequent Switzerland references, see Oscar Baumann, *In Deutsch-Ostafrika während des Aufstandes, Reise der Dr. Hans Meyer'schen Expedition in Usambara* (Wien: Eduard Hölzel, 1890), 77. In his 1888 explorations of northern Usambara, Baumann claims that the Switzerland references are misplaced, at least insofar as they are applied to the northern tier of West Usambara. See also Johannes Buchwald, "Aus dem deutsch-ostafrikanischen Schutzgebiete. Beitrag zur Gliederung der Vegetation von West-Usambara," *Mitteilungen aus den deutschen Schutzgebieten* 9 (1896): 229; Clement Gillman, Rhodes House Library Manuscript Collection, MSS.Afr.S.1175, vol. 6, Diaries, February 1920, 82. Gillman compares the Shume region of the West Usambara plateau to Swiss or Bavarian regions.

24. Baumann, "Karte von Usambara," *Petermanns geographische Mitteilungen* 35.11 (1889): 257–61. Baumann's map labels as "unresearched" the Shume region and the southeastern slopes of the West Usambaras.

25. Oscar Baumann, "Usambara," *Petermanns geographische Mitteilungen* 2 (1889): 41–47; also see chapter 5, "Usambara," in *Usambara und seine Nachbargebiete* (Berlin: Dietrich Reimer, 1891): 162–97.

26. Baumann, *In Deutsch-Ostafrika*, 104.

27. Baumann, "Usambara," 47.

28. Th. Siebenlist, *Forstwirtschaft in Deutsch Ostafrika* (Berlin: Verlagsbuchhandlung Paul Parey, 1914), 39.

29. Siebenlist, *Forstwirtschaft*, 3–4.

30. See Henry Lowood, "The Calculating Forester: Quantification, Cameral Science and the Emergence of Scientific Forestry Management in Germany," in *The Quantifying Spirit in the 18th Century*, ed. Tore Fraengsmyr, J. L. Heilbron, and Robin E. Rider (Berkeley: University of California Press, 1990), 315–42.

31. See, for example, R. E. Moreau, *The Bird Fauna of Africa and Its Islands* (London: Academic Press, 1966); "Pleistocene Climatic Changes and the Distribution of Life in East Africa," *Journal of Ecology* 21 (1933): 415–35; "Some Eco-climatic Data for Closed Evergreen Forest in Tropical Africa," *Journal of the Linnean Society* (Zool.) 39.265 (March 8, 1935): 285–93; "A Synecological Study of Usambara, Tanganyika Territory with Particular Reference to Birds," *Journal of Ecology* 23.1 (1935): 1–43; "Climatic Classification from the Standpoint of East African Biology," *Journal of Ecology* 26 (1938): 467–96.

32. Kingdon, *Island Africa*, 138.

33. William Rodgers suggests that these views may be stereotypical, given that, to his knowledge, there has been "no quantitative study of forest resource use by village communities anywhere in eastern Africa." "The Conservation of the Forest Resources of Eastern Africa: Past Influences, Present Practices and Future Needs," in Lovett and Wasser, *Biogeography*, 297.

Chapter 2

1. For a discussion of the chronology of agriculture's spread in Africa south of the Sahara, see Jan Vansina, "A Slow Revolution: Farming in Subequatorial Africa," *Azania* 29–30 (1994–95): 16–17.

2. Geoffrey Milne, "Essays in Applied Pedology: 1. Soil Type and Soil Management in Relation to Plantation Agriculture in East Usambara," *East African Agricultural Journal* 3.1 (1937): 8–9. Milne points out the paradox of finding luxuriant forests growing on such impoverished soils.

3. For an overview of East African environmental history, see James Giblin and Gregory Maddox, introduction to *Custodians of the Land: Ecology and Culture in the History of Tanzania*, ed. Gregory Maddox, James Giblin, and Isaria N. Kimambo (London: James Currey, 1996), 1–14. For an early examination of the social and economic interaction of East African herders and farmers, see J. L. Berntsen, "The Maasai and Their Neighbors: Variables and Interaction," *African Economic History* 2 (1976): 1–11; and Richard Waller, "Interaction and Identity on the Periphery: The Trans-Mara Maasai," *International Journal of African Historical Studies* 17 (1984): 243–84.

4. For a good synthesis of the debates and an overview of Bantu language classification, see, respectively, J. E. G. Sutton, "The Growth of Farming and the Bantu Settlement on and South of the Equator: Editor's Introduction," *Azania* 29–30 (1994–95): 1–14; and Derek Nurse, "'Historical' Classifications of the Bantu Languages," in the same volume, 65–81.

5. See Jan Vansina, "New Linguistic Evidence and 'The Bantu Expansion,'" *Journal of African History* 36 (1995): 173–96; Christopher Ehret, *An African Classical Age: Eastern and Southern Africa in World History, 1000 B.C. to A.D. 400* (Charlottesville: University of Virginia Press, 1998); and David Schoenbrun, *A Green Place, A Good Place: Agrarian Change, Gender, and Social Identity in the Great Lakes Region to the 15th Century* (Portsmouth, N.H.: Heinemann, 1998).

6. Jan Vansina, "New Linguistic Evidence," 191–92.

7. For autochthonous agricultural arrangements that preceded and accompanied the Bantu expansion, see Christopher Ehret, *African Classical Age*. Millet and sorghum are grains native to northeast Africa and were likely domesticated there. For Vansina's explanation of three phases of agriculture's spread, see "A Slow Revolution," 17.

8. See David Taylor and Robert Marchant, "Human Impact in the Interlacustrine Region: Long-Term Pollen Records from the Rukiga Highlands," *Azania* 29–30 (1994–95): 283–95. For deforestation on the western side of Lake Victoria during the Bantu expansion, see Peter Schmidt, "Historical Ecology and Landscape Transformation in Eastern Equatorial Africa," in *Historical Ecology: Cultural Knowledge and Changing Landscapes*, ed. Carol Crumley (Santa Fe, N.M.: School of American Research Press, 1994), 108–9. For Great Lakes origins of the East African Bantu expansion, see also Christopher Ehret, *An African Classical Age*, chapter 6.

9. Ehret, 184–89.

10. Peter Schmidt, *Iron Technology in East Africa: Symbolism, Science and Archaeology* (Bloomington: Indiana University Press, 1997), 170–72.

11. For an early analysis of the Bantu expansion into Usambara and Pare highlands, see Robert Soper, "Iron Age Sites in Northeastern Tanzania," *Azania* 2 (1967): 19–36. More recently, see Peter Schmidt, "Eastern Expressions of the 'Mwitu' Tradition: Early Iron Age Industry of the Usambara Mountains, Tanzania," *Nyame Akuma* 30 (1988): 36–37; and David Collett, "The Spread of Early Iron Producing Communities in Eastern and Southern Africa: Volume 1" (Ph.D. thesis, Cambridge University, 1985). On page 131, Collett argues that the Mwitu tradition is expressed in unity of furnace brick motifs and furnace types, and that it was part of a particular migration. For the relationship between agricultural practice and Bantu language spread, see Jan Vansina, "A Slow Revolution," 15–26. Although Nkese and other sites suggest that the Upland Bantu expansion was revolutionary in its ability to exploit mountain forest soils, the archaeological database for these settlements of the first millennium A.D. remains rudimentary. Until more sites are excavated and analyzed, the character and rapidity of mountain deforestation and regeneration and the consequences on forest ecology, for example, cannot be fully determined. Archaeological and linguistic analyses for more recent settlements do reveal, however, that Nkese and its sister sites represent only the beginning of a series of complex movements of East Africans into and out of these mountain regions, where, over time, they developed more individualized environmental and cultural adaptations.

12. For a similar description of Taita, see Bill Bravman, *Making Ethnic Ways: Communities and Their Transformations in Taita, Kenya 1800–1950* (Portsmouth, N.H.: Heinemann, 1998), 33.

13. Usambara Interview Transcripts (hereafter UIT), Sefu Mjenga, at Mbwei, 1/16/92, 65–66.

14. Isaria N. Kimambo suggests in "Environmental Control and Hunger in the Mountains and Plains of Northeastern Tanzania," in Maddox, Giblin, and Kimambo,

Custodians, 74 and 82, that iron smelted in the South Pare mountains was made available to smiths in West Usambara for forging, but no smelting occurred in the Usambaras themselves. If this is true, pressure on West Usambara's forest resources would have been lighter than in neighboring Upare. N. Thomas Hakansson argues for the regional renown of Pare smiths and for iron ore abundance in "Rulers and Rainmakers in Precolonial South Pare, Tanzania: The Role of Exchange and Ritual Experts in Political Centralization," *Ethnology* 37.3 (Summer 1998): 269–70. Hakansson also argues for seventeenth-century migrations from Taita to Upare, ibid., 268.

15. For Taita, see Bravman, 31, but I wonder about Bravman's taking the stories from the seventeenth and eighteenth centuries at face value. For Taitans migrating to Mlalo in the nineteenth century, see UIT, Ali Gembe and son Shemboza bin Shemndola, at Mlalo, 1/18/92, 5.

16. Soper, "Iron Age."

17. For *Musa*'s antiquity in the northeastern Tanzania highlands, see Gerda Rossel, "Musa and Ensete in Africa: Taxonomy, Nomenclature and Uses," *Azania* 29–30 (1994–95): 135 and 144. For various arrival dates of banana in East Africa, see J. S. Wigboldus, "The Spread of Crops into Sub-equatorial Africa during the Early Iron Age," *Azania* 29–30 (1994–95): 123–25; and E. De Langhe, R. Swennen, and D. Vuylsteke, "Plantain in the Early Bantu World," 147–60. In *An African Classical Age,* Ehret places banana importation early in the first millennium A.D., 278.

18. Rossel, "Musa," 135.

19. De Langhe, Swennen, and Vuylsteke, "Plantain," 149.

20. For other uses, ibid., 143–44.

21. Otto Warburg, "Die Kulturpflanzen Usambaras," *Mitteilungen aus den deutschen Schutzgebieten* 7 (1894): 175–80.

22. The American crops would have become available sometime after 1500. For an excellent overview of nineteenth-century agricultural practice at Mlalo and Kitivo, see Warburg, "Die Kulturpflanzen," 142. For introductions of exotic cultigens during the Early Iron Age, see J. S. Wigboldus, "Spread," 121–29.

23. East African "hill-furrow irrigation" is similar in design to systems in Afghanistan, Pakistan, and Nepal. The technique occurs in many East African highland zones. See W. M. Adams, T. Potkanski, and J. E. G. Sutton, "Indigenous Farmer-Managed Irrigation in Sonjo, Tanzania," *Geographical Journal* 160 (1994): 19.

24. Adams, Potkanski, and Sutton, "Indigenous," 19. For explorer descriptions of hill-furrow irrigation, see Oscar Baumann, *In Deutsch-Ostafrika während des Aufstandes, Reise der Dr. Hans Meyer'schen Expedition in Usambara* (Wien: Eduard Hölzel, 1890), 84; Warburg, "Die Kulturpflanzen," 84.

25. See J. E. G. Sutton, "Irrigation and Soil-conservation in African Agricultural History. With a Reconsideration of the Inyanga Terracing (Zimbabwe) and Engaruka Irrigation Works (Tanzania)," *Journal of African History* 25 (1984): 25–41; and "Towards a History of Cultivating the Fields," *Azania* 24 (1989): 98–112. Soil salinization or extended drought, or both, may have been the culprit.

26. William M. Adams and David M. Anderson, "Irrigation before Development: Indigenous and Induced Change in Agricultural Water Management in East Africa," *African Affairs* 87 (1988): 525. For northeastern Tanzania in particular, see Kimambo, "Environmental Control," 72–73.

27. N. Thomas Hakansson, "Irrigation, Population Pressure, and Exchange in Pre-Colonial Pare of Tanzania," in *Research in Economic Anthropology*, vol. 16, ed. Barry Isaac (Greenwich, Conn.: JAI Press, 1995), 315–16.

28. See Adams, Potkanski, and Sutton, "Indigenous," 18–19, for discussion of technical terminology. For descriptions of indigenous irrigation systems, see UIT, Japhet Kalata, at Mlalo, 12/23/91, 1–2; Ali Gembe and son Shemboza bin Shemndola, at Mlalo, 1/18/92, 6; Kasisi Kuambaza Shezia, at Mlalo, 1/18/92, 9; Bakari Panduka, Abdallah Mdoe, Musa Athumani, Ahamadi Rashidi Kidumi, at Kitivo, Mng'aro, 2/8/92, 13.

29. For an examination of the political repercussions of the Mbugu entrance into Usambara, see Steven Feierman, *The Shambaa Kingdom: A History* (Madison: University of Wisconsin Press, 1974), chapter 3.

30. Known currently as the Wambugu, the elders refer to their ancestors as the Vamaa. Some Wambugu still speak a language which has been classified as a branch of Southern Cushitic in Derek Nurse, "Extinct Southern Cushitic Communities in East Africa," in *Cushitic—Omotic. Papers from the International Symposium on Cushitic and Omotic Languages, Cologne, January 6–9, 1986*, ed. Marianne Bechaus-Gerst and Fritz Serzisko (Hamburg: Helmut Buske Verlag, 1988), 93–104; see also A. N. Tucker and M. A. Bryan, "The Vamaa Anomaly," *Bulletin of the School of Oriental and African Studies* 37 (1974): 188–207; and Morris Goodman, "The Strange Case of Vamaa," in *Pidginization and Creolization of Languages*, ed. Dell Hymes (Cambridge: Cambridge University Press, 1971), 243–54.

31. Ehret, *African Classical*, 190.

32. Sharon Nicholson, "Environmental Change within the Historical Period," in *The Physical Geography of Africa*, ed. W. M. Adams, A. S. Goudie, and A. R. Orme (Oxford: Oxford University Press, 1996), 80.

33. For linguistic and historical ties to Upare, see E. C. Green, "The Wambugu of Usambara (with Notes on Kimbugu)," *Tanzania Notes and Records* 61 (1963): 176. Green describes a "colony" of Vamaa still residing in North Pare and occasional Mshitu ceremonies in South Pare. See also B. D. Copland, "A Note on the Origin of the Mbugu with a Text," *Zeitschrift für Eingeborenen-Sprachen* 24 (1933–34): 243; Tucker and Bryan, "Vamaa Anomaly," 190; UIT, Seuya and Baharia, at Magamba, 3/12/92, 2–3 and 11; T. Mganga, at Kwefingo, 29/3/92, 13; Dominique Ndala, at Batai (Magamba), 21; Salim Kadala at Mshangai, 27/4/92, 27.

34. UIT informants recall these lineage names as follows: the Londo (Ombweni), Ombeji, Gonja, Nkandu, Ngarito Ngarire, and Kwangwana. Feierman, *Shambaa Kingdom*, chap. 3, and E. C. Green, "Wambugu of Usambara," also note lineage names in their treatments of Vamaa history. Informants claimed that the Shambaa then had no

cattle and that the Vamaa purchased their rights of residence with cattle. UIT, Seuya and Baharia, 3/12/92, 2.

35. Feierman, *Shambaa Kingdom*. For Shambaa agriculture see chapter 1, and for Vamaa/Shambaa relations during the eighteenth century, chapters 2 and 3.

36. UIT, Seuya and Baharia, 3/12/92, 3; Dominique Ndala, at Batai, 4/92, 21; T. Mganga, 14. These glades may have been conditioned by buffalo, bush buck, and other ungulates common in central plateau forests until the 1940s.

37. For evidence of burning forest to create pasture, see B. D. Copland, "A Note on the Origin of the Mbugu with a Text," 244; UIT, Paulo Mwavoa and Mlango Msasu, at Kinko, 3/3/92, 39; T. Mganga, 14. Mzee Mganga claims that the Vamaa never cleared forest to create pasture. The presence in the mountains of the Soil Erosion Control and Afforestation Project (SECAP), run cooperatively by the Tanzanian government and the German government's aid agency, Gesellschaft für technische Zusammenarbeit, complicated testimony. Informants were often reluctant to admit any practice, such as burning fields or cultivation on steep slopes, which the project prohibited.

38. UIT, Mkanda Shusha, at Mshangai, 2/92, 25.

39. Oscar Baumann, "Usambara," *Petermanns geographische Mitteilungen* 2 (1889): 47; UIT, T. Mganga, 14 and 20; Seuya and Baharia, 1/23/92, 11.

40. UIT, T. Mganga, 16. This feature might have become more common during the late nineteenth century. Place names in central Usambara also indicate the former presence of large bomas, especially around Kwai, Mshangai, and Malibwi.

41. UIT, Seuya and Baharia, 1/23/92, 9–10. The elders also cite infanticide as a common practice.

42. Ibid., 11. Gregory Maddox (personal communication) also notes herd culling and the availability of meat through regular ritual slaughter of animals. UIT, Seuya and Baharia, 1/23/92, 7.

43. Steven Feierman, *Peasant Intellectuals: Anthropology and History in Tanzania* (Madison: University of Wisconsin Press, 1990), 49; and *Shambaa Kingdom*, 155; UIT, T. Mganga, 20.

44. UIT, T. Mganga, 20.

45. Informant used the Swahili word *jangwa* to describe an area without adequate grazing.

46. UIT, M. Shusha, 25; my translation.

47. UIT, Paulo Mwavoa and Mlango Msasu, at Kinko, 3/92, 39.

48. UIT, T. Mganga, 14; P. Mwavoa and M. Msasu, 39. This is a pattern of temporary absorption characteristic of Maasai relations with Bantu speakers in Transmara, Kenya; see Richard Waller, "Interaction and Identity," 243–84.

49. For reclusiveness, see Green, "Wambugu of Usambara," 175. For an example of interactions between pastoralists and farmers in East Africa, see J. L. Berntsen, "Maasai and Their Neighbors."

50. UIT, T. Mganga, 19; D. Ndala, 21 and 22; Mkanda Shusha, 27. For honey production in East African forest ecology, see R. H. Blackburn, "Honey in Okiek Person-

ality, Culture and Society" (Ph.D. diss., Michigan State University, 1971), chaps. 1 and 2.

51. UIT, T. Mganga, 17–18 and 20.

52. UIT, T. Mganga, 17–18; M. Shusha, 27. Once mixed with maize, honey could be stored for months until needed; see also Blackburn, "Honey in Okiek Personality," chap. 3, for honey-related economic relations between Okiek (highland forest) and Maasai (plains).

53. This conceptualization of environmental degradation draws heavily on Michael Mortimer, *Roots in the African Dust: Sustaining the Drylands* (Cambridge: Cambridge University Press, 1998), 125–39.

54. For three excellent works on crises in the region, see Richard Waller, "Emutai: Crisis and Response in Maasailand 1883–1902," in *The Ecology of Survival: Case Studies from Northeast African History*, ed., Douglas Johnson and David Anderson (Boulder: Westview Press, 1988), 73–114; Charles Ambler, *Kenyan Communities in the Age of Imperialism: The Central Region in the Late Nineteenth Century* (New Haven: Yale University Press, 1988); and James Giblin, *The Politics of Environmental Control in Northeastern Tanzania, 1840–1940* (Philadelphia: University of Pennsylvania Press, 1992).

55. Jonathon Glassman, *Feasts and Riot: Revelry, Rebellion, and Popular Consciousness on the Swahili Coast, 1856–1888* (Portsmouth, N.H.: Heinemann Books, 1995), 80.

56. For an analysis of the commodity trade on Zanzibar, see Abdul Sheriff, *Slaves, Spices and Ivory: Integration of an East African Commercial Empire in the World Economy* (London: James Currey, 1987). Frederick Cooper analyzes the nineteenth-century plantation economy on the mainland coast of Kenya and Tanzania in *Plantation Slavery on the East Coast of Africa* (Portsmouth, N.H.: Heinemann Books, 1997). For an examination of the nineteenth-century political economy in Usambara, see Steven Feierman, *Peasant Intellectuals*, chaps. 2, 3, and 4. James Giblin analyzes similar processes in Uzigua with special attention to their ecological effects in *Politics of Environmental Control*. Marcia Wright looks at the personal stories of women displaced by the slave trade in *Strategies of Slaves and Women: Life Stories from East/Central Africa* (London: James Currey, 1993).

57. UIT, Jafeth Kalata, at Mlalo, 3/13/92, 23. In "Environmental Control," 71, Kimambo explains that njaa can denote either a killing famine (a rare phenomenon in the northeastern Tanzania highlands) or a situation of chronic hunger and impoverishment which drives communities to find ways to control their environments.

58. I believe it likely that long-standing patterns of soil erosion in the mountains made the vitivo attractive during the early nineteenth century. The settlements mentioned above are directly downstream from Mlalo and Bumbuli/Vuga, centers of dense population and intensive agriculture.

59. Oscar Baumann, *Usambara und seine Nachbargebiete: Allgemeine Darstellung des nordöstlichen Deutsch-Ostafrika und seiner Bewohner auf Grund einer im Auftrage der Deutsch-Ostafrikanischen Gesellschaft im Jahre 1890 ausgeführten Reise* (Berlin: Dietrich Reimer, 1891), 172. Feierman, *Shambaa Kingdom*, 126–30, argues that these colonies operated as ivory collection stations and trading posts throughout the eighteenth century. Whatever

the case, they served as refuges for those fleeing famine in Ukambani over much of the course of the nineteenth century. For a discussion of nineteenth-century Kamba migrations, see Ambler, *Kenyan Communities*.

60. See Baumann, *Usambara*, 175, for Iloikop Maasai settlement at Vuruni. For Mtaarwanda, see Feierman, *Shambaa Kingdom*, 125.

61. Tanzania National Archive (hereafter TNA) Sec. 24732, Geoffrey Milne, "Report on a Soil Reconnaissance in the Neighbourhood of Kitivo, Lushoto District, Tanganyika Territory, and in adjacent Highlands, September–October 1937," 13.

62. TNA Sec. 24732, Milne, "Report," 11. For climatic data, see S. E. Nicholson, "Environmental Change," 82. Warburg, "Die Kulturpflanzen," 141, notes cultivation of sorghum by Kamba at Kitivo, and that surpluses were sold in mountain markets. Baumann, *In Deutsch-Ostafrika*, 166, also notes the importance of *mtama*, which can be translated as either sorghum or millet. Warburg, "Die Kulturpflanzen," 135 for maize and 140 for rice.

63. For conflict in the 1840s and earlier, see Johann Ludwig Krapf, *Reisen in Ostafrika ausgeführt in den Jahren 1837–1855* (Stuttgart: F. A. Brockhaus Kimm.-Gesch., GmbH., Abt. Antiquarium, 1964), 122. For oral evidence of later abandonment, see Baumann, *Usambara*, 170.

64. For a detailed description of the politics of the Kilindi succession struggle, see Feierman, *Shambaa Kingdom*, chap. 6.

65. See Christopher Conte, "Nature Reorganized: Ecological History in the Plateau Forests of West Usambara Mountains, c. 1850–1935," in *Custodians of the Land: Ecology and Culture in the History of Tanzania*, ed. Gregory Maddox, James Giblin, and Isaria N. Kimambo (London: James Currey, 1996): 96–122. For detailed discussion of Kilindi history during the late nineteenth century, see Feierman, *Peasant Intellectuals*, chap. 4.

66. Baumann, *Usambara*, 173.

67. Johannes Buchwald, "Aus dem deutsch-ostafrikanischen Schutzgebiete. Beitrag zur Gliederung der Vegetation von West-Usambara," *Mitteilungen aus den deutschen Schutzgebieten* 9 (1896): 223; "Westusambara, die Vegetation und der wirtschaftliche Werth des Landes," *Der Tropenpflanzer, Zeitschrift für tropische Landwirtschaft* 1 (1897): 84.

68. Baumann, *Usambara*, 177.

69. Baumann, *In Deutsch-Ostafrika*, 77.

70. Abdallah bin Hemedi 'l Ajjemy, *The Kilindi* (Nairobi: East African Literature Bureau, 1963), 236–37.

71. Feierman, *Shambaa Kingdom*, 193.

72. Baumann, *In Deutsch-Ostafrika*, 75.

73. Ibid., 78.

74. Ibid., 168. Because he traversed the northerly side of the West Usambara massif, Baumann may well have been mistaken in this assumption.

75. The following description of Mlalo's agriculture is based on Warburg, "Die Kulturpflanzen," 131–99. Warburg's article is based on Carl Hölst's extensive botanical inventories for West Usambara.

76. Warburg, "Die Kulturpflanzen," 176; UIT, Kalata, 23.

77. For a detailed description of rice production in German East Africa generally and Kitivo in particular, see Dr. K. Braun, "Der Reis in Deutsch-Ostafrika," *Berichte über Land- und Forstwirtschaft in Deutsch-Ostafrika* 3 (1907): 167–217.

78. Buchwald, "Westusambara," 88. At Tewe, within walking distance of Mlalo on the northern side of the Shagai forest, ironsmiths produced iron famous throughout Usambara.

79. J. E. G. Sutton, "Towards a History of Cultivating the Fields," *Azania* 24 (1989): 111. For an argument on stress at Mlalo, see Patrick Fleuret, "Farm and Market: A Study of Society and Agriculture in Tanzania" (Ph.D. diss., University of California at Santa Barbara, 1978), 44.

80. UIT, Seuya and Baharia, 3/12/92, 3; Salim Kadala, 28.

81. UIT, Salim Kadala, 29; Dr. Neubaur, "Die Besiedelungsfähigkeit von Westusambara," *Zeitschrift für tropische Landwirtschaft* 6 (1902): 504.

82. UIT, Paulo Mwavoa and Mlango Msasu, at Kinko, 3/3/92, 39.

83. UIT, T. Mganga, 16; D. Ndala, 21; M. Shusha, 27; S. Kadala, 28; P. Mwavoa and M. Msasu, 39. For effects on the Maasai, see Richard Waller, "Emutai."

84. E. Eick, "Bericht über meine Reise ins Kwai und Masumbailand (Usambara) vom 12. bis 16. März 1896," *Mitteilungen aus den deutschen Schutzgebieten* 9.3 (1896): 187; Copland, "A Note on the Origin," 244; UIT, Kadala, 29.

85. UIT, T. Mganga, 16; P. Mwavoa and M. Msasu, 38.

86. For Mbugu refugees, see Feierman, *Shambaa Kingdom*, 166; for battles against Maasai and Germans, see chapter 3.

87. C. J. W. Pitt-Schenkel, "Some Important Communities of Warm Temperate Rain Forest at Magamba, West Usambara, Tanganyika Territory," *Journal of Ecology* 26 (1938): 60.

88. Ernst Johanssen, "Die Mission unter den Vamaa," *Nachrichten aus der ostafrikanischen Mission* 8 (1894): 25; Br. Becker, "Die Vamaakinder," *Nachrichten aus der ostafrikanischen Mission* 8 (1894): 98; Oskar Baumann, "Usambara," 49.

89. Eick, "Berichte," 186.

90. Ernst Johanssen, "Missionsarbeit unter den Wambugu," *Nachrichten aus der ostafrikansichen Mission* 11 (1897): 126.

91. Hans Schabel, "Tanganyika Forestry under German Colonial Administration, 1891–1919," *Forest and Conservation History* 34.3 (1990): 131.

92. Geoffrey Milne, "Essays in Applied Pedology," 9.

Chapter 3

1. For a discussion of how precolonial plantations functioned in the lower Pangani Valley, see Jonathan Glassman, *Feasts and Riot: Revelry, Rebellion, and Popular Consciousness on the Swahili Coast, 1856–1888* (Portsmouth, N.H.: Heinemann Books, 1995), chapter 3.

2. For the cultural context of the superiority complex, see Michael Adas, *Machines as the Measure of Men: Science, Technology and Ideologies of Western Dominance* (Ithaca: Cornell University Press, 1989), chapter 5.

3. Personal observation, October 1996.

4. Amani's scientists have published in many prestigious scientific journals. However, Amani-based research has appeared consistently in two publications. For the German era, see especially *Der Tropenpflanzer: Zeitschrift für tropische Landswirtschaft*, and for the British colonial era, see *East African Agricultural and Forestry Journal*.

5. See Alfred Crosby, *Ecological Imperialism: The Biological Expansion of Europe* (Cambridge: Cambridge University Press, 1986).

6. John Mackenzie, "Introduction," in *Imperialism and the Natural World*, ed. John Mackenzie (Manchester, U.K.: Manchester University Press, 1990), 6.

7. For a discussion of this complex process, see John Iliffe, *A Modern History of Tanganyika* (Cambridge: Cambridge University Press, 1979), chapter 4. More recently, see Juhani Koponen, *Development for Exploitation: German Colonial Policies in Mainland Tanzania, 1884–1914* (Helsinki: Finnish Historical Society, Studia Historica 49, 1994); and Glassman, *Feasts and Riot*.

8. Daniel R. Headrick, *Tentacles of Progress: Technology Transfer in the Age of Imperialism* (Oxford: Oxford University Press, 1988), 212–19.

9. Adolf Engler, *Über die Gliederung der Vegetation von Usambara und der angrenzenden Gebiet*, Abhandlungen der Königlichen Akademie der Wissenschaften zu Berlin, 1894 Physikalische Abhandlungen, 1 (Berlin: Verlag der Akademie der Wissenschaften, 1894) 6.

10. Lucille Brockway, *Science and Colonial Expansion: The Role of the British Botanical Gardens* (New York: Academic Press, 1979), 177–80. The fibers from sisal leaves are used in making rope and other woven products.

11. Ibid., 179–80.

12. For sisal in German East Africa, see J. Vosseler, "Sisal im Usambaragebirge," *Der Pflanzer* 2 (1906): 339–47. For ecological change, see Christopher Conte, "Transformations along the Gradient" (Ph.D. diss., Michigan State University, 1995), 29–30.

13. For a discussion, see Paolo Pallidino and Michael Worboys, "Science and Imperialism," *Isis* 74 (1993): 91–102. For German botany and empire, see Eugene Cittadino, *Nature as the Laboratory: Darwinian Plant Ecology in the German Empire, 1880–1900* (Cambridge: Cambridge University Press, 1990).

14. For example, see Helge Kjekshus, *Ecology Control and Economic Development in East African History: The Case of Tanganyika, 1850–1950*, 2nd ed. (London: James Currey, 1996); Leroy Vail, "Ecology and History: The Example of Eastern Zambia," *Journal of Southern African Studies* 3.2 (1977): 130–55; Ramachandra Guha and Madhav Gadgil, *This Fissured Land* (Berkeley: University of California Press, 1992).

15. For example, see Richard Grove, *Green Imperialism: Colonial Expansion, Tropical Island Edens and the Origins of Environmentalism, 1600–1860* (Cambridge: Cambridge University Press, 1995); and Detlaf Bald and Gerhild Bald, *Das Forschungsinstitut Amani:*

Wirtschaft und Wissenschaft in der deutschen Kolonialpolitik Ostafrika 1900–1918 (Munich: Weltforum-Verlag, 1972). For a critique of environmental history's approach to imperialism, see John MacKenzie, "Empire and the Ecological Apocalypse: The Historiography of the Imperial Environment," in *Ecology of Empire: Environmental History of Settler Societies*, ed. Tom Griffiths and Libby Robin (Seattle: University of Washington Press, 1997), 218–24. For exemplary studies of indigenous land-use practice, see James Fairhead and Melissa Leach, *Misreading the Landscape: Society and Ecology in a Forest-Savanna Mosaic*, African Studies Series 90 (Cambridge: Cambridge University Press, 1996); James McCann, *People of the Plow: An Agricultural History of Ethiopia, 1800–1990* (Madison: University of Wisconsin Press, 1995); and Ian Scoones, "The Dynamics of Soil Fertility Change: Historical Perspectives on Soil Fertility Change from Zimbabwe," *Geographical Journal* 163 (July 1997): 161–69.

16. E. Eick, "Bericht über meine Reise ins Kwai und Masumbailand (Usambara) vom 12. bis 16. März 1896," *Mitteilungen aus den deutschen Schutzgebieten* 9.3 (1896): 186. For earlier description of the area, see Oscar Baumann, *In Deutsch-Ostafrika während des Aufstandes, Reise der Dr. Hans Meyer'schen Expedition in Usambara* (Wien: Eduard Hölzel, 1890), 154–55.

17. For the reference to Switzerland, see Johannes Buchwald, "Aus dem deutschostafrikanischen Schutzgebiete. Beitrag zur Gliederung der Vegetation von West-Usambara," *Mitteilungen aus den deutschen Schutzgebieten* 9 (1896): 229.

18. Christopher Conte, "Nature Reorganized: Ecological History in the Plateau Forests of the West Usambara Mountains, c. 1850–1935," in *Custodians of the Land: Ecology and Culture in the History of Tanzania*, ed. Gregory Maddox, James Giblin, and Isaria N. Kimambo (London: James Currey, 1996), 105.

19. Ibid.

20. Usambara Interview Transcripts (hereafter UIT), Mbega Mavoa, at Malibwi, 41.

21. See UIT, Baharia and Seuya, at Magamba, 3/12/92, 1.

22. Herman Paasche, *Deutsch Ostafrika* (Grossenworden [Nieder-Elbe]: Rüsch'she Verlagsbuchhandlung, 1927), 247.

23. Dr. Neubaur, "Die Besiedelungsfähigkeit von Westusambara," *Der Tropenpflanzer: Zeitschrift für tropische Landswirtschaft* 6 (1902): 500.

24. UIT, Athumani Senavuri, at Kwemekame, 10/96.

25. Teichmann, "Auszüge aus den Jahresberichten der Bezirksämter und Militärstationen für die Zeit vom 1. Juli 1900 bis 30. Juni 1901, 2. Bezirksamt Wilhelmstal (West Usambara)," *Berichte über Land- und Forstwirtschaft in Deutsch-Ostafrika* 1 (1903): 27–38. See also reports from Gare and Kwai in the same volume.

26. John Iliffe, *A Modern History of Tanganyika* (Cambridge: Cambridge University Press, 1979), 126.

27. Chr. Hedde, "Auszüge aus den Jahresberichten der Bezirkämter und Militärstationen für die Zeit vom 1. Juli 1900 bis 30. Juni 1901, 3. Privatpflanzungen in West-Usambara. Asiedelung am Mkusu, den 12. Juni 1901," *Berichte über Land- und Forstwirtschaft in Deutsch-Ostafrika* 1 (1903): 45–46.

28. Dr. Richard Hindorf, "Eine Versuchsstation für Tropenkulturen in Usambara," *Der Tropenpflanzer: Zeitschrift für tropische Landwirtschaft* 2.5 (1898): 137–42.

29. TNA G8/37, "Report from Kwai to the Imperial Government," 11/24/1900, Agricultural Station Kwai, 1898–1901, 29 (my translation).

30. Ibid.

31. Paasche, *Deutsch Ostafrika,* 250–51.

32. UIT, D. Ndala, 23.

33. UIT, T. Mganga, 13; F. Baharia and Seuya, 6; D. Ndala, 23.

34. UIT, T. Mganga, 13.

35. UIT, Baharia and Seuya, 1/23/92, 7.

36. On milk production, see Neubaur, "Die Besiedelungsfähigkeit," 498; on meat processing, see Paasche, *Deutsch Ostafrika,* 252. Paasche's account is based on a 1905 trip. In the Tanzanian National Museum there is an exhibit dedicated to Illich's meat production operation at Kwai. See also Neubaur, "Die Besiedelungsfähigkeit," 502–5.

37. TNA 72/21/1, Deceased Estates—Non-Natives, A.D.O., Lushoto, to Chief Secretary, Dar es Salaam, 2/8/21.

38. TNA 4/309/29, Kwai—Complaints of Mr. J. T. Woodcock, concerning estate boundaries, D.O., Lushoto (R. E. Seymour), to P.C., Tanga, 11/18/36 (confidential), 67.

39. TNA 4/309/29, "Précis of Papers Relating to Mr. Woodcock's Complaint Regarding Survey of Kwai, P. H. Hutchinson, Land Surveyor, 3/5/37," Kwai (Mr. J. T. Woodcock), Usambara District, 81. A 1937 survey found that the second survey did in fact correspond to the farm's boundaries of 1911.

40. TNA 4/309/29, "Précis," Kwai (Mr. J. T. Woodcock), Usambara District, 81.

41. TNA 3/309/29, J. T. Woodcock, Kwai, to P.C., Tanga, 1/6/31, 1; D.O., Lushoto (R. E. Seymour), to P.C., Tanga, 6/15/36, 58, Kwai (Mr. J. T. Woodcock), Usambara District. File contains the minutes for the district water board meeting of 9/1/32.

42. TNA 4/309/29, J. T. Woodcock, Kwai, to P.C., Tanga, 1/9/31, Kwai (Mr. J. T. Woodcock), Usambara District, 2.

43. TNA 4/309/29, D.O., Lushoto (Hartnoll), to P.C., Tanga, 2/26/31, Kwai (Mr. J. T. Woodcock), Usambara District, 13.

44. TNA 4/309/29, Superintendent of Police, Lushoto, A. G. de Villiers, to Superintendent of Police, Tanga, 9/9/36, Kwai (Mr. J. T. Woodcock), Usambara District, n.p. The superintendent notes: "Since the big cattle *shauri* [affair] people will not go and work for Mr. Woodcock and some complete one *kipandi* [work card] only and some not even that; leaving behind unfinished *kipandi*s. He does not beat natives but is always quarrelling with boys; accusing them of thefts which allegations are untrue and in consequence boys leave and will not return as they are afraid of being taken to the Boma on frivolous charges."

45. TNA 4/309/29, Sub-Magistrate, Lushoto (A. V. Hartnoll), to P.C., Tanga, 5/21/31, "First Class case no. 13 of 1931, Rex vs. Mr. J. T. Woodcock;" Chief Secretary to Mr. Woodcock, 4/16/36, Kwai (Mr. J. T. Woodcock), Usambara District, 18 and 56.

46. TNA 4/303/29, G. W. Lock, District Agricultural Officer, Lushoto, to D.O.,

Lushoto, 10/4/33, Complaints by Mr. J. T. Woodcock against the D.O. Lushoto, Kwai (Mr. J. T. Woodcock), Usambara District, n.p.

47. TNA 4/309/29, D.O., Lushoto (Callaghan), to Lands Officer, Dar es Salaam, 2/3/34, Kwai (Mr. J. T. Woodcock), Usambara District, 37.

48. TNA 4/309/29, D.O., Lushoto (R. E. Seymour), to P.C., Tanga, 10/19/34, Kwai (Mr. J. T. Woodcock), Usambara District, 43. Seymour mistakenly uses "Shambaa." Kwai area was in 1933 occupied mostly by Mbugu herders and Pare cultivators.

49. TNA 4/309/29, A.D.O., Lushoto, E. J. W. Carlton, to D.O., Lushoto, 26/6/35, Kwai (Mr. J. T. Woodcock), Usambara District, 48.

50. TNA 4/309/29, "Comments and Observations on the complaints by Mr. J. T. Woodcock by A. R. Mill Chief Inspector of Police at Kwai Farm at 9:45 am 9/21/36," Kwai (Mr. J. T. Woodcock), Usambara District, n.p.

51. TNA 4/309/29, A.D.O. in Charge of Labour, Muheza, R. C. Jerrard, to Labour Office, Provincial Administration, Muhesa, Tanga, 6/19/37, Kwai (Mr. J. T. Woodcock), Usambara District, n.p.

52. TNA 4/303/29, D.C., Lushoto, R. Thomas, to P.C, Tanga, 7/9/53, Complaints by Mr. J. T. Woodcock against the D.O., Lushoto, Kwai (Mr. J. T. Woodcock), Usambara District, 32.

53. "Verdict of Murder in New Inquest on Farm Case," *Tanganyika Standard*, May 18, 1955.

54. Bald and Bald, *Das Forschungsinstitut Amani*, 5.

55. Richard Drayton, *Nature's Government: Science, Imperial Britain and the 'Improvement' of the World* (New Haven: Yale University Press, 2000), 193–201. Of course, the idea was central to German forestry practice from the eighteenth century.

56. Otto Warburg, "Die Notwendigkeit einer Versuchsstation für Tropenkulturen in Usambara und ihre Kosten," *Der Tropenpflanzer: Zeitschrift für tropische Landwirtschaft* 2 (1898): 184.

57. Adolf Engler, *Über die Gliederung der Vegetation von Usambara und der angrenzenden Gebiete*, Abhandlungen der Königlichen Akademie der Wissenschaften zu Berlin, 1894, Physikalische Abhandlungen, 1 (Berlin: Verlag der Akademie der Wissenschaften, 1894), 7.

58. For an excellent bibliography detailing the history of these efforts, see Stig Johansson, "Conservation in the East Usambara Mountains—A Partly Annotated Bibliography of Selected Published and Non-Published Material," Working Paper 22 (Tanga, Tanzania: East Usambara Catchment Forest Project, 1996).

59. Engler, *Gliederung*, 43–75.

60. Ibid., 48. Engler, citing Hölst's observations, notes African tendencies to employ long-fallow and intercropping techniques using bananas and maize. This practice led observers to make the mistaken claim of wild banana plants occurring in Urwald zones, when they were actually seeing the remnants of banana plantings in forest fallows.

61. Otto Warburg, "Die Kulturpflanzen Usambaras," *Mitteilungen aus den deutschen Schutzgebieten* 7 (1894): 131–99.

62. See Carl Hölst, "Der Landbau der Eingeborenen von Usambara," *Deutsche Kolonialzeitung* 6.9 (1893): 113–14; 6.10, 128–30. For an exposition on the rice growing techniques on the plains below the West Usambaras, see K. Braun, "Der Reis in Deutsch-Ostafrika," *Berichte über Land- und Forstwirtschaft in Deutsch-Ostafrika* 3 (1907): 167–217.

63. Richard Hindorf, "Die Versuchsstation für Tropenkulturen in Usambara," *Der Tropenpflanzer: Zeitschrift für tropische Landwirtschaft* 5 (1901): 268–69.

64. Franz Stuhlman, "Übersicht über Land- und Forstwirtschaft in Deutsch-Ostafrika im Berichtsjahre vom 1. Juli 1900 bis 30. Juni 1901," *Berichte über Land- und Forstwirtschaft in Deutsch-Ostafrika* 1 (1903): 11–12. See also L. Sander, "Usambara," *Der Tropenpflanzer: Zeitschrift für tropische Landwirtschaft* 7.5 (1903): 203.

65. Hindorf, "Die Versuchsstation" (1901), 270.

66. "Dr. Stuhlmann über die wirtschaftliche Entwickelung Deutsch-Ostafrikas," *Der Tropenpflanzer: Zeitschrift für tropische Landwirtschaft* 2 (1898): 119–25.

67. Stuhlmann, "Übersicht," 15–16. Station scientists and their assistants planned and planted out a 300 ha botanical garden with tropical plants collected by Stuhlman and others.

68. Cittadino, *Nature*, 136.

69. Bald and Bald, *Amani*, 51–53.

70. For the economic vision, see Otto Warburg, "Die Notwendigkeit"; Hindorf, "Die Versuchsstation" (1901); and Walter Busse, "Zur Frage der tropischen Versuchsstation in Usambara," *Der Tropenpflanzer: Zeitschrift für tropische Landwirtschaft* 5 (1901): 270–73.

71. TNA 2588, German Staff at Amani, n.p.

72. One of the visitors went so far as to call Amani a tropical Kew Gardens. See Drayton, *Nature's Government*, 254.

73. Bald and Bald, *Amani*, 72; ibid., 88–89.

74. Geoffrey Milne, "Essays in Applied Pedology: 1. Soil Type and Soil Management in Relation to Plantation Agriculture in East Usambara," *East African Agricultural Journal* 3.1 (1937): 8–9.

75. Bald and Bald, *Amani*, 41–42.

76. Adolf Engler, "Bemerkungen über Schonung und verständige Ausnutzung der einzelnen Vegetationsformen Deutsch-Ostafrikas," *Berichte über Land- und Forstwirtschaft in Deutsch-Ostafrika* 2 (1904): 3.

77. See Warburg, "Die Notwendigkeit," 184–85; for soil fertility, see Sander, "Usambara," 207.

78. For an excellent description of the degradation process, see G. Milne, "Essays," 16.

79. Th. Siebenlist, *Forstwirtschaft in Deutsch-Ostafrika* (Berlin: Verlagsbuchhandlung Paul Parey, 1914), 54.

80. Bald and Bald, *Amani*, 71.

81. TNA 2588, Director of Ag. A. C. MacDonald to the D.A.Q.M.G., G.H.Q., Dar es Salaam, 9/27/16, German Staff at Amani, n.p., first letter in file.

82. D. Sheil, "Naturalized and Invasive Plant Species in the Evergreen Forests of the East Usambara Mountains, Tanzania," *African Journal of Ecology* 32 (1994), 66–69.

83. Bald and Bald, *Amani*, 90–92. Regarding cinchona, in 1902 Zimmerman had brought cinchona from Buitenzorg and planted it in the northern part of the colony. By 1906–7, the trees had produced cinchona bark. During the war, Amani provided instructions on how to produce quinine tablets, which were, according to the Balds, "just as good as the ones from Germany." Braun, Amani's assistant director, developed instructions for troops in the field to produce quinine tablets with bark taken from Amani.

84. TNA 2588, Director of Ag. A. C. MacDonald to the D.A.Q.M.G., G.H.Q., Dar es Salaam. 9/27/16, German Staff at Amani, n.p, first letter in file.

85. TNA 2588 Leechman, Director, Amani Institute, and Acting Director of Ag. to Chief Secretary, DSM, German Staff at Amani, 1/14/20, 9.

86. TNA 3132, volume 1, D. Prain, Royal Botanic Gardens, Kew, June 28, 1920, "Observations relative to the future of the Amani Institute," Amani Institute, 2.

87. TNA 3132, volume 1, Leechman, Director, Amani to Chief Secretary, DSM, November 1920, Amani Institute, 3.

88. TNA 3132 contains a number of sets of correspondences that highlight Leechman's futile battle to keep Amani open. See Leechman to Hon. Chief Sec, 10/17/21, forwarded by Wolf, Director of Agriculture, 31/10/21, n.p.; Wolfe, Director of Agriculture, to Chief Sec. 31/10/21, n.p.; Covering, H. Wolfe, Deputy Director of Agriculture, to Hon. Chief Sec., DSM, 1/12/22, 47; "Report on the Re-Establishment of a Research Institute at Amani, in the Tanganyika Territory to Serve the East African Dependencies," Sd. Edward North, Governor, Kenya, to The right Honourable Winston Churchill, PC, MF Secretary of State for the Colonies, Downing Street, London, S.W., 3/2/22, page 59; A. H. Kirby, Director of Agriculture, Dar es Salaam, to Hon Chief Secretary, DSM, 5/26/22, 61.

89. British Colonial Office (hereafter CO) 822/14/1, East Africa Agricultural Station Progress Reports, 1929, 16–19.

90. Geoffrey Milne, "Notes on Soil Conditions and Two East African Vegetation Types," *Journal of Ecology* 25 (1937): 254–58; and "A Soil Reconnaissance Journey through Parts of Tanganyika Territory. December 1935–February 1936," *Journal of Ecology* 35 (1947): 192–265. R. E. Moreau, "Pleistocene Climatic Changes and the Distribution of Life in East Africa." *Journal of Ecology* 21 (1933): 415–35; and "A Synecological Study of Usambara, Tanganyika Territory with Particular Reference to Birds," *Journal of Ecology* 23.1 (1935): 1–43.

91. CO 822/22/4, Sir William Furse to Germal Creasy, Secretary, Colonial Advisory Council of Agriculture and Animal Health, 3/11/30, East Africa Agricultural Station Future Development and Progress, 1930, 144–45.

92. CO 822/22/4, Edward Grigg, Governor of Kenya, to Sec. of State for Colonies, Lord Passfield, P.C., 5/12/30, East Africa Agricultural Station Future Development and Progress, 1930.

93. CO 822/22/4, Colonial Advisory Council of Agriculture and Animal Health, "Report of Sub Committee on East African Agricultural Research Station, Amani," 8/13/30, East Africa Agricultural Station Future Development and Progress, 1930, 81.

94. TNA, Secretariat 27184, Director of Agriculture, Wakefield, to Chief Secretary, 7/28/9, 2.

95. CO 822/108/17, "Note on the reasons which led to the Conference of Directors of Ag., 1940, to agree that Amani was unsuitable as a center for the direction and coordination of long term agricultural research in East Africa," East African Agricultural Research Institute, Future Of. 1943, 22.

96. CO 822/114/6, G. Hill, Director of the East African Agricultural Station, to the Chief Sec., Governor's Conference Nairobi, 4/24/44, East African Agricultural Research Institute, Future Of, 1944, n.p.

97. This comes through in Geoffrey Milne Rhodes House, MSS, Brit. Empire. S.457, vol. 4, A. G. Hill, Director East African Ag. Research Station Amani Tanga Territory, to Milne, 6/5/38, 58; and Milne to Hill, 60.

Chapter 4

1. Melissa Leach and Robin Mearns, eds., *The Lie of the Land: Challenging Received Wisdom on the African Environment* (London: The International African Institute, 1996); James Fairhead and Melissa Leach, *Misreading the African Landscape: Society and Ecology in a Forest-Savanna Mosaic,* African Studies Series 90 (Cambridge: Cambridge University Press, 1996).

2. William Newmark, *Conserving Biodiversity in East African Forests: A Study of the Eastern Arc Mountains* (New York: Springer-Verlag, 2002), tables 2.1 and 4.3.

3. This seems to be the case in many tropical forests; see Leslie E. Sponsel, Thomas N. Headland, and Robert C. Bailey, "Anthropological Perspectives on the Causes, Consequences and Solutions of Deforestation," in *Tropical Deforestation: The Human Dimension,* ed. Leslie E. Sponsel, Thomas N. Headland, and Robert C. Bailey (New York: Columbia University Press, 1996), chapter 1.

4. Johannes Buchwald, "Aus dem deutsch-ostafrikanischen Schutzgebiete. Beitrag zur Gliederung der Vegetation von West-Usambara," *Mitteilungen aus den deutschen Schutz-gebieten* 9 (1896): 213–33. Carl Hölst found cedars in the thousands on the same plateau regions. See Adolf Engler, *Über die Gliederung der Vegetation von Usambara und der angrenzenden Gebiete,* Abhandlungen der Königlichen Akademie der Wissenschaften zu Berlin, 1894, Physikalische Abhandlungen, 1 (Berlin: Verlag der Akademie der Wissenschaften, 1894), 68.

5. Juhani Koponen, *Development for Exploitation: German Colonial Policies in Mainland Tanzania, 1884–1914* (Helsinki: Finnish Historical Society, Studia Historica 49, 1994), 205.

6. See, for example, Brunhoff, "Auszüge aus den Berichten der Bezirksamter, Militärstationen und anderer Dienststellen über die wirtschaftliche Entwicklung im

Berichtsjahre vom 1. April bis 31. März 1903. Bezirk Wilhelmstal," *Berichte über Land- und Forstwirtschaft in Deutsch-Ostafrika* 2 (1903): 41–46.

7. Adolf Engler, "Bemerkungen über Schonung und verständige Ausnutzung der einzelnen Vegetationsformen Deutsch-Ostafrikas," *Berichte über Land- und Forstwirtschaft in Deutsch-Ostafrika* 2 (1904): 3. For an excellent description of the degradation process, see Geoffrey Milne, "Essays in Applied Pedology: 1. Soil Type and Soil Management in Relation to Plantation Agriculture in East Usambara," *East African Agricultural Journal* 3.1 (1937): 16.

8. Th. Siebenlist, *Forstwirtschaft in Deutsch-Ostafrika* (Berlin: Verlagsbuchhandlung Paul Parey, 1914), 54.

9. Geoffrey Milne, "Essays," 8–9. In the 1930s, Milne found that on coffee clearings of twenty-five to forty years, forest recovery had either stopped altogether or had been significantly retarded.

10. Th. Siebenlist, *Forstwirtschaft,* 48 and 50 (my translation).

11. Ibid., 9–10.

12. Ibid., 7. For statistics on size, location, and ownership of Usambara plantations, see Franz Stuhlman, "Übersicht über Land- und Forstwirtschaft in Deutsch-Ostafrika im Berichtsjahre vom 1. Juli 1900 bis 30. Juni 1901," *Berichte über Land- und Forstwirtschaft in Deutsch-Ostafrika* 1 (1903): 11–12; Stuhlman reports six West Usambara plantations with 1.2 million coffee trees and East Usambara plantations holding almost 4 million trees.

13. Siebenlist, *Forstwirtschaft,* 7–10.

14. See Henry Lowood, "The Calculating Forester: Quantification, Cameral Science and the Emergence of Scientific Forestry Management in Germany," in *The Quantifying Spirit in the 18th Century,* ed. Tore Fraengsmyr, J. L. Heilbron, and Robin E. Rider (Berkeley: University of California Press, 1990): 315–42.

15. Stuhlman, "Übersicht," 22. For the orderly forests, see also Teichman, "Auszüge aus den Jahresberichten der Bezirksämter und Militärstationen für die Zeit vom 1. Juli 1900 bis 30. Juni 1901, 4. Forstliche Versuche im Bezirk Wihelmstal," *Berichte über Land- und Forstwirtschaft in Deutsch-Ostafrika* 1 (1903): 53.

16. Lushoto Office of Natural Resources Files (hereafter LF) 11/B/1/3, A. S. Adamson, forester, Shume Station, Safari Reports for Shume Reserve for 12/19/21 to 12/23/21, 8/14/22 to 8/19/22, 7/13/21 to 7/18/21. Recutting the boundary line involved finding the German markers and clearing the underbrush between them. Sisal, aloe, or eucalyptus were often planted as markers of the boundaries.

17. LF 11/B/1/3, A. S. Adamson, Safari Report for Shume Reserve for 8/14/22 to 8/19/22, 3.

18. R. S. Troup, *Colonial Forest Administration* (Oxford: Oxford University Press, 1940), 127.

19. See, for example, H. M. Gardner, "East African Pencil Cedar," *Empire Forestry Journal* 5 (1926): 39–53.

20. TNA 2796, D. K. S. Grant to Chief Secretary, Tanganyika Territory, 1/24/21, Forest Concessions, 9.

21. Tanganyika Territory, *Third Annual Report of the Forest Department, Tanganyika Territory* (Dar es Salaam: Government Printer, 1923), 2; Tanganyika Territory, *Fourth Annual Report of the Forest Department, Tanganyika Territory* (Dar es Salaam: Government Printer, 1924), 4.

22. The "squatter system" was an adaptation of the system, popular with the British forestry service in India, called *Juming* or *Taungyar*. For early attempts to institute such a system in the Usambaras, see TNA 3046/10, "Forest Department Annual Report 1921," n.p.

23. In 1925, hut and poll taxes were 10/– per year each.

24. Tanganyika Territory, *Seventh Annual Report of the Forest Department, Tanganyika Territory* (Dar es Salaam: Government Printer, 1927), 3.

25. Tanganyika Territory, *Thirteenth Annual Report of the Forest Department, Tanganyika Territory* (Dar es Salaam: Government Printer, 1933), 8.

26. Usambara Interview Transcripts (hereafter UIT), Mkanda Shusha, at Mshangai, 5/93, 24.

27. LF 11/B/1/3, Conservator of Forests to the Assistant Conservator of Forests, Magamba, 5/27/30, 15.

28. For grazing violations, see LF 11/B/1/3, Assistant Conservator of Forests to D. A. Fletcher, Forester, Shume, 6/19/30. For the ban on grazing, see Tanganyika Territory, *Fifteenth Annual Report of the Forest Department, Tanganyika Territory* (Dar es Salaam: Government Printer, 1935), 4.

29. *Nzerengembe* is the name of a tree (wild olive) often used as firewood.

30. LF 11/B/1/3, D. A. Fletcher, Forester, Shume, to Assistant Conservator of Forests, Lushoto, 8/30/35, 64.

31. LF 11/B/1/3, Assistant Conservator of Forests, Lushoto, to District Officer, Lushoto, 10/17/35, "Boundary Dispute at Nzeragembei," 70.

32. LF 11/B/1/3, Forester, Shume, to Assistant Conservator of Forests, Lushoto, 16/11/35, 69.

33. LF 11/B/1/3, District Officer R. E. Seymour to Assistant Conservator of Forests, Lushoto, 19/10/34. The D.O. also had reason to support Mbugu claims in light of a difficult land dispute between a British settler and Wambugu at nearby Kwai.

34. LF 11/B/1/3, Assistant Conservator of Forests to D.O., Lushoto, 10/25/35.

35. LF 11/B/1/3, Forester Fletcher to Assistant Conservator of Forests, Lushoto, 10/28/35, 69.

36. UIT, M. Shusha, 24 and 27; T. Mganga, at Kwefingo, 3/92, 17. Mganga notes that the livestock market at Kwekanga, the main livestock market in Usambara until the 1970s, began in 1928. The *mnada* (livestock market) was regularly attended by Maasai livestock buyers from the plains, and during the late 1920s the Wambugu began to sell animals for cash.

37. LF 11/B/1/3, Forester Fletcher to Assistant Conservator of Forests, Lushoto, 28/9/35, 69.

38. UIT, Paulo Mwavoa and Mlango Msasu, at Kinko, 3/3/92, 45.

39. UIT, Shusha, 29.

40. UIT, Hoseni Kisimbo, at Malibwi, 1/2/92, 62.

41. UIT, Athumani Shemweta, Athumani Kikoi, Abeid Athumani, and Hasani Mlimahadala, at Kwedeghe, 1/92, 72a.

42. UIT, Juma Zahabu, at Handei, 3/92, 27. Cedar was prized because of its ability to resist termite infestations.

43. Ibid., 28. For migrations from Malindi to Lukozi, see UIT, Salehe Jambia, Juma Sebarua, and Peter Kaniki, at Lukozi, 3/17/92; TNA 74/6, Forester, Shume to D.C., Lushoto, 12/15/51, Squatters and Graziers, 1950–53, 20; and "District Team Meeting 11/20/53, Destocking at Shume," n.p. For aerial evidence, see TNA 4/5/4-D, "Minutes of Meeting of the Advisory District Committee, 10/22/54," Lushoto District Committee, 230.

44. TNA 74/6A, "Squatters," Forester, Shume, to D.C., Lushoto, 12/15/51, 20.

45. UIT, Mtee Nyangusi, at Magamba, 5/92, 38.

46. LF 11/B/1/5/2/G, Lushoto Forest Office, Manager, Shagai Mill, to Divisional Forest Officer, Lushoto, 7/12/50, 37.

47. Ibid.

48. TNA 74/6A, "Squatters," D.C., Lushoto, to the Conservator of Forests, Morogoro, and P.C., Tanga, 2/1/52, 37.

49. LF 11/B/1/5/2/G, Lushoto Forest Office, Manager, Shagai Mill to Divisional Forest Officer, Lushoto, 7/12/50, 37. TNA 4/962/15, Tanga Forest Division, Annual Report for the Year Ended 31st December 1954, 86 and 90.

50. UIT, Nyangusi, 38.

51. Tanganyika Territory, *Thirty-First Annual Report of the Forest Department for the Year Ending 31st December 1951, Tanganyika Territory* (Dar es Salaam: Government Printer, 1952), 24; A. J. Lubango, Chief Forester, Magamba Forest Reserve, personal communication.

52. For TFLC's failure, see TNA 270/EA/2, correspondence between the Acting Conservator of Forests and the Chief Secretary and between the General Manger, TLFC, and the Acting Conservator of Forests, Tanganyika Forests and Lumber Co. Ltd.

53. LF 11/B/1/5/2/G, Divisional Forest Officer C.W. D. Kermode to Conservator of Forests, Morogoro, 9/21/50, 17.

54. LF 11/B/1/5/2/G, Conservator of Forests, Northern Circle, to the Chief Conservator of Forests, Morogoro, 4/6/54, 284.

55. LF 11/B/1/5/2/G, Provincial Forest Officer to Grewal Sawmills, 1/12/54, 222.

56. LF 11/B/1/5/2/G, Provincial Forest Officer to Grewal Sawmills, 3/11/55, 230.

57. LF 11/B/1/5/2/G, Grewal Saw Mills to Chief Conservator of Forests, Morogoro, 6/6/57, 339.

58. LF 11/B/1/5/2/G, Provincial Forest Officer, Lushoto, to Chief Conservator of Forests, Morogoro, RE: Relaxation of Sustained Yield on Podo in W. Usambara, Concessions at Shume/Magamba and Shagayu, 10/25/57, 340.

59. TNA 74/19/B, "Safari Report, Tanga Province, 7/7/52," Research Utilization Section, 30a.

60. Ibid.

61. Lubango, personal communication.

62. TNA 270/A/20/TD, Annual Report, 1950, Tanga Division, n.p.

63. LF 11/B/1/5/2/G, Forester, Magamba to Conservator of Forests, Lushoto, 11/18/60, "Quarterly Report for July–Sept. 1960, Magamba Charge"; for the Grewal monthly cut in 1954, see LF 11/B/1/5/2/G, Provincial Forest Officer to Grewal Sawmills, 1/12/54; for description of Kisii see UIT, Musa Paulo, at Coasti (Magamba), 4/92.

64. For a definition of "sustained yield," see R. S. Troup, *Forestry and State Control* (Oxford: Clarendon Press, 1938), 9–11.

65. TNA 41577, vol. 2, Dr. Eggeling, Conservator of Forests, Tanganyika Territory, to Hon. Member for Agriculture and Natural Resources, 1/10/51, "Development Plans: Forest Dep.," Forest Policy, 119.

66. TNA 41577, vol. 2, Confidential Minute, Member for Lands and Mines to Member for Agriculture and Natural Resources, 6/7/54, Forest Policy, 163.

67. The species that predominate in East Usambara's humid evergreen forests include *Cephalosphaera usambarensis, Parineri excelsa, Allanblackia stuhlmannii, Piptadenia buchananii, Macaranga usambarensis,* and *Nyriathae arboreus.*

68. J. P. Farler, "The Usambara Country in East Africa," *Proceedings of the Royal Geographical Society* 1.2 (1879): 81–97.

69. TNA 304/L2/402, Eastern Usambara—Land Survey, 1955–56, 66.

70. For a good description of the complex rainfall patterns in East Usambara, see A. C. Hamilton, "The Climate of the East Usambaras," in *Forest Conservation in the East Usambara Mountains, Tanzania,* ed. A. C. Hamilton and R. Bensted-Smith (Gland, Switzerland: IUCN, 1989), 97–102.

71. Peter Schmidt, "Early Exploitation and Settlement in the Usambara Mountains," in Hamilton and Bensted-Smith, *Forest Conservation,* 76–77.

72. A. C. Hamilton, "History of Resource Utilization and Management: The Precolonial Period," in Hamilton and Bensted-Smith, *Forest Conservation,* 35.

73. A. C. Hamilton, "Climate," 99.

74. TNA 25842, Forester, Morogoro to Chief Secretary, 2/8/40, Mvule Timber Concessions—Tanga Province, 9.

75. Power over Public Lands was vested in the colonial governor. They were, in essence, the places where Africans could legally reside and farm.

76. TNA 25842, Forester, Morogoro, to Chief Secretary, 2/8/40, Mvule Timber Concessions—Tanga Province, 9.

77. Ibid.

78. TNA 7315, Custodian of Enemy Property to Land Officer, 11/17/23, Native Reserves on the Ngambo Estate, 1.

79. British Colonial Office (hereafter CO) 822/79/17, East African Agricultural Research Station, A. Sir Frank Stockdale's Report and B. Programme of Work, 1937, 27.

80. TNA 304/L2/402, 1955–56, Eastern Usambara— Land Survey, 80–81.
81. TNA Sec. 12077, Conservator of Forests, Grant, to Lands Officer 12/1/32, The Forests Ordinance, 79–80.
82. Otto Warburg, "Die Notwendigkeit einer Versuchsstation für Tropenkulturen in Usambara und ihre Kosten," *Der Tropenpflanzer: Zeitschrift für tropische Landwirtschaft* 2 (1898): 184–85.
83. CO 691/127/10, Harold Mann, "Report on Tea Cultivation in the Tanganyika Territory and Its Development" (published on behalf of the Government of the Tanganyika Territory by the Crown Agents for the Colonies, 1933), 12–16.
84. Ibid.
85. TNA 26664, "Note of a Meeting in the Room of Acting Administrative Secretary on Saturday, 4/2/39," Development of Usambaras, 3.
86. LF 32B, "Confidential Memorandum on the Potentialities of the Eastern Usambaras for Small Holdings, 1939, Reconnaissance Survey from March 3rd to March 10th undertaken by Bonavia, D.C., Lushoto, assisted by Davie, Senior Agricultural Officer, and Gillman, Agricultural Officer, Lushoto." Land Utilization and Forest Survey, East Usambara. paragraph 9, n.p.
87. In CO 691/127/10, For the Secretary of State, Plymouth to Gov. Tan. Terr., 4/22/33, Report of the Tea Expert, 13, Nowell, Amani Director, is quoted as arguing that the principal menace to the forests appears to lie in the possibility of tea production.
88. Clement Gillman, Rhodes House MSS.Afr.S.1175, vol. 6, *Diaries*, March 7, 1920, 13–14.
89. Ibid., 96.
90. Ibid., May 17–20, 1935, 60. Here Gillman describes the view eastward across the Lwengera Valley from Vugiri.
91. Clement Gillman, "Water Consultant's Report, No. 6, A Reconnaissance Survey of the Hydrology of Tanganyika Territory in Its Geographical Settings" (Tanganyika Territory, 1940), 71.
92. Geoffrey Milne, "Essays in Applied Pedology: 1. Soil Type and Soil Management in Relation to Plantation Agriculture in East Usambara," *East African Agricultural Journal* 3.1 (1937): 7.
93. Ibid., 8.
94. Ibid., 9. For another report based on the same data, see CO 822/79/14, "Soil Conditions at Kwamkoro and Sangarawe," East African Agricultural Research Station, Kwamkoro Estate, 1937, 38–45.
95. R. E. Moreau, "A Synecological Study of Usambara, Tanganyika Territory, with Particular Reference to Birds," *Journal of Ecology* 23.1 (1935), 1–43. For a comprehensive presentation of Moreau's work, see *The Bird Fauna of Africa and Its Islands* (London: Academic Press, 1966).
96. A. C. Hamilton and I. V. Mwasha, "History of Resource Utilization and Management after Independence," in *Forest Conservation in the East Usambara Mountains, Tanzania*, ed. A. C. Hamilton and R. Bensted-Smith (Gland, Switzerland: IUCN, 1989), 42.

97. LF, 32B, B. H. Winstanley D.O., Muheza to P.C., Tanga, 8/25/53, "Land Utilization–East Usambara," Land Utilization and Forest Survey, East Usambara, 1.

98. TNA 304/L2/402, F. D. Dowsett, B. Gilchrist, and D. H. Drennan, "Report of the East Usambara Land Utilization Survey," 2.

99. Ibid.

100. Ibid., 3.

101. Ibid., 48–49. The "Report" does not mention the 1939 survey, but seems to have been a confidential memo entitled, "Memorandum on the Potentialities of the East Usambaras for Small Holdings, Reconnaissance Survey from March 3rd to March 10th Undertaken by Bonavia assisted by Davie, Herring, and Gillman (A.O.)," found in LF 32B, Land Utilization and Forest Survey, East Usambara.

102. TNA 304/L2/402, Dowsett, Gilchrist, and Drennan, "Report," 70–72.

103. LF 32B, Chief Conservator of Forests to Member for Agriculture and Natural Resources, Dar es Salaam (Secretariat), 5/9/56, n.p.

Chapter 5

1. United Republic of Tanzania, *Report of the Presidential Commission of Inquiry into Land Matters, Volume I, Land Policy and Land Tenure Structure,* Ministry of Lands, Housing and Urban Development, Government of the United Republic of Tanzania (Dar es Salaam: United Republic of Tanzania). The report notes that, eventually, in 1928, the ordinance was amended to give customary law titles a statutory recognition. The definition of the right of occupancy was extended to include for the first time the title of a native or of a native community lawfully using or occupying land in accordance with native law and custom. Since then, customary law titles have come to be called "deemed rights of occupancy."

2. British Colonial Office (CO) 691/95/10, "Alleged Alienation of Large Areas of Land to Non-Natives and Alienation of Land to Non-Natives," Memo by Governor, 8.

3. Steven Feierman, *Peasant Intellectuals: Anthropology and History in Tanzania* (Madison: University of Wisconsin Press, 1990), 127.

4. UIT, Kasisi and Kuambaza Sheiza, at Mlalo, 1/18/92, 10; Juma Kingazi Kimako, Hoseni Hamsini, Salimu Shekulwavu, at Shita, 2/13/92, 18; Jafeth Kalata, at Mlalo, 3/13/92, 23.

5. Ernst Johanssen, "Missionsarbeit unter den Wambugu," *Nachrichten aus der ostafrikanischen Mission* 11 (1897): 126.

6. Feierman, *Peasant Intellectuals,* 130. This was the decade's second rinderpest outbreak.

7. K. Braun, "Der Reis in Deutsch-Ostafrika," *Berichte über Land- und Forstwirtschaft in Deutsch-Ostafrika* 3 (1907): 177–79.

8. For a description of the rubber boom in Central Africa, see Adam Hochschild, *King Leopold's Ghost: A Story of Greed, Terror, and Heroism in Colonial Africa* (Boston: Houghton Mifflin, 1998).

9. Juhani Koponen, *Development for Exploitation: German Colonial Policies in Mainland Tanzania, 1884–1914* (Helsinki: Finnish Historical Society, Studia Historica 49, 1994), 433. Tanzania National Archive (hereafter TNA) 1733/10 and 1733/28, Annual Reports for Usambara District for the years 1920 and 1924, respectively. In 1920, some 17,000 acres of former rubber plantation land lay unused.

10. For Lwengera, see Clement Gillman, Rhodes House MSS.Afr.S.1175, vol. 13, Diaries. See R. E. Moreau, "A Synecological Study of Usambara, Tanganyika Territory, with Particular Reference to Birds," *Journal of Ecology* 23.1 (1935), 14–15, for East Usambara lowlands, and 31, for Mlalo's kitivo. See also TNA 24732, Geoffrey Milne, "Report on a Soil Reconnaissance in the Neighbourhood of Kitivo, Lushoto District, Tanganyika Territory, and in Adjacent (West Usambara) Highlands, September–October 1937," Mimeo, East African Agricultural Research Station, Amani, n.d., 8.

11. C. W. Guillebaud, *An Economic Survey of the Sisal Industry of Tanganyika*, 3rd ed. (Digswell Place, U.K.: James Nisbet and Co. Ltd., 1966), 8 and 9. Kapepwa Tambila, "A Plantation Labour Magnet: The Tanga Case," in *Migrant Labour in Tanzania during the Colonial Period: Case Studies of Recruitment and Conditions of Labour in the Sisal Industry*, ed. Walter Rodney, Kapepwa Tambila, and Laurent Sabo (Hamburg: Institut für Afrika-Kunde, 1983), 29–30. Pangani Valley sisal plantations could be anywhere from 1,200 to 3,000 hectares.

12. TNA 1733/11, Annual Report, Usambara District, 1925, 7. Neither census data nor annual reports, at least the ones I have seen, provide numbers of migrant workers specifically for West Usambara, but for figures from Tanga Province, see Tambila, "Plantation Labour," 31.

13. TNA 1733/11, Annual Report, Usambara District, 1925, 21.

14. Tambila, "Plantation Labour," 30; for hazardous conditions, see 33–42.

15. This definition and the discussion which follows comes from TNA 24732, Geoffrey Milne, "Report," 2–25.

16. Ibid., 11–12.

17. Ibid., 14.

18. UIT, Kalata, 2; Musa Sembe, at Lunguza, 2/8/92, 15; Bakari Panduka, Abdallah Mdoe, Musa Athumani, Ahamadi Rashidi Kidumi, at Kitivo, Mng'aro, 2/8/92, 15. The last group argues that many of the kitivo settlers had worked at the coast and thus had developed some resistance to malaria.

19. TNA 24732, "Report," 15.

20. TNA 4/183/2, vol. 1, Census, 1931.

21. TNA 72/21/1, "Deceased Estates, Non-Native," A.D.O., Lushoto, to Chief Secretary, Dar es Salaam, 2/8/21.

22. Land which remained in continuous cultivation for seven years could be designated as Public Land.

23. TNA 1733/25, Annual Report, Usambara District, 1923.

24. Ibid.

25. TNA 1733/11, Annual Report, Usambara District, 1925, 6. In the same report, see "Regulations Issued under the Native Authority Ordinance."

26. For a discussion of Kilindi power and political legitimacy in Usambara, see Feierman, *Peasant Intellectuals,* chap. 3.

27. TNA 1733/11, "Regulations Issued under the Native Authority Ordinance," Annual Report, Usambara District, 1925.

28. Feierman, *Peasant Intellectuals,* 146.

29. TNA 4/6/2, Acting P.C. to D.O., Lushoto, 8/1/33, Native Administration—Usambara District, 70.

30. TNA 4/6/2, Acting D.O., Lushoto (C. M. Coke), to P.C., Tanga 8/3/34, Native Administration—Usambara District, 93.

31. TNA 1733/25, Annual Report for Usambara District, May 30, 1921; 1733/28, Annual Report, Usambara District, 1924; TNA 72/62/6, vol. 1, Annual Report, Usambara District, Lushoto Division, 1937; TNA 72/62/6, vol. 1, Annual Report, Lushoto Division, Korogwe District, 1938; TNA 72/62/6, Korogwe District, Annual Report, 1939. For dominance of maize, see also R. E. Moreau, "A Synecological Study of Usambara, Tanganyika Territory, with Particular Reference to Birds," *Journal of Ecology* 23 (1935): 31.

32. Patrick Fleuret, "Farm and Market: A Study of Society and Agriculture in Tanzania" (Ph.D. diss., University of California at Santa Barbara, 1978), 86.

33. UIT, Sheiza, 8; Sabuni Mbilu and Epiphan John Mntangi, at Kwemashai (near Gare), 2/23/92, 41; Mashambo Mavoo, at Kirete (near Kwai), 2/21/92, 47.

34. Fleuret, in "Farm and Market," 92, cites the senior agricultural officer for the Northeast Circle district, who reported that 800 tons of maize had been exported to sisal estates alone. One must remember, however, that Usambara included South Pare and part of the present-day Handeni district, so the 800 tons did not come exclusively from Usambara. Indeed, cash was readily available in the mountains: hut and poll taxes for 1923–24 topped half a million shillings; TNA 1733/28, Annual Report for Usambara District, 1924.

35. TNA 1733/11, Usambara District, Annual Report, 1925, 9.

36. TNA 72/5/4, M. Mailer, Mombo Estate, to Admin. Officer in Charge, Lushoto, 11/14/25, Complaints: Water Supply and Disputes, 22.

37. G. W. Lock, *Sisal: Thirty Years' Sisal Research in Tanzania* (London: Longmans, Green and Co., 1962), 295.

38. TNA 72/5/4, A.O. in Charge to Akidas Kayambo and Bernard of Mombo and Vuga, 11/25/25, Complaints: Water Supply and Disputes, 1.

39. For irrigation history, see UIT, Kalata, 1–2; Rajabu Shemzinghwa, at Mlalo, 12/28/91, 4; Ali Gembe and son Shemboza bin Shemndola, at Mlalo, old town, 1/18/92, 6; Sheiza, 9.

40. TNA 72/5/4, M. Mailer, Mombo Estate, to D.O., Lushoto, 4/12/28, 43; and Kitala cha Kinyassi, Vuga, to D.O. in Charge, Lushoto, 5/12/28, Complaints: Water Supply and Disputes, 48.

41. TNA 72/5/4, J. Gleiss, Pastor, Vuga Mission to D.O., Lushoto, 7/19/30, 65 and J. Gleiss to D.O., Lushoto, 10/1/30, Complaints: Water Supply and Disputes, 66.

42. TNA 72/5/6, D.O. Hartnoll, Lushoto, to Hon. Land Officer, D.S.M., 11/6/30, Usambara Water Board, 109.

43. Feierman, *Peasant Intellectuals,* 126–27.

44. TNA 4/107/7, D.O., Lushoto, to Secretary, Department of Lands and Mines, Dar es Salaam, 3/31/36. Boundary Disputes Bethel Misson, Vuga vs. Natives, 1936.

45. TNA 4/107/4, D.O., Lushoto, to P.C. Tanga, 8/8/32, Boundary Disputes, Mponde Estate, 1932.

46. TNA 72/5/30, Zumbe Salim Mjata, Mgwashi, to A.D.O., Lushoto, 2/4/35, Water and Irrigation, 38–39.

47. TNA 72/5/30, D.O., Lushoto, to Kimweri Magogo, Vuga, 8/8/35, Water and Irrigation, 39. Correspondence suggests that this was a large project and that labor consisted of scores of tax defaulters. Milne, in the 1937 report cited above, describes a large abandoned furrow, six feet deep and four feet across and over a kilometer long.

48. TNA 4/651/2, P.C. (F. Langland) to D.O., Lushoto (Callaghan), 10/31/33 "Concerning land for lease along the Mlola river, Land Lushoto," 193.

49. TNA 4/651/2, P.C., Tanga, to D.O., Lushoto, 12/4/33; and for presence of Shambaa farmers, see A.D.O. to D.O., 11/28/33, Land Files.

50. Ibid., D.O., Lushoto, to P.C., Tanga, 12/8/33.

51. Ibid., 2, P.C., Tanga, to Land Office, Dar es Salaam, n.d.

52. TNA 24732, Milne, "Report," 7.

53. For land pressure and food shortages, see UIT, Gembe and Shemndola, 6. The informants suggested that pressure on land was such that the chief considered expelling all people of Taita descent from the Mlalo Basin.

54. See David Anderson, "Depression, Dust Bowl, Demography, and Drought: The Colonial State and Soil Conservation in East Africa during the 1930s," *African Affairs* 83 (1984): 321–44.

55. See Christopher Conte, "Transformations along the Gradient: Ecological Change in the Mountains and Plains of Northeastern Tanzania's West Usambara Mountains, c. 1860–1970" (Ph.D. diss., Michigan State University, 1995), chap. 3.

56. For general comments on ecological problems made at the meeting, see C. W. Hobley, "Soil Erosion: A Problem in Human Geography: A Paper Read at the Afternoon Meeting of the Society on 8 May 1933," *Geographical Review* 82 (1933): 139–46. Those commenting included C. F. M. Swynnerton, Tanganyika Territory director of tsetse research, and Grantham, member of Tanganyika Territory Soil Erosion Commission.

57. A. M. Champion, "Soil Erosion in Africa: A Paper Read at the Afternoon Meeting of the Society on 8 May 1933 by Mr. C. W. Hobley on behalf of A. M. Champion," *Geographical Review* 82 (1933): 135.

58. Ibid., 135 and 140.

59. Anderson, "Depression," 323.

60. TNA 4/1071, "Minutes of the First Meeting of the Standing Committee on Soil Erosion Appointed by His Excellency the Acting Governor. Held at the Secretariat, Dar es Salaam, June 15th, 1931, Soil Erosion, 1931–38. Those present: Director of the East Africa Agricultural Research Station, W. Nowell; Director of Agriculture, E. Harrison; Acting Director of Public Works, C. U. Stevenson; Acting Director of Veterinary Services, H. E. Hornby; Director of Geological Survey, E. O. Teale; Conservator of Forests, D. K. S. Grant; Chief Engineer of Railways, C. Gillman.

61. TNA 4/1071, "Memorandum on Soil Erosion," E. Harrison, Director of Agriculture, Tanganyika Territory, 1937, Soil Erosion, 1931–38, 3.

62. For a complete list of Gillman's scholarly work, see B. S. Hoyle, *Gillman of Tanganyika 1882–1946* (Brookfield, Vt.: Gower Publishing, 1987), 424–28.

63. Clement Gillman, "A Population Map of Tanganyika Territory," *Geographical Review* 26 (1936): 353–75.

64. Ibid., 355.

65. Clement Gillman, "Problems of Land Utilisation in Tanganyika Territory," *South African Geographical Journal* 20 (1938): 14.

66. Gillman, "Population Map," 373.

67. Clement Gillman, Rhodes House MSS.Afr.S.1175, vol. 6, Diaries, Amani, 4/1/29, 96.

68. See Geoffrey Milne, "Essays in Applied Pedology: 1. Soil Type and Soil Management in Relation to Plantation Agriculture in East Usambara," *East African Agricultural Journal* 3.1 (1937): 7–20. For an overview of Amani-based research, see H. H. Storey, *Basic Research in Agriculture: A Brief History of Research at Amani 1928–1947* (Nairobi: East African Standard, 1951).

69. Clement Gillman, review of *The Rape of the Earth* by G. V. Jacks and R. O. Whyte, *Tanganyika Notes and Records* 8 (1939): 104.

70. Gillman, "Population Map," 373.

71. Ibid.

72. Gillman, Rhodes House MSS.Afr.S.1175, vol. 12, Diaries, 98; "Reconnaissance," 135; "Population Map," 359.

73. TNA 4/1071, D.O. (Seymour), Lushoto, to P.C., Tanga, 1/25/37, Soil Erosion, 1931–38, 29.

74. TNA 24732, Milne, "Report," 7.

75. Geoffrey Milne, *A Provisional Soil Map of East Africa* (Amani, Tanganyika: East African Agricultural Research Station, 1936). For previous journey to the West Usambaras, see Rhodes House MSS, British Empire, S.457, vol. 2, "Report on a Journey to West Usambara, 3rd to 16th November, 1930"; and MSS, British Empire, S.457, vol. 2, Milne to Director, E. A. Ag. Research Station, Amani, 6/7/34.

76. TNA 24732, Milne, "Report," 28–29.

77. Ibid., 29.

78. Ibid., 37.

79. Ibid., 30.

80. Ibid., 39.

81. Ibid., 43.

82. TNA 24732, Provincial Commissioner, Tanga, to Chief Secretary, Dar es Salaam, 5/16/38, Report on Soil Reconnaissance by Govt. Chemist Milne.

83. Ibid., Director of Agriculture to Chief Secretary, 6/6/38.

84. Ibid., Acting Chief Secretary to P.C., Tanga, 6/28/38. Milne's report was published in 1944, after his death; see Geoffrey Milne, "Soils in Relation to the Native Population in West Usambara," *Geography* 29 (1944): 107–13.

85. For the director of agriculture's perspective, see Rhodes House MSS, British Empire, S.457, vol. 4, Director of Ag., Morogoro, to A. G. Hill, Director, East African Ag. Research Station, 4/25/38, 59. Clement Gillman embraced Milne's report and decried the departmental jealousy that diminished its power. See Rhodes House MSS, British Empire, S.457, vol. 4, C. Gillman to Hill, Director, East African Agricultural Research Station, February 10, 1944, 51. The report was published as "A Soil Reconnaissance Journey through Parts of Tanganyika Territory. December 1935–February 1936," *Journal of Ecology* 35.1 and 35.2 (1947): 192–265.

86. Patrick Fleuret, "Farm and Market," 98–99; UIT, Gembe and Shemndola, 6. Hassani Kinyassi, the Mlalo subchief, certainly worried over population pressures. The old men relate an incident which occurred during 1935, when Kinyassi called a meeting of the Taita (Kenya) migrants residing at Mlalo in order to ask them to return to Kenya. "However, when he saw how many of them came to the baraza he was rather shocked and the wazee convinced him that since so many had been born at Mlalo and likely knew not where in Taita to return to, they should be allowed to remain at Mlalo."

87. Dezu formed part of a broader designation of lineage communal lands known as *Tundui*.

88. TNA 4/269/6, "Addendum to Monthly Report for August 1947," Mlalo Basin Rehabilitation Scheme, n.p.; see also UIT, Hasain Singano Mbuguni, Musa Hasani, Mbwana Omari Shemzighwa, at Mlalo, 1/3/92, 19.

89. TNA 4/269/5, vol. 1, Hans Cory, "Report to Provincial Commissioner, Tanga 8/31/46," Mlalo Rehabilitation/Development Scheme, n.p.

90. Daniel E. Vasey, *An Ecological History of Agriculture: 10,000 BC–AD 10,000* (Ames, Iowa: Iowa State University Press, 1992), 52. Numerous Mlalo informants remember cassava as a key to survival during drought; see UIT, Hemedi Ngereza, at Mlalo, 3/19/92, 22; Kimako et al., 16; Panduka et al., 13.

91. For discussions of the cultural and political context of Chankola's famine, see Conte, "Transformations," 143–56; and Feierman, *Peasant Intellectuals*, 147–49.

92. TNA 4/6/2, Usambara District, D.O. (J. L. Fairclough), Lushoto, to P.C., Tanga, Tanga Province 2/30/40, Native Administration, 149.

93. Ibid., 173. His fears are not unfounded, considering the Mbiru tax revolt in the nearby Pare Mountains.

94. UIT, Mbuguni et al., 19; Ngereza, 21b.

95. TNA 4/6/2, D.O., Lushoto (K. B. A. Dobson), to the District Commissioner, Korogwe District, Korogwe, 11/29/40, Native Administration, 181.

96. Ibid., D.O., Lushoto (Dobson), to D.C., Korogwe, 1/5/42, "Administration of Mlalo Zumbeate," 206.

97. Ibid., P.C., Tanga (Bonavia), to D.C., Korogwe, 2/7/42, "Mlalo Subchiefdom," 208.

98. Ibid., A.D.O., Lushoto (Dobson), to D.C., Korogwe, 5/19/42, "Commission on the Jumbes of Mlalo," 224.

99. Ibid., D.O., Korogwe, to P.C., Tanga Province, 7/29/42, "Appointment of New Zumbe for Mlalo Zumbeate," 233.

100. Feierman, *Peasant Intellectuals*, 140.

101. UIT, Kalata, 2; Shemzinghwa, 4; Gembe and Shemndola, 6; Kimako et al., 17–18; Athumani Shemweta, joined by Athumani Kikoi, Abeid Athumani, and Hasani Mlimahadala, at Kwedeghe, 1/21/92, 71. For an alternative view, see Ngereza, 21a. Mzee Ngereza argues that Chankola was a scapegoat and that poor farming practices caused the famine.

102. UIT, Shemweta et al., 71.

103. UIT, Shemzinghwa, 4. For other similar arguments for the famine's cause, see Kimako et al., 18; Ali Gembe and Shemdola, 6.

104. Ibid.

105. See Feierman, *Peasant Intellectuals*, chaps. 3 and 4.

106. TNA 72/62/6, vol. 3, "Report for 1944," Reports, District Annual.

107. UIT, Gembe and Shemdola, 18; K. Mdoe, 20; Amina Kitindu Mdoe, at old Mlalo, 1/18/92, 8.

108. UIT, K. Mdoe, 20.

109. UIT, A. Mdoe, 8. For information on the *Mbiru* tax revolt in the Pare Mountains, see Isaria N. Kimambo, *Penetration and Protest in Tanzania: The Impact of the World Economy on the Pare, 1860–1960* (London: James Currey, 1991), chap. 6.

110. UIT, A. Mdoe, 8. For evidence of further Pare influence, see TNA 4/269/6, Appendix A to Quarterly Report ending 12/31/46, Mlalo Basin Rehabilitation Scheme.

111. TNA 72/62/6, vol. 3, D.O., C. C. de Rosemund, "Lushoto Division–Korogwe District, Annual Report, 1946," Reports–District Annual, 207b.

112. Ibid.

113. In *Peasant Intellectuals*, Feierman argues that the Mlalo crisis reflects a larger pattern in Usambara's politics in which "intellectuals" begin to challenge Kilindi legitimacy as Native Authorities and to shape the political discourse. There is certainly a great deal of evidence to the effect that the chama participated in resistance to the Mlalo Basin Rehabilitation Scheme (1946–49). Like Feierman, I would argue that the chama represented an amalgamation of elders and younger, educated men. However, I believe their support grew more from the droughts of the 1940s in northern Usambara than from their "discursive" abilities.

114. UIT, A. Mdoe, 8.
115. TNA 72/62/6, vol. 3, D.O. C. C. de Rosemund, "Lushoto Division–Korogwe District, Annual Report, 1946," Reports–District Annual, 207b.
116. UIT, Kalata, 2.
117. TNA 13079, P.C., Tanga, to Chief Sec., "Report on food position," 12/30/43, Food Shortages.
118. TNA 72/62/6, vol. 3, See Annual Reports for 1944, 1945 and 1946, Reports–District Annual.
119. The Provincial Committee consisted of the provincial commissioner, Tanga; district commissioner, Korogwe; district officer, Lushoto; senior medical officer, Tanga; provincial education officer, Lushoto; assistant conservator of forests, Lushoto; senior agricultural officer, Lushoto; provincial veterinary officer, Tanga; and the paramount chief of the Wasambaa.
120. TNA 72/3/25, H. Cory to P.C., Tanga, 8/31/46, "Report on 2–month stay at Mlalo," Mlalo Basin Rehabilitation Scheme, Correspondence and Reports. Cory pointed out to the Provincial Commissioner farmers' firm grasp of the concept of fallow.
121. For further discussion of East African indigenous irrigation systems, see W. M. Adams, T. Potkanski, and J. E. G. Sutton, "Indigenous Farmer-Managed Irrigation in Sonjo, Tanzania," *Geographical Journal* 160 (1994): 17–32; Patrick Fleuret, "The Social Organisation of Water Control in the Taita Hills, Kenya," *American Ethnologist* 12 (1985): 103–18; David Anderson, "Agriculture and Irrigation Technology at Lake Baringo," *Azania* 24 (1989): 89–97; F. T. Masao, "The Irrigation System in Uchagga: An Ethno-historical Approach," *Tanzania Notes and Records* 75 (1974): 1–8; and J. E. G. Sutton, "Irrigation and Soil-conservation in African Agricultural History. With a Reconsideration of the Inyanga Terracing (Zimbabwe) and Engaruka Irrigation Works (Tanzania)," *Journal of African History* 25 (1984): 25–41. For a report on irrigation during njaa ya Chankola, see TNA 4/269/5, vol. 1, Extract from Burrow's report titled, "The Mlalo Basin, A Rural Sociological Survey Covering 14 Days in the Field," 8/24/46, Mlalo Basin Rehabilitation Scheme, 196.
122. For a few examples, see UIT, Mavoo, 48; Ngereza, 22; Mwanakombo Shechambo and Mama Majuma Lukindo, at Mlalo, 2/26/92, 17.
123. UIT, Mavoo, 48.
124. TNA 72/3/25, vol. 1, F. J. Nutmann, "A Study of the Mlalo Basin—An Area Forming Part of the W. Usambara Development Scheme," 9/6/45, Mlalo Basin Rehabilitation Scheme, 14b.
125. TNA 72/62/6, vol. 3, "Lushoto Division—Korogwe District, Annual Report, 1944," Reports–District Annual, 201.
126. UIT, Panduka et al., 15.
127. TNA 72/3/25, H. Cory to P.C., Tanga, 8/31/46, "Report on 2–month stay at Mlalo," Mlalo Basin Rehabilitation Scheme, Correspondence and Reports.
128. UIT, Panduka et al., 13.

129. TNA 72/3/25, H. Cory to P.C., Tanga, 8/31/46, "Report on 2–month stay at Mlalo," Mlalo Basin Rehabilitation Scheme, Correspondence and Reports.

130. TNA 4/269/5, vol. 1, "Extract from Burrow's report titled, 'The Mlalo Basin, A Rural Sociological Survey covering 14 days in the field, 8/24/46,'" Mlalo Basin Rehabilitation Scheme, 199.

131. TNA 72/3/25, H. Cory to P.C., Tanga, 8/31/46, "Report on 2–month stay at Mlalo," Mlalo Basin Rehabilitation Scheme, Correspondence and Reports.

132. Ibid. Cory reported that in 1946 women carried out most of the work connected with irrigation areas. This suggests a paucity of the exclusively male labor informants equate with irrigation works.

133. UIT, Shemzinghwa, 4.

Chapter 6

1. John Lonsdale and David Low, "Introduction: Towards the New Order, 1945–1963," in *History of East Africa*, ed. D. A. Low and A. Smith, eds., vol. 3 (Oxford: Oxford University Press, 1976), 1–63. For a description of the ecological and political ramifications of the process in central Kenya, see David Throup, *Economic and Social Origins of Mau Mau, 1945–53* (London: James Currey, 1988), 140–63. For the politics of the second colonial occupation in the West Usambaras, see Steven Feierman's excellent discussion of the anti-erosion projects in *Peasant Intellectuals: Anthropology and History in Tanzania* (Madison: University of Wisconsin Press, 1990), chapter 7.

2. John Iliffe, *A Modern History of Tanganyika* (Cambridge: Cambridge University Press, 1979), 474.

3. Clifford Geertz, *Agricultural Involution: The Process of Ecological Change in Indonesia* (Berkeley: University of California Press, 1966).

4. TNA 72/3/25, F. J. Nutman, "A Study of the Mlalo Basin—An Area Forming Part of the W. Usambara Development Scheme, 6 September 1945," (hereafter "Nutman Report"), Mlalo Basin Rehabilitation Scheme (hereafter MBRS), 14 (a-g).

5. TNA 72/3/25, "Nutman Report," 14c–f.

6. TNA 72/3/25, "Minutes of Provincial Committee Convened to Discuss Dr. Nutman's 'Study of the Mlalo Basin.' Held at Lushoto on 10th and 11 December, 1945," MBRS, 40–51.

7. TNA 72/3/25, S. A. Linton, Senior Agricultural Officer, Lushoto, to P.C., Tanga, December 3, 1945, MBRS, 21.

8. TNA 72/3/25, H. J. Van Rensberg, "Land Utilization and Soil Conservation Scheme for the Western Usambaras, 11/7/45," MBRS, 17.

9. TNA 72/3/25, H. J. Van Rensberg, "Land Utilization and Soil Conservation Scheme for the Western Usambaras, 11/7/45," MBRS, 17c. Van Rensberg suggests bench terraces, grass strips planted along stream courses and hill contours, and tie ridging.

10. TNA 72/3/25, Provincial Committee to Chief Sec., 12/29/45, "Meeting to Discuss Nutman's Scheme," MBRS, 22a.

11. TNA 4/269/5, vol. 1, "Precis of the Various Suggested Schemes for the Rehabilitation of the Mlalo Basin 3/16/46," MBRS, 42; TNA 72/3/25, "Land Utilization in West Usambara, by F. J. Nutman, 3/12/45," MBRS, 18.

12. TNA 72/3/25, Provincial Committee to Chief Secretary, 12/29/45, MBRS, 22a. Kitivo and Lwengera are lowland areas directly adjacent to the massif on the northwestern and southeastern sides respectively.

13. TNA 72/3/25, R. W. R. Miller, Director of Agricultural Production, to Chief Secretary, 2/6/46, MBRS, 26a; TNA 25576, "Tanganyika Territory Soil Conservation Report for 1945–46," Soil Conservation Reports, Tanganyika Territory, 46a.

14. TNA 72/3/25, "Extract from Burrows, 'The Mlalo Basin: A Rural Sociological Study Covering 14 Days in the Field, 8/24/46,'" MBRS, 64a.

15. TNA 4/269/5, vol. 1, Cory to Hartnoll, P.C., Tanga, 2/6/46, MBRS, 135. D.C. Korogwe to Cory, 137. For Cory's report see chapter 5, note 133.

16. TNA 4/269/5, vol. 1, A.V. Hartnoll, P.C., Tanga, to R. A. J. Maguire, Acting Administrative Secretary, Dar es Salaam, 7/19/46, MBRS.

17. Usambara Interview Transcripts (hereafter UIT), Hemedi Ngereza, at Mlalo, 1/25/92, para. 6, para. 13; Juma Zahabu, at Handei, 3/26/92, 30; Japhet Kalata, at Mlalo, 12/23/91, 2.

18. TNA 72/62/9B, J. B. Clegg, Mlalo Scheme—Monthly Reports, July 1946, 2.

19. TNA 72/62/9A, Reports—Mlalo Scheme—Quarterly Reports, for the period ending 12/31/46, 1.

20. TNA 72/3/25, D.O., Lushoto (Rosemond), to D.C., Korogwe, 10/11/46, MBRS, 57. The ex-Jumbe of Shita, the location where the demonstration project would be laid out, claimed that there was no land shortage in the Basin and rejected the government's ideas about agricultural reform. Mlalo, he claimed, had always been eroded.

21. TNA 72/3/25, D.O., Lushoto (Rosemond) to D.C., Korogwe, 10/11/46, MBRS, 57.

22. TNA 72/62/9B, J. B. Clegg, Mlalo Scheme—Monthly Reports, August 1946, 3a.

23. TNA 72/62/9A, Reports—Mlalo Scheme—Quarterly Reports, for the period ending 12/31/46, 1.

24. TNA 72/62/9B, J. B. Clegg, Mlalo Scheme—Monthly Reports, October 1946, p. 5A; for out migration, see TNA 4/269/6, "Mlalo Scheme, Annual Report," 12/20/46, Mlalo Basin Rehabilitation Scheme, Reports, Monthly and Quarterly.

25. TNA 72/62/9B, J. B. Clegg, Mlalo Scheme—Monthly Reports, October 1946, 5a.

26. TNA 4/269/5, vol. 1, "Land Utilization Rules," 11/20/46, MBRS, 211–12.

27. TNA 72/3/25 "Mlalo," F. H. Jackson, A.D.O. Korogwe, "Report on Activities in Connection with Mlalo Basin Rehabilitation Scheme 12/8/47–6/1/48," 122a.

28. TNA 72/62/9B, "Short Interim Report on Activities in Connection with the Mlalo Rehabilitation Scheme 11/28/47–12/20/47," Mlalo Scheme—Monthly Reports, 20.

29. TNA 4/269/6, J. B. Clegg, "Mlalo Basin Rehabilitation Scheme, Progress Report, January 1948," Mlalo Basin Rehabilitation Scheme, Reports, Monthly and Quarterly, 113a, c.

30. TNA 4/269/6, "Mlalo Basin Rehabilitation Scheme Report for Year Ending 12/31/48," Mlalo Basin Rehabilitation Scheme, Reports, Monthly and Quarterly.

31. TNA 72/62/9B, "Monthly Report for July 1948," Mlalo Scheme—Monthly Reports, 28.

32. TNA 72/62/9B, J. B. Clegg, "Monthly Report for September 1948," Mlalo Scheme—Monthly Reports, 29.

33. TNA 72/62/9B, J. B. Clegg, "Monthly Report for April 1948," Mlalo Scheme, Monthly Reports, 25.

34. TNA 72/62/9B, J. B. Clegg "Monthly Report for March 1949," and "Monthly Report for May 1949," "David Mwakosya, Monthly Report for June 1949," Mlalo Scheme, Monthly Reports, 35, 35, 37.

35. Discussion of Clegg's final report comes from: TNA 4/269/5 vol. 1, J. B. Clegg, "Report of the Mlalo Rehabilitation Scheme," 10/29/49, MBRS, 145–52.

36. Piers Blaikie, *The Political Economy of Soil Erosion in Developing Countries* (New York: Longman, 1985), 53.

37. UIT, Sabuni Mbilu and John Mntangi Epiphan, at Kwemashai, 2/23/92, 43.

38. UIT, Athumani Shemweta, Athumani Kikoi, Abeid Athumani, and Hasani Mlimahadala, at Kwedeghe, 1/21/92, 72.

39. UIT, Salim Saguti, Asmani Mdoe, and Juma Msagati, at Nyasa (Mlalo), 1/29/92 (interview not recorded).

40. UIT, Rajabu Shemzinghwa, at Mlalo, 12/28/91, 5; TNA 4/962/15, "Annual Report, Agriculture, Tanga Province, 1954," 1954 Annual Reports by Departmental Officers, 137; TNA 4/962, D.C., Lushoto, to Provincer, Tanga, 1/23/57, Annual Reports for Tanga Province and Districts, 1956, 17; TNA 72/3/2, vol. 4, "Monthly Reports," for July 1956, January 1957, June 1957; and Annual Report, Lushoto District, June 1958, Agricultural Reports, Lushoto, 78.

41. TNA 72/61/6, vol. 3, "Lushoto Annual Report for 1953," Annual Reports, Lushoto District, 84.

42. TNA 72/3/2, vol. 4, Field Officer (McGregor) to Provincial Agricultural Officer, Tanga, 6/28/56, Agricultural Reports. Lushoto, n.p., notes 189,700 kilos of rice sold on local markets in June alone. In same file, see also Monthly Report, Lushoto District (Plains), July 1956 (E. C. Green), n.p.; Green reports 147,842 kilos sold on local markets, "with considerable quantities sold outside official markets."

43. By the 1950s, hybrid maize strains had appeared in Usambara. They yielded more per acre but were less drought-resistant than local varieties. See UIT, Kasisi and Kuambaza Shezia, at Mlalo, 1/8/92, 8; Khadija Mdoe, at Mlalo, 2/26/92, 20.

44. UIT, Zahabu, 28.

45. TNA 72/US/28, R. H. Gower, "Safari Reports," 11/12/50 and 1/29/51, Usambara Scheme: Safari Reports, 16.

46. TNA 72/62/6, vol. 3, "Annual Reports," for 1950, 1951, 1953 and 1954, Annual Reports, Lushoto District.

47. TNA 72/62/6, vol. 3, "Annual Report," 1951, Annual Reports, Lushoto District.

48. TNA 72/62/6, vol. 3, "Annual Report," 1950, Annual Reports, Lushoto District, D.C. notes "slow drain of population from West to East Usambara"; Fleuret, "Farm and Market," 100.

49. TNA 72/62/6, vol. 3, "Annual Report," 1950, Annual Reports, Lushoto District.

50. TNA 72/US/63, Chant (D.O., Lushoto) and Drennan (A.O., Lushoto), Report on the Usambara Scheme, 2/7/53, n.p. Report estimates that 43,000 acres of mountains were available for the African population. Given the 2.5 percent rate of population increase, the authors argue that only mass emigration of people and livestock to uninhabited territories or the transformation of peasant cultivators to industrial laborers will solve the long term problems in the Usambaras. See also TNA 72/US/53, D.C., Lushoto (W. MacMillan), "Origins, Principles and Progress, 1950," Annual and Half-Annual Reports of Usambara Scheme, n.p.

51. TNA 4/269/12, D.C., Lushoto (MacMillan) to P.C., Tanga, 1/3/50, Ruvu/Pangani Agricultural Development Plan, n.p.

52. TNA 72/US/53, D.C., Lushoto (W. MacMillan), "Origins, Principles and Progress, 1950," Annual and Half-Annual Reports of Usambara Scheme, n.p.

53. For discussion of Hehe ridging, see A. H. Pike, "Soil Conservation among the Matenge Tribe," *Tanzania Notes and Records* 6 (1938): 79–81. Mlalo farmers had protested against the systems during the MBRS.

54. Wattle tree bark was sold for use in the manufacture of tannin, a product used in leather tanning. Once it has been cut, wattle regenerates from coppices.

55. TNA 72/US/34, Gibbons, "Field Report," 12/51, Usambara Scheme: Field Officers Safaris and Reports, 1.

56. TNA 72/US/53, C.S. Kernahan, executive director, Usambara Scheme, "Report for June 1953," Annual and Half-Annual Reports of Usambara Scheme, n.p. Kernahan notes here the intention of converting from maize to banana cultivation on sloped land.

57. TNA 72/US/53, C.S. Kernahan, executive director, Usambara Scheme, "Report for June 1953," Annual and Half-Annual Reports of Usambara Scheme, n.p.; TNA 72/US/41, A. O. Chant, no date [but likely 4/10/52], "Report on the Usambara Scheme," Copies of Articles and Records Concerning Usambara Scheme: from Other Sources, n.p.

58. TNA 72/61/6, vol. 3, "Annual Report, 1950," Lushoto Annual Reports, and TNA 72/US/28, Gower, "Safari Notes," 9/21/50, Usambara Scheme, Safari Reports, 2.

59. Ibid.

60. TNA 72/US/53, Gower, "Usambara Scheme, Annual Report, 1951," Annual and Half-Annual Reports of Usambara Scheme.

61. For instances of resistance, see TNA 72/US/41, vol. 2, Implementation of Scheme Rules, for example, D.C., Lushoto, to Dr. Friberg, Lutheran Mission, Bumbuli,

9/1/53, 1; D.C., Lushoto, to R. Bolsted, Vuga Mission Press, 12/14/55, 20; R. Bolsted to D.C., Lushoto, 12/17/55, 22; and in same file, see, "Extract from Minutes of the District Committee," 2/6/56, 23. TNA 72/US/45, C. M. Kapalenga, reports for 1/52–6/54; also see reports for 2/29/52, 3/27/52, April 1952, May 1952, Usambara Scheme: Safari and Monthly Reports, n.p.; TNA 72/US/30, vol. 3, Silcocks, "Monthly Reports" from April 1956 to June 1958; also see reports from 9/4/56, 12/7/56, Usambara Scheme: Monthly Reports, n.p.

62. See the monthly reports from TNA series 72/US for numerous reports on the number of acres ridged and terraced.

63. UIT, Ngereza, 13.

64. Ibid., 12.

65. TNA 4/962, "Lushoto District Annual Reports" for 1954 and 1956, District and Provincial Annual Reports, 94 and 96.

66. UIT, Ngereza, 12.

67. UIT, Shemzinghwa, 4; Mshirhiri Hippoliti, at Gare Mission, 12/31/91; TNA 72/US/68 Senior Field Officer to Mr. Raymond Shemhunge, Field Assistant, Mbaramo, Usambara Scheme Staff, n.p.

68. TNA 72/US/68, "Usambara Scheme Staff: Dismissal Threats and Requests for Retirement of Wakauzi," Usambara Scheme Staff. See entire file, which contains numerous letters from instructors requesting leave, retirement, and transfers.

69. TNA 72/US/30, vol. 3, Silcocks, "Monthly Reports" from April 1956 to June 1958, Usambara Scheme: Monthly Reports, 10b, 11, 14, 21, and 23.

70. TNA 72/3/2, vol. 4, "Usambara Scheme Annual Report, 1958," Agricultural Reports, Lushoto, n.p.

71. TNA 72/US/63, Chant and Drennan, Report on the Usambara Scheme, 7/2/53, n.p.

72. TNA 72/US/56, "Areas for Preservation under Ordinance no. 12/1954," 6/16/54, Notes on Soil Conservation, Land Use, Areas for Preservation, 12.

73. TNA 72/US/63, Chant and Drennan, Report on the Usambara Scheme, 7/2/53; TNA 72/US/62, Usambara Scheme: Plains Expansion and Resettlement, Handeni Preserve, 6.

74. TNA 72/US/62, "Report on Inspection of Northern Handeni Area, 6–7 October, 1953," Usambara Scheme: Plains Expansion and Resettlement, Handeni Preserve, 6.

75. TNA 72/US/60, "Estimates" for 7/1/55 to 6/30/56, no date, Usambara Scheme: Financial, Scheme Estimates, 1954–55, n.p.

76. TNA 72/US/75, P.A.O., Tanga (Drennan) to P.C., Tanga, 5/19/58, Usambara Scheme: Irrigation Scheme Mng'aro Area, 20.

77. Feierman, *Peasant Intellectuals*, 189–90.

78. Ibid., 203.

79. UIT, Rajabu Shemzinghwa, at Mlalo, 12/28/91, 5.

80. One difference in the extent of degradation may lie in the depopulation

trends on southern Usambara in the nineteenth century, a process that seemed not to affect the northern tier.

81. UIT, Juma Kingazi Kimako, Hoseni Hamsini, Salimu Shekulwavu, at Shita, 2/13/92, 17; Salehe Jambia, Juma Sebarua, and Peter Kaniki, at Lukozi, 3/17/92, 70; Kalata, 24; Zahabu, 30b.

82. UIT, Kalata, 25; Domitila Epimark and Mshirhiri Hippoliti, at Gare Mission, 1/7/92, 35.

83. TNA 72/US/8, D.C., J. W. Sword, Lushoto, to P.C., Tanga, 2/4/56, Landslides, Mbaramo, n.p.

84. Personal communication with Sufian Shekoloa of Mlalo.

85. For an explanation of this concept, see Michael Mortimer, *Roots in the African Dust: Sustaining the Drylands* (Cambridge: Cambridge University Press, 1998), 128–39; see also Ian Scoones, "The Dynamics of Soil Fertility Change: Historical Perspectives on Environmental Transformation from Zimbabwe," *Geographical Journal* 163 (1997): 161–69.

86. TNA 72/US/34, Gibbons, "Field Report," December 1951, [Bumbuli], Usambara Scheme: Field Officers Safaris and Reports, 1; TNA 72/US/56, "Notes on a Visit to West Usambara by Pasture Research Officer, 3/9/53 to 3/13/53," Notes on Soil Conservation, Land Use, Areas for Preservation, 3a; TNA 72/3/2, vol. 4, "Monthly Report for August 1958," 62 [landslides in vicinity of Vuga], Agricultural Reports, Lushoto; TNA 72/US/41, "Report," 4/10/52, Copies of articles and records concerning Usambara Scheme: from other sources.

Chapter 7

1. R. E. Moreau, *The Bird Fauna of Africa and Its Islands* (London: Academic Press, 1966).

2. For discussions of Eastern Arc Mountain forests, see J. C. Lovett, "Eastern Arc Moist Forest Flora," in *Biogeography and Ecology of the Rain Forests of Eastern Africa*, ed. Jon C. Lovett and Samuel K. Wasser (Cambridge: Cambridge University Press, 1993), 33–55; William Newmark, "Forest Area, Fragmentation, and Loss in the Eastern Arc Mountains: Implications for the Conservation of Biological Diversity," *Journal of East African Natural History* 87 (1998): 1–8; A. W. Diamond, "Reserves as Oceanic Islands: Lessons for Conserving Some East African Montane Forests," *African Journal of Ecology* 19.1–2 (1981): 21–25; A. C. Hamilton, "The Quaternary History of African Forests: Its Relevance to Conservation," *African Journal of Ecology* 19 (1981): 1–6; and F. White, "The History of the Afromontane Archipelago and the Scientific Need for Its Conservation," *African Journal of Ecology* 19 (1981): 33–54. For Usambara biological research, see, for example, D. Sheil, "Naturalized and Invasive Plant Species in the Evergreen Forests of the East Usambara Mountains, Tanzania," *African Journal of Ecology* 32 (1994), 66–71; W. A. Rodgers and K. M. Homewood, "Species Richness and Endemism in the Usambara Mountain Forests, Tanzania," *Biological Journal of the Linnean Society* 18 (1982),

197–242. See also the technical papers of the East Usambara Conservation and Management Project at http://www.metsa.fi/eng/tat/usambara/public/tech/.

3. J. C. Lovett, "Tanzania Forest Law," in *Environmental Law and Policy in Africa*, ed. B. Chaytor and K. Gray (The Hague: Kluwer Law International, forthcoming).

4. UIT, Mtee Nyangusi, at Magamba, 5/92, 39.

5. UIT, Musa Paulo, at Coasti (Magamba), 4/92, 41–42.

6. UIT, Salehe Jambia, Juma Sebarua, and Peter Kaniki, at Lukozi, 3/92, 67–68. This group proved very elusive: while admitting that bribes played a role in the amount of land one received, they dismissed the idea that anyone in Lukozi came from the Mlalo Basin. For a more cynical account, see UIT, Nyangusi, 38–39.

7. UIT, Jambia et al., 67–68; Nyangusi, 37–38; and Paulo, 41–42.

8. UIT, Nyangusi, 38–39.

9. Based on numerous studies of changing conditions of African latosols, Björn Lundgren charts a time sequence of changing soil conditions before, during, and after forest clearance. Lundgren has made an extensive study of these conditions at two forest sites in West Usambara, Shume-Magamba and Mazumbai. See Björn Lundgren, "Soil Conditions and Nutrient Cycling under Natural and Plantation Forests in the Tanzanian Highlands," *Reports in Forest Ecology and Forest Soils* 31 (Uppsala: Department of Forest Soils, Swedish University of Agricultural Sciences, 1978), 204–8. For soil deterioration of Usambara forest soils after clearing, see Lill Lundgren and Björn Lundgren, "Rainfall Interception and Evaporation in the Mazumbai Forest Reserve, West Usambara Mts., Tanzania and Their Importance in the Assessment of Land Potential," *Geografiska Annaler* 61 A (1979): 173–74.

10. B. Lundgren, "Soil Conditions," 32. For degradation at Lukozi, see also W. A. Rodgers, "The Conservation of the Forest Resources of Eastern Africa: Past Influences, Present Practices and Future Needs," in *Biogeography and Ecology of the Rainforests of Eastern Africa*, ed. Jon C. Lovett and Samuel K. Wasser (Cambridge: Cambridge University Press, 1993), 300.

11. UIT, Nyangusi, 38–39; Paulo, 41–42; Jambia et al., 69–70.

12. This information is gleaned from a number of hikes through the area and conversations with farmers now using it, and from UIT, Paulo, 41–42; Domitila Epimark and M. Hippoliti, at Gare Mission, 1/92, 34. For the more general tendency of Usambara farmers to cultivate stream valley alluvium, see Tanzania National Archive (hereafter TNA) Sec. 24732, Geoffrey Milne, "Report on a Soil Reconnaissance in the Neighbourhood of Kitivo, Lushoto District, Tanganyika Territory, and in Adjacent (West Usambara) Highlands, September–October 1937," Mimeo, East African Agricultural Research Station, Amani, n.d., 36–37.

13. Lundgren, "Soil Conditions," 227–28.

14. Ibid., 227; Lubango, personal communication.

15. Lubango, personal communication.

16. A. C. Hamilton and I. V. Mwasha, "History of Resource Utilization and Management after Independence," in *Forest Conservation in the East Usambara Mountains, Tan-*

zania, ed. A. C. Hamilton and R. Bensted-Smith (Gland, Switzerland: IUCN, 1989), 52.

17. Hamilton and Mwasha, 48.

18. Newmark, *Conserving Biodiversity,* 24–25.

19. Pierre Binggeli, "The Ecology of *Maesopsis* Invasion and Dynamics of the Evergreen Forest of the East Usambaras, and Their Implications for Forest Conservation and Forestry Practice," in Hamilton and Bensted-Smith, *Forest Conservation,* 275–76.

20. Hamilton and Mwasha, 51.

21. Ibid.

22. Newmark, *Conserving Biodiversity,* 22–23.

23. Ibid., 23.

24. Ibid., 121.

25. Stig Johansson and Richard Sandy, "Protected Areas and Public Lands: Land Use in the East Usambara Mountains," East Usambara Catchment Forest Project, Technical Paper 28 (Vantaa, Finland: Finnish Forest and Park Service, 1995).

26. Lists of administrative and working papers are available at: http://www.metsa.fi/eng/tat/usambara/public/, for biodiversity surveys, see: www.frontier.ac.uk/forms/East_Usambara_Biodiversity_Surveys.pdf. A number of documents from the East Usambara Conservation and Management Programme can be downloaded from: http://www.easternarc.org/html/eucamp.html.

27. http://www.gtz.de/themen/projekt.asp, 1.

28. Roderick Neuman, "Primitive Ideas: Protected Area Buffer Zones and the Politics of Land in Africa," in *Producing Nature and Poverty in Africa,* ed. Vigdis Broch-Due and Richard A. Schroeder (Uppsala, Sweden: Nordiska Africainstitutet, 2000), 220–21.

Bibliography

Oral Interviews

The author, along with Peter Mlimahadala and Sufian Shekoloa, conducted interviews in 1991–92 and in 1996 in West Usambara. Transcripts are written in Kiswahili and available upon request from the author. The tapes are in the possession of the author. References herein are to Usambara Interview Transcripts or UIT.

Archives, Libraries, and Manuscript Collections Consulted

East Usambara Catchment Forestry Project, Tanga, Tanzania
Lutheran Mission Archives, Wuppertal, Germany
Lushoto District, Office of Natural Resources, Lushoto, Tanzania
Lushoto District, Silvicultural Research Center, Library, Lushoto, Tanzania
Public Records Office, London
Rhodes House Library Manuscript Collection, Oxford
Tanzania National Archives, Dar es Salaam, Tanzania

Articles and Books

Adams, William M., and David M. Anderson. "Irrigation before Development: Indigenous and Induced Change in Agricultural Water Management in East Africa." *African Affairs* 87 (1988): 519–35.

Adams, W. M., T. Potkanski, and J. E. G. Sutton, "Indigenous Farmer-Managed Irrigation in Sonjo, Tanzania." *Geographical Journal* 160 (1994): 17–32.

Adas, Michael. *Machines as the Measure of Men: Science, Technology and Ideologies of Western Dominance.* Ithaca: Cornell University Press, 1989.

Ambler, Charles. *Kenyan Communities in the Age of Imperialism: The Central Region in the Late Nineteenth Century.* New Haven: Yale University Press, 1988.

Anderson, David. "Depression, Dust Bowl, Demography, and Drought: The Colonial State and Soil Conservation in East Africa during the 1930s." *African Affairs* 83 (1984): 321–44.

———. "Agriculture and Irrigation Technology at Lake Baringo." *Azania* 24 (1989): 89–97.

Bald, Detlaf, and Gerhild Bald. *Das Forschungsinstitut Amani: Wirtschaft und Wissenschaft in der deutschen Kolonialpolitik Ostafrika 1900–1918.* Munich: Weltforum-Verlag, 1972.

Baumann, Oscar. "Karte von Usambara." *Petermanns geographische Mitteilungen* 35.11 (1889): 257–61.

———. "Usambara." *Petermanns geographische Mitteilungen* 35.11 (1889): 41–47.

———. *In Deutsch-Ostafrika während des Aufstandes, Reise der Dr. Hans Meyer'schen Expedition in Usambara*. Wien und Olmütz: Eduard Hölzel, 1890.

———. *Usambara und seine Nachbargebiete. Allgemeine Darstellung des nordöstlichen Deutsch-Ostafrika und seiner Bewohner auf Grund einer im Auftrage der Deutsch-Ostafrikanischen Gesellschaft im Jahre 1890 ausgeführten Reise*. Berlin: Dietrich Reimer, 1891.

Becker, Br. "Die Vamaakinder," *Nachrichten aus der ostafrikanischen Mission* 9 (1895): 98–102.

Berntsen, J. L. "The Maasai and Their Neighbors: Variables and Interaction." *African Economic History* 2 (1976): 1–11.

bin Hemedi 'l Ajjemy, Abdallah. *The Kilindi*. Nairobi: East African Literature Bureau, 1963.

Binggeli, Pierre. "The Ecology of *Maesopsis* Invasion and Dynamics of the Evergreen Forest of the East Usambaras, and Their Implications for Forest Conservation and Forestry Practice." In *Forest Conservation in the East Usambara Mountains Tanzania*, edited by A. C. Hamilton and R. Bensted-Smith, 269–300. Gland, Switzerland: IUCN, 1989.

Blackburn, R. H. "Honey in Okiek Personality, Culture and Society." Ph.D. diss., Michigan State University, 1971.

Blaikie, Piers. *The Political Economy of Soil Erosion in Developing Countries*. New York: Longman, 1985.

Braun, K. "Der Reis in Deutsch-Ostafrika." *Berichte über Land- und Forstwirtschaft in Deutsch-Ostafrika* 3 (1907): 167–217.

Bravman, Bill. *Making Ethnic Ways: Communities and Their Transformations in Taita, Kenya 1800–1950*. Portsmouth, N.H.: Heinemann, 1998.

Brockway, Lucille. *Science and Colonial Expansion: The Role of the British Botanical Gardens*. New York: Academic Press, 1979.

Brunhoff. "Auszüge aus den Berichten der Bezirksamter, Militärstationen und anderer Dienststellen über die wirtschaftliche Entwicklung im Berichtsjahre vom 1. April bis 31. März 1903. Bezirk Wilhelmstal." *Berichte über Land- und Forstwirtschaft in Deutsch-Ostafrika* 2 (1903): 41–46.

Buchwald, Johannes. "Aus dem deutsch-ostafrikanischen Schutzgebiete. Beitrag zur Gliederung der Vegetation von West-Usambara." *Mitteilungen aus den deutschen Schutzgebieten* 9 (1896): 213–33.

———. "Westusambara, die Vegetation und der wirtschaftliche Werth des Landes." *Der Tropenpflanzer: Zeitschrift für tropische Landwirtschaft* 1 (1897): 82–85.

Busse, Walter. "Zur Frage der tropischen Versuchsstation in Usambara." *Der Tropenpflanzer: Zeitschrift für tropische Landwirtschaft* 5 (1901): 270–73.

Champion, A. M. "Soil Erosion in Africa: A Paper Read at the Afternoon Meeting of the Society on 8 May 1933 by Mr. C. W. Hobley on behalf of A. M. Champion." *Geographical Journal* 82 (1933): 130–39.

Cittadino, Eugene. *Nature as the Laboratory: Darwinian Plant Ecology in the German Empire, 1880–1900*. Cambridge: Cambridge University Press, 1990.

Collett, David. "The Spread of Early Iron Producing Communities in Eastern and Southern Africa: Volume 1." Ph.D. thesis, Cambridge University, 1985.

Conte, Christopher. "Nature Reorganized: Ecological History in the Plateau Forests of the West Usambara Mountains, c. 1850–1935." In *Custodians of the Land: Ecology and Culture in the History of Tanzania*, edited by Gregory Maddox, James Giblin, and Isaria N. Kimambo, 96–122. London: James Currey, 1996.
———. "Transformations along the Gradient: Ecological Change in the Mountains and Plains of Northeastern Tanzania's West Usambara Mountains, c. 1860–1970." Ph.D. diss., Michigan State University, 1995.
———. "Colonial Science and Ecological Change: Tanzania's Mlalo Basin, 1888–1946." *Environmental History* 4.2 (1999): 220–44.
Cooper, Frederick. *Plantation Slavery on the East Coast of Africa.* Portsmouth, N.H.: Heinemann Books, 1997.
Copland, B. D. "A Note on the Origin of the Mbugu with a Text." *Zeitschrift für Eingeborenen-Sprachen* 24 (1933–34): 241–44.
Crosby, Alfred. *Ecological Imperialism: The Biological Expansion of Europe.* Cambridge: Cambridge University Press, 1986.
De Langhe, E., R. Swennen, and D. Vuylsteke. "Plantain in the Early Bantu World." *Azania* 29–30 (1996): 147–60.
Diamond, A. W. "Reserves as Oceanic Islands: Lessons for Conserving Some East African Montane Forests." *African Journal of Ecology* 19.1–2 (1981): 21–25.
Dobson, E. B. "Land Tenure of the Wasambaa." *Tanganyika Notes and Records* 10 (1940): 1–27.
Drayton, Richard. *Nature's Government: Science, Imperial Britain and the 'Improvement' of the World.* New Haven: Yale University Press, 2000.
"Dr. Stuhlmann über die wirtschaftliche Entwickelung Deutsch-Ostafrikas," *Der Tropenpflanzer: Zeitschrift für tropische Landwirtschaft* 2 (1898): 119–25.
Ehret, Christopher. *An African Classical Age: Eastern and Southern Africa in World History, 1000 B.C. to A.D. 400.* Charlottesville: University of Virginia Press, 1998.
Eick, E. "Bericht über meine Reise ins Kwai und Masumbailand (Usambara) vom 12. bis 16. März 1896." *Mitteilungen aus den deutschen Schutzgebieten* 9.3 (1896): 184–88.
Engler, Adolf, *Über die Gliederung der Vegetation von Usambara und der angrenzenden Gebiete.* Abhandlungen der Königlichen Akademie der Wissenschaften zu Berlin; 1894, Physikalische Abhandlungen, 1. Berlin: Verlag der Akademie der Wissenschaften, 1894.
———. "Bemerkungen über Schonung und verständige Ausnutzung der einzelnen Vegetationsformen Deutsch-Ostafrikas." *Berichte über Land- und Forstwirtschaft in Deutsch-Ostafrika* 2 (1904): 1–7.
Fairhead, James, and Melissa Leach. *Misreading the Landscape: Society and Ecology in a Forest-Savanna Mosaic.* African Studies Series 90. Cambridge: Cambridge University Press, 1996.
Farler, J. P. "The Usambara Country in East Africa." *Proceedings of the Royal Geographical Society* 1.2 (1879): 81–97.
Feierman, Steven. *The Shambaa Kingdom: A History.* Madison: University of Wisconsin Press, 1974.
———. *Peasant Intellectuals: Anthropology and History in Tanzania.* Madison: University of Wisconsin Press, 1990.
Fleuret, Patrick. "Farm and Market: A Study of Society and Agriculture in Tanzania." Ph.D. diss., University of California at Santa Barbara, 1978.

———. "The Social Organisation of Water Control in the Taita Hills, Kenya." *American Ethnologist* 12 (1985): 103–18.
Flores, Dan. "Nature's Children: Environmental History as Natural History." In *The Natural West: Environmental History in the Great Plains and Rocky Mountains*. Norman: University of Oklahoma Press, 2001.
Fraengsmyr, Tore, J. L. Heilbron, and Robin E. Rider, eds. *The Quantifying Spirit in the Eighteenth Century*. Berkeley: University of California Press, 1990.
Gardner, H. M. "East African Pencil Cedar." *Empire Forestry Journal* 5 (1926): 39–53.
Geertz, Clifford. *Agricultural Involution: The Process of Ecological Change in Indonesia*. Berkeley: University of California Press, 1966.
Giblin, James. *The Politics of Environmental Control in Northeastern Tanzania, 1840–1940*. Philadelphia: University of Pennsylvania Press, 1992.
Gillman, Clement. "A Population Map of Tanganyika Territory." *Geographical Review* 26 (1936): 353–75.
———. "Problems of Land Utilisation in Tanganyika Territory." *South African Geographical Journal* 20 (1938): 12–20.
———. Review of *The Rape of the Earth* (G. V. Jacks and R. O. Whyte). *Tanganyika Notes and Records* 8 (1939): 104.
———. "Water Consultant's Report, No. 6, A Reconnaissance Survey of the Hydrology of Tanganyika Territory in Its Geographical Settings." Tanganyika Territory, 1940.
Glassman, Jonathon. *Feasts and Riot: Revelry, Rebellion, and Popular Consciousness on the Swahili Coast, 1856–1888*. Portsmouth, N.H.: Heinemann Books, 1995.
Goodman, Morris. "The Strange Case of Vamaa." In *Pidginization and Creolization of Languages*, edited by Dell Hymes, 243–54. Cambridge: Cambridge University Press, 1971.
Green, E. C. "The Wambugu of Usambara (with Notes on Kimbugu)." *Tanzania Notes and Records* 61 (1963): 175–89.
Grove, Richard. *Green Imperialism: Colonial Expansion, Tropical Island Edens and the Origins of Environmentalism, 1600–1860*. Cambridge: Cambridge University Press, 1995.
Guha, Ramachandra, and Madhav Gadgil. *This Fissured Land*. Berkeley: University of California Press, 1992.
Gullebaud, C. W. *An Economic Survey of the Sisal Industry of Tanganyika*, 3rd ed. Digswell Place, U.K.: James Nisbet and Co. Ltd., 1966.
Hakansson, N. Thomas. "Irrigation, Population Pressure, and Exchange in Pre-colonial Pare of Tanzania." In *Research in Economic Anthropology*, vol. 16, edited by Barry Isaac, 297–323. Greenwich, Conn.: JAI Press, 1995.
———. "Rulers and Rainmakers in Pre-colonial South Pare: The Role of Exchange and Ritual Experts in Political Fragmentation." *Ethnology* 37.3 (Summer 1998): 263–83.
Hamilton, A. C. "The Quaternary History of African Forests: Its Relevance to Conservation." *African Journal of Ecology* 19 (1981): 1–6
———. "The Climate of the East Usambaras." In *Forest Conservation in the East Usambara Mountains, Tanzania*, edited by A. C. Hamilton and R. Bensted-Smith, 97–102. Gland, Switzerland: IUCN, 1989.

———. "History of Resource Utilization and Management: The Precolonial Period." In *Forest Conservation in the East Usambara Mountains, Tanzania*, edited by A. C. Hamilton and R. Bensted-Smith, 35–37. Gland, Switzerland: IUCN, 1989.

Hamilton, A. C., and R. Bensted-Smith, eds. *Forest Conservation in the East Usambara Mountains, Tanzania*. Gland, Switzerland: IUCN, 1989.

Hamilton, A. C., and I. V. Mwasha. "History of Resource Utilization and Management after Independence." In *Forest Conservation in the East Usambara Mountains, Tanzania*, edited by A. C. Hamilton and R. Bensted-Smith, 45–56. Gland, Switzerland: IUCN, 1989.

Headrick, Daniel R. *Tentacles of Progress: Technology Transfer in the Age of Imperialism*. Oxford, U.K.: Oxford University Press, 1988.

Hedde, Chr. "Auszüge aus den Jahresberichten der Bezirkämter und Militärstationen für die Zeit vom 1. Juli 1900 bis 30. Juni 1901, 3. Privatpflanzungen in West-Usambara. Asiedelung am Mkusu, den 12. Juni 1901." *Berichte über Land- und Forstwirtschaft in Deutsch-Ostafrika* 1 (1903): 45–46.

Hindorf, Richard. "Eine Versuchsstation für Tropenkulturen in Usambara." *Der Tropenpflanzer: Zeitschrift für tropische Landwirtschaft* 2.5 (1898): 137–42.

———. "Die Versuchsstation für Tropenkulturen in Usambara." *Der Tropenpflanzer: Zeitschrift für tropische Landwirtschaft* 5 (1901): 266–70.

Hobley, C. W. "Soil Erosion: A Problem in Human Geography: A paper read at the Afternoon Meeting of the Society on 8 May 1933." *Geographical Review* 82 (1933): 139–46.

Hochschild, Adam. *King Leopold's Ghost: A Story of Greed, Terror, and Heroism in Colonial Africa*. Boston: Houghton Mifflin, 1998.

Hölst, Carl. "Der Landbau der Eingeborenen von Usambara." *Deutsche Kolonialzeitung* 6.9 (1893): 113–14; 6.10: 128–30.

Hoyle, B. S. *Gillman of Tanganyika 1882–1946*. Brookfield, Vt.: Gower Publishing, 1987.

Iliffe, John. *A Modern History of Tanganyika*. Cambridge, U.K.: Cambridge University Press, 1979.

Johanssen, Ernst. "Die Mission unter den Vamaa." *Nachrichten aus der ostafrikanischen Mission* 8 (1894): 24–26.

———. "Missionsarbeit unter den Wambugu," *Nachrichten aus der ostafrikanischen Mission* 11 (1897): 124–27.

Johansson, Stig. "Conservation in the East Usambara Mountains—A Partly Annotated Bibliography of Selected Published and Non-Published Material," Working Paper 22. Tanga, Tanzania: East Usambara Catchment Forest Project, 1996.

Kaoneka, A. R. S., and B. Soldberg. "Forestry Related Land Use in the West Usambara Mountains, Tanzania." *Agriculture, Ecosystems and Environment* 49 (1994): 207–15.

Kimambo, Isaria N. "Environmental Control and Hunger in the Mountains and Plains of Northeastern Tanzania." In *Custodians of the Land: Ecology and Culture in the History of Tanzania*, edited by Gregory Maddox, James Giblin, and Isaria N. Kimambo, 71–95. London: James Currey, 1996.

———. *Penetration and Protest in Tanzania: The Impact of the World Economy on the Pare, 1860–1960*. London: James Currey, 1991.

Kingdon, Jonathan. *Island Africa: The Evolution of Africa's Rare Animals and Plants*. Princeton, N.J.: Princeton University Press, 1989.

Kjekshus, Helge. *Ecology Control and Economic Development in East African History: The Case of Tanganyika, 1850–1950*, 2nd ed. London: James Currey, 1996.

Koponen, Juhani. *Development for Exploitation: German Colonial Policies in Mainland Tanzania, 1884–1914*. Helsinki: Finnish Historical Society, Studia Historica 49, 1994.

Krapf, Johann Ludwig. *Reisen in Ostafrika ausgeführt in den Jahren 1837–1855*. Stuttgart: F. A. Brockhaus Kimm.-Gesch., GmbH., Abt. Antiquarium, 1964.

———. *Travels, Researches, and Missionary Labours During an Eighteen Years' Residence in Eastern Africa*. London: Frank Cass and Co. Ltd, 1968; orig. ed., London: Trübner, 1860.

Leach, Melissa, and Robin Mearns, eds. *The Lie of the Land: Challenging Received Wisdom on the African Environment*. London: The International African Institute, 1996.

Lock, G. W. *Sisal: Thirty Years' Sisal Research in Tanzania*. London: Longmans, Green and Co., 1962.

Lonsdale, John, and David Low, "Introduction: Towards the New Order, 1945–1963." In *History of East Africa*, vol. 3, edited by D. A. Low and A. Smith, 1–63. Oxford: Oxford University Press, 1976.

Lovett, J. C. "Climatic History and Forest Distribution in Eastern Africa" and "Eastern Arc Moist Forest Flora." In *Biogeography and Ecology of the Rain Forests of Eastern Africa*, edited by Jon C. Lovett and Samuel K. Wasser, 23–29 and 33–55. Cambridge: Cambridge University Press, 1993.

———. "Tanzania Forest Law." In *Environmental Law and Policy in Africa*, edited by B. Chaytor and K. Gray. The Hague: Kluwer Law International, forthcoming.

Lowood, Henry. "The Calculating Forester: Quantification, Cameral Science and the Emergence of Scientific Forestry Management in Germany." In *The Quantifying Spirit in the 18th Century*, edited by Tore Fraengsmyr, J. L. Heilbron, and Robin E. Rider, 315–42. Berkeley: University of California Press, 1990.

Lundgren, Björn. "Soil Conditions and Nutrient Cycling under Natural and Plantation Forests in the Tanzanian Highlands." *Reports in Forest Ecology and Forest Soils 31*. Uppsala: Department of Forest Soils, Swedish University of Agricultural Sciences, 1978.

Lundgren, Lill, and Björn Lundgren. "Rainfall Interception and Evaporation in the Mazumbai Forest Reserve, West Usambara Mts., Tanzania and Their Importance in the Assessment of Land Potential." *Geografiska Annaler* 61 A (1979): 157–78.

Mackenzie, John. "Introduction." In *Imperialism and the Natural World*, edited by John Mackenzie. Manchester, U.K.: Manchester University Press, 1990.

———. "Empire and the Ecological Apocalypse: The Historiography of the Imperial Environment." In *Ecology of Empire: The Environmental History of Settler Societies*, edited by Tom Griffiths and Libby Robin. Seattle: University of Washington Press, 1997.

Maddox, Gregory and James Giblin. "Introduction." In *Custodians of the Land: Ecology and Culture in the History of Tanzania*, edited by Gregory Maddox, James Giblin, and Isaria N. Kimambo, 1–14. London: James Currey, 1996.

Masao, F. T. "The Irrigation System in Uchagga: An Ethno-historical Approach." *Tanzania Notes and Records* 75 (1974): 1–8

McCann, James. *People of the Plow: An Agricultural History of Ethiopia, 1800–1990*. Madison: University of Wisconsin Press, 1995.

Milne, Geoffrey. *A Provisional Soil Map of East Africa*. Amani, Tanganyika: East African Agricultural Research Station, 1936.

———. "Essays in Applied Pedology: 1. - Soil Type and Soil Management in Relation to Plantation Agriculture in East Usambara." *East African Agricultural Journal* 3.1 (1937): 7–20.

———. "Notes on Soil Conditions and Two East African Vegetation Types." *Journal of Ecology* 25 (1937): 254–58.

———. "Soils in Relation to the Native Population in West Usambara." *Geography* 29 (1944): 107–13.

———. "A Soil Reconnaissance Journey through Parts of Tanganyika Territory. December 1935–February 1936." *Journal of Ecology* 35.1 and 35.2 (1947): 192–265.

Moreau, R. E. "Pleistocene Climatic Changes and the Distribution of Life in East Africa," *Journal of Ecology* 21 (1933): 415–35.

———. "Some Eco-climatic Data for Closed Evergreen Forest in Tropical Africa." *Journal of the Linnean Society* (Zool.) 39.265 (8 March 1935): 285–93.

———. "A Synecological Study of Usambara, Tanganyika Territory, with Particular Reference to Birds." *Journal of Ecology* 23.1 (1935): 1–43.

———. "Climatic Classification from the Standpoint of East African Biology." *Journal of Ecology* 26 (1938): 467–96.

———. *The Bird Fauna of Africa and Its Islands*. London: Academic Press, 1966.

Mortimer, Michael. *Roots in the African Dust: Sustaining the Drylands*. Cambridge, U.K.: Cambridge University Press, 1998.

Nature. Volume 405 (11 May 2000).

Neubaur, Dr. "Die Besiedelungsfähigkeit von Westusambara." *Der Tropenpflanzer: Zeitschrift für tropische Landwirtschaft* 6 (1902): 496–513.

Neuman, Roderick. "Primitive Ideas: Protected Area Buffer Zones and the Politics of Land in Africa." In *Producing Nature and Poverty in Africa*, edited by Vigdis Broch-Due and Richard A. Schroeder, 220–42. Uppsala, Sweden: Nordiska Africainstitutet, 2000.

Newmark, William. "Forest Area, Fragmentation, and Loss in the Eastern Arc Mountains: Implications for the Conservation of Biological Diversity." *Journal of East African Natural History* 87 (1998): 1–8.

———. *Conserving Biodiversity in East African Forests: A Study of the Eastern Arc Mountains*. New York: Springer-Verlag, 2002.

Nicholson, Sharon. "Environmental Change within the Historical Period." In *The Physical Geography of Africa*, edited by W. M. Adams, A. S. Goudie, and A. R. Orme, 60–75. Oxford: Oxford University Press, 1996.

Nurse, Derek. "Extinct Southern Cushitic Communities in East Africa." In *Cushitic—Omotic. Papers from the International Symposium on Cushitic and Omotic Languages, Cologne, January 6–9, 1986*, edited by Marianne Bechaus-Gerst and Fritz Serzisko, 93–104. Hamburg: Helmut Buske Verlag, 1988.

———. "'Historical' Classifications of the Bantu Languages." *Azania* 29–30 (1994–95): 63–81.

Paasche, Herman. *Deutsch Ostafrika*. Grossenworden (Nieder-Elbe): Rüsch'she Verlagsbuchhandlung, 1927.

Pallidino, Paolo, and Michael Worboys. "Science and Imperialism." *Isis* 74 (1993): 91–102.

Pike, A. H. "Soil Conservation among the Matenge Tribe." *Tanzania Notes and Records* 6 (1938): 79–81.

Pitt-Schenkel, C. J. W. "Some Important Communities of Warm Temperate Rain Forest at Magamba, West Usambara, Tanganyika Territory." *Journal of Ecology* 26 (1938): 50–81.

Rodgers, W. A. "The Conservation of the Forest Resources of Eastern Africa: Past Influences, Present Practices and Future Needs." In *Biogeography and Ecology of the Rainforests of Eastern Africa*, edited by Jon C. Lovett and Samuel K. Wasser, 283–331. Cambridge, U.K.: Cambridge University Press, 1993.

Rodgers, W. A., and K. M. Homewood. "Species Richness and Endemism in the Usambara Mountain Forests, Tanzania." *Biological Journal of the Linnean Society* 18 (1982): 197–242.

Rossel, Gerda. "Musa and Ensete in Africa: Taxonomy, Nomenclature and Uses." *Azania* 29–30 (1994–95): 130–46.

Russell, Emily. *People and the Land through Time: Linking Ecology and History*. New Haven: Yale University Press, 1997.

Sander, L. "Usambara." *Der Tropenpflanzer: Zeitschrift für tropische Landwirtschaft* 7.5 (1903): 202–10.

Schabel, Hans. "Tanganyika Forestry under German Colonial Administration, 1891–1919." *Forest and Conservation History* 34.3 (1990): 130–141.

Schmidt, Peter. "Eastern Expressions of the 'Mwitu' Tradition: Early Iron Age Industry of the Usambara Mountains, Tanzania." *Nyame Akuma* 30 (1988): 36–37.

———. "Early Exploitation and Settlement in the Usambara Mountains." In *Forest Conservation in the East Usambara Mountains, Tanzania*, edited by A.C. Hamilton and R. Bensted-Smith, 75–78. Gland, Switzerland: IUCN, 1989.

———. "Historical Ecology and Landscape Transformation in Eastern Equatorial Africa." In *Historical Ecology: Cultural Knowledge and Changing Landscapes*, edited by Carol Crumley, 99–126. Santa Fe, N.M.: School of American Research Press, 1994.

———. *Iron Technology in East Africa: Symbolism, Science and Archaeology*. Bloomington: Indiana University Press, 1997.

Schoenbrun, David. "We Are What We Eat: Ancient Agriculture between the Great Lakes." *Journal of African History* 34 (1993): 1–31.

———. *A Green Place, A Good Place: Agrarian Change, Gender, and Social Identity in the Great Lakes Region to the 15th Century*. Portsmouth, N.H.: Heinemann, 1998.

Scoones, Ian. "The Dynamics of Soil Fertility Change: Historical Perspectives on Environmental Transformation from Zimbabwe." *Geographical Journal* 163 (July 1997): 161–69.

Sheil, D. "Naturalized and Invasive Plant Species in the Evergreen Forests of the East Usambara Mountains, Tanzania." *African Journal of Ecology* 32 (1994): 66–71.

Sheriff, Abdul. *Slaves, Spices and Ivory: Integration of an East African Commercial Empire in the World Economy*. London: James Currey, 1987.

Siebenlist, Th. *Forstwirtschaft in Deutsch-Ostafrika*. Berlin: Verlagsbuchhandlung Paul Parey, 1914.

Soper, Robert. "Iron Age Sites in Northeastern Tanzania." *Azania* 2 (1967): 19–36.

Sponsel, Leslie E., Thomas N. Headland, and Robert C. Bailey. "Anthropological Perspectives on the Causes, Consequences and Solutions of Deforestation." In *Tropical*

Deforestation: The Human Dimension, edited by Leslie Sponsel et al., 3–52. New York: Columbia University Press, 1996.

Stanford, Craig. *Significant Others: The Ape-Human Continuum and the Quest for Human Nature*. New York: Basic Books, 2001.

Storey, H. H. *Basic Research in Agriculture: A Brief History of Research at Amani 1928–1947*. Nairobi: East African Standard, 1951.

Stuhlman, Franz. "Übersicht über Land- und Forstwirtschaft in Deutsch-Ostafrika im Berichtsjahre vom 1. Juli 1900 bis 30. Juni 1901." *Berichte über Land- und Forstwirtschaft in Deutsch-Ostafrika* 1 (1903): 1–22.

Sutton, J. E. G. "Irrigation and Soil-conservation in African Agricultural History. With a Reconsideration of the Inyanga Terracing (Zimbabwe) and Engaruka Irrigation Works (Tanzania)." *Journal of African History* 25 (1984): 25–41.

———. "Towards a History of Cultivating the Fields." *Azania* 24 (1989): 98–112.

———. "The Growth of Farming and the Bantu Settlement on and South of the Equator: Editor's Introduction." *Azania* 29–30 (1994–95): 1–14.

Tambila, Kapepwa. "A Plantation Labour Magnet: The Tanga Case." In *Migrant Labour in Tanzania during the Colonial Period: Case Studies of Recruitment and Conditions of Labour in the Sisal Industry*, edited by Walter Rodney, Kapepwa Tambila, and Laurent Sabo. Hamburg: Institut für Afrika-Kunde, 1983.

Tanganyika Territory. *The Third Annual Report of the Forest Department, Tanganyika Territory*. Dar es Salaam: Government Printer, 1923.

———. *The Fourth Annual Report of the Forest Department, Tanganyika Territory*. Dar es Salaam: Government Printer, 1924.

———. *The Seventh Annual Report of the Forest Department, Tanganyika Territory*. Dar es Salaam: Government Printer, 1927.

———. *The Thirteenth Annual Report of the Forest Department, Tanganyika Territory*. Dar es Salaam: Government Printer, 1933.

———. *The Fifteenth Annual Report of the Forest Department, Tanganyika Territory*. Dar es Salaam: Government Printer, 1935.

———. *The Thirty-First Annual Report of the Forest Department, Tanganyika Territory*. Dar es Salaam: Government Printer, 1952.

Taylor, David, and Robert Marchant. "Human Impact in the Interlacustrine Region: Long-Term Pollen Records from the Rukiga Highlands." *Azania* 29–30 (1994–95): 283–95.

Teichmann. "Auszüge aus den Jahresberichten der Bezirksämter und Militärstationen für die Zeit vom 1. Juli 1900 bis 30. Juni 1901, 2. Bezirksamt Wilhelmstal (West Usambara)." *Berichte über Land- und Forstwirtschaft in Deutsch-Ostafrika* 1 (1903): 27–38.

———. "Auszüge aus den Jahresberichten der Bezirksämter und Militärstationen für die Zeit vom 1. Juli 1900 bis 30. Juni 1901, 4. Forstliche Versuche im Bezirk Wihelmstal." *Berichte über Land- und Forstwirtschaft in Deutsch-Ostafrika* 1 (1903): 53.

Throup, David. *Economic and Social Origins of Mau Mau, 1945–53*. London: James Currey, 1988.

Tilman, David. "Causes, Consequences and Ethics of Biodiversity." *Nature* 405 (11 May 2000), 208–11.

Troup, R. S. *Forestry and State Control*. Oxford: Clarendon Press, 1938.

———. *Colonial Forest Administration*. Oxford: Oxford University Press, 1940.
Tucker, A. N., and M. A. Bryan. "The Vamaa Anomaly." *Bulletin of the School of Oriental and African Studies* 37 (1974): 188–207.
United Republic of Tanzania, *Report of the Presidential Commission of Inquiry into Land Matters, Volume I, Land Policy and Land Tenure Structure*. The Ministry of Lands, Housing and Urban Development, Government of the United Republic of Tanzania. Dar es Salaam: United Republic of Tanzania.
Vail, Leroy. "Ecology and History: The Example of Eastern Zambia." *Journal of Southern African Studies* 3.2 (1977): 130–55.
Vansina, Jan. "A Slow Revolution: Farming in Subequatorial Africa." *Azania* 29–30 (1994–95): 15–26.
———. "New Linguistic Evidence and 'The Bantu Expansion.'" *Journal of African History* 36 (1995): 173–96.
Vasey, Daniel E. *An Ecological History of Agriculture: 10,000 BC–AD 10,000*. Ames: Iowa State University Press, 1992.
Vosseler, J. "Sisal im Usambaragebirge." *Der Pflanzer* 2 (1906): 339–47.
Waller, Richard. "Interaction and Identity on the Periphery: The Trans-Mara Maasai." *International Journal of African History Studies* 17 (1984): 243–84.
———. "Emutai: Crisis and Response in Maasailand 1883–1902." In *The Ecology of Survival: Case Studies from Northeast African History*, edited by Douglas Johnson and David Anderson, 73–114. Boulder: Westview Press, 1988.
Warburg, Otto. "Die Kulturpflanzen Usambaras." *Mitteilungen aus den deutschen Schutzgebieten* 7 (1894): 131–99.
———. "Die Notwendigkeit einer Versuchsstation für Tropenkulturen in Usambara und ihre Kosten." *Der Tropenpflanzer: Zeitschrift für tropische Landwirtschaft* 2 (1898): 180–86.
Wasser, Samuel, and Jon Lovett. "Introduction." In *Biogeography and Ecology of the Rain Forests of Eastern Africa*, edited by Jon C. Lovett and Samuel K. Wasser, 3–6. Cambridge, U.K.: Cambridge University Press, 1993.
White, F. "The History of the Afromontane Archipelago and the Scientific Need for Its Conservation." *African Journal of Ecology* 19 (1981): 33–54.
Wigboldus, J. S. "The Spread of Crops into Sub-equatorial Africa during the Early Iron Age." *Azania* 29–30 (1994-95): 121–46.
Wright, Marcia. *Strategies of Slaves and Women: Life Stories from East/Central Africa*. London: James Currey, 1993.

Index

Adamson, A. S., 76
agriculture
    expansion of, 9
    highland, 21–23, 37 (*see also* Mwitu)
    involution, 127
    settlers, by, 13
    small-scale, 2–3
    subsistence, 19
Agriculture Department, 13, 82, 90–91
akida, 103
Amani
    Botanical Garden, 60, 62
    Institute for Biological Research, 13, 15, 43–47, 55–66, 87, 149–50, 157, 160
    See also East African Agricultural Research Station (EAARS)
Arusha, 159

Balangai, 84
banana, 23–24, 36, 105, 141. *See also* ensete (false banana)
Bantu
    culture, 9
    languages, 8, 19–20, 22–23
    Upland, 20
Baumann, Oscar, 34–36
Berlin Botanical Museum, 15, 57, 73
Berlin Conference, 44
Bethel Mission, 36
biological diversity, 7, 73
biology, conservation, 7
Bismarck, Otto von, 44
black wattle, 82
Blaikie, Piers, 134
Boma, 29
botanical gardens
    Amani, 60, 62
    Buitenzorg, 45
botany
    economic, 12–13, 56–57, 60

    research, 13, 45, 58
    systematic, 58
Braun, Karl, 63, 98
Brockway, Lucile, 46
Buchwald, Johannes, 72
Buitenzorg Botanical Garden, 45
Bumbuli, 34–35

cabbage, 49
Callaghan, 53
camphor
    East African, 72, 74–75, 84, 88, 152
    Japanese, 75
cardamom, 155
cassava, 24, 116, 133
cedar, 72, 74, 152
Cephalosphaera, 155
chama, 120, 132
Chankola (Ali Mashina), 116–21, 130–32. *See also* njaa ya Chankola
Chlorophora excelsa, 88
Church Missionary Society, 11
cinchona, 90
Clegg, J. B., 130–34
climate, 3, 5, 6, 8–9
cloves, 32
coffee, 4, 12, 60–61, 73, 87
Colonial Advisory Council for Agriculture and Animal Health (CACAAH), 65
Colonial Development and Welfare Act, 126
conservation, environmental, 15–16, 18
Convention for Biodiversity, 150
Cory, Hans, 130
crops
    cash (*see* cardamom; tobacco)
    plantation, 12, 41 (*see also* coffee; rubber; sisal; tea)
    subsistence (*see* banana; maize; millet; potato; sorghum)
Crosby, Alfred, 43

Cushites, 9
    language of, 9–10, 27–28
    southern, 27–28
custodian of (ex-)enemy property, 52, 99, 101

dau, 123–24, 135
deforestation, 9, 20, 68–95, 152–57
degradation
    environmental, 3, 110
    land, 31, 114
de Rosemund, C. C., 120
Der Tropenpflanzer, 60
Deutsch-Ostafrika Gesellschaft (DOAG). See German East Africa Society
dezu, 115
Dobson, K. B. A., 117–18
Dowsett, F. D., 94
Drennan, D. H. 94

East African Agricultural Research Station (EAARS), 62–65, 90. *See also* Amani
East African highlands, 3–4
East Coast Fever (ECF), 50, 81
Eastern Arc Mountains, 1, 4–9, 15, 18, 23, 45, 69, 71, 87, 150
East Usambara Area Management Programme, 157
East Usambara Conservation and Development (EUCD) project, 157
East Usambara Conservation and Management Programme (EUCAMP), 157
ecological imperialism, 43
ecology
    changes in, 9
    degradation of, 3, 31
    forest, 9
Ehret, Christopher, 23, 27
Eick, 47–50
Engaruka, 24
Engler, Adolf, 15, 57–60, 73, 93
ensete (false banana), 24. *See also* banana
environmental change, 4
    control, 3
    degradation, 31
estates, 73, 90. *See also* Balangai; Kwamkoro; Mombo; Ngambi; Ngua; Sakarre

Fairclough, J. L., 117
Fairhead, James, 70–71
famine, 10, 32–37, 96–125. *See also* njaa ya Chankola; njaa ya mchele
Farler, J. P., 87
Feierman, Steven, 10, 28, 97, 144
forest
    communities, 5
    conservation, 5, 69, 81, 89
    deforestation, 9, 20, 68–95, 152–57
    ecology, 5–6, 9, 29
    ecosystem, 4
    evolution, 7
    exotic, 10
    Gare Mission, 153
    highland, 28–29, 93
    history, 7, 68–95
    indigenous, 2
    labor, 78–79 (*see also* squatters)
    plantation, 3
    preservation, 7, 11, 155–57
    reserves, 82–83
    secondary, 11
    tropical, 13–14
    value 4
Forest Department, 14
Forest Ordinance (1921), 77
Forest Ordinance (1956), 94
forestry
    colonial, 73
    German, 73
    ideology, 14
    science, 74

Gare Mission, 153
Geertz, Clifford, 127
geology, 5
German East Africa Protectorate, 44–46
German East Africa Society, 12, 44, 47–49
Germany, colonialism, 11, 41–47, 149
Gibbons, W. D., 141
Gilchrist, B., 94
Gillman, Clement, 90, 109–11, 114
Gillman, Harold, 113
Gonja, 23
Government Land, 96
Gower, R. H., 141
Grant, D. K. S., 78
Great Britain, 11

Greenway, Arthur, 65
Grewal and Co., 83–84

Hakansson, Thomas, 25
Hartnoll, 53
Hehe ridges, 132–34, 140–43, 146
herders, 10
highlands, East African, 3–4
Hindorf, Richard, 46, 59
historiography, 19
Hohenfriedberg, 36
Hölst, Carl, 36–37, 57
Homo sapiens, 7, 17
honey, 30
horticulture, 22, 24
hyrax, 6

Iliffe, John, 127
Illich, Ludwig, 50–51
imperialism, 11
Indian Ocean, 5
intensification, agricultural, 123
intercropping, 123
iron
    forging, 9
    furnaces, 20
    smelting, 9
    Pare smiths (Washana), 22
    working, 19, 20–22
irrigation, hill furrow, 24–25, 106

Jackson, F. H., 132
Johanssen, Ernst, 39
Juniperus procera, 72, 74, 152

Kamba settlements, 33
Kasigau, 22
Kauzeni, 107
Kenya, Mount, 20
Keudel, 50
Kew Gardens, 45
Khaya nyasica, 156
Kilimanjaro, Mount, 1, 20
Kilindi, 28, 33–35, 103–5, 106
Kingdon, Jonathan, 6
Kinyassi, Hassani, 116–21, 132
Kisii, 85. *See also* pit sawing
Kitivo, 105, 124
kitivo (vitivo pl.), 22, 37, 98–101, 124

Korogwe, 49
Krapf, Johan Ludwig, 11–12
Kwai Farm, 13, 41, 46–55, 66
Kwamkoro, 90–91, 155
Kwekanga market, 81
Kwemekame, 42

labor, forest, 78–79. *See also* squatters
Laikipia Plateau, 27
land tenure, 115
land-use systems, 18
Land Utilization Survey, 94
Lands Office, 52–53
Lands Ordinance (1923), 96–97
Lands Ordinance (1928), 97
laterization, 92
Leach, Melissa, 70–71
Leechman, Alleyne, 63–64
Lukozi Valley, 82, 152–53
Lundgren, Björn, 153
Lushoto District Development Committee, 139, 143–44
Lwengera Valley, 33, 72, 87, 99

Maasai, 10, 27, 48
MacDonald, A. C., 62
Maesopsis, 155
Magamba, 51, 74–75
    Forest Reserve, 38
mahogany, 88–89
maize, 24, 26, 101, 105, 116, 141
malaria, 12
Malindi, 130
Mann, Harold, 90, 94
Manumba, 100
markets
    local, 134–35
    Mlalo, 37
Mashina, Ali. *See* Chankola (Ali Mashina)
Mazinde, 34
Mbaramo, 101, 117, 124, 141, 146
Mbaru, 35
Mbugu (Wambugu pl.), 9–10, 12, 14, 27–30, 37–39, 47–55, 74–76, 78–82, 87, 95
Mdando River, 108
Mearns, Robin, 70
Mesozoic era, 5
microenvironments, 21

millet, 116
Milne, Geoffrey, 91, 94, 100, 108, 111–14
Milicia excelsa, 156
Mkomazi Plain, 22
Mkussu River, 50
Mkuzi River, 106–7
Mlalo, 22, 24–25, 34, 37–38, 82, 97–98, 101–2, 108, 112, 114, 116
Mlalo Basin Rehabilitation Scheme, 117, 126–34
Mlimahadala, 39
Mlimahadala, Kadala, 81
Mlola, 35–36, 137, 139, 141
modernization, 18
Mombo
    experimental station, 49
    sisal estate, 106
    subchiefdom, 106
monoculture, 3
monsoon, 5
Moreau, R. E., 93–94, 150
Mtai Forest Reserve, 88
Muheza District, 94
mvule, 88
Mwakosa, David, 142
Mwangoi, 130–31
Mwitu, 9, 20 (*see also* agriculture: highland)

Native Authorities, 140
Native Foodstuffs Ordinance, 121
natural history, 4–7, 148
Natural Resources Management and Buffer Zone Development Programme, 157
Neuman, Roderick, 159
Newtonia buchananii, 156
Ngambo, 94
Ngua, 94
Nguu, 8
njaa ya Chankola, 116–24, 126–27, 145
njaa ya mchele, 98
Nkese, 20–22
North Pare, 8, 20
Nutman, F. J., 65, 128
Nyamwezi, 50
Nzerengembe, 80–81

Ocotea usambarensis. *See* camphor: East African

oral history, 9
oral traditions, 10

Pangani Valley, 45, 99–100
    slave trade, 32–33
pastoralism, 10, 27–30, 78, 79. *See also* Mbugu (Wambugu pl.)
Peters, Carl, 44
pit sawing, 85, 156
Pitt-Schenkel, C. J. W., 38
plantain, 23–24
plantations (*see* coffee; forest; rubber; sisal; tea)
Pleistocene epoch, 5–6
podocarpus, 72, 84, 152
Podocarpus spp. See podocarpus
Polhill, R. M., 150
potato, 24, 49, 105, 116
    sweet, 105
Prain, D., 64
Private Land, 96, 102
Provincial Committee, 128–30
Public Land, 79–80, 83, 87–89, 96–102, 111, 152, 155

rainfall, 5, 10
    long rains, 5
    regime, 18
    short rains, 5
rain forest, 3, 59
rain shadow, 5
rice, 24, 98, 101
Rift Valley, 9, 10, 25, 27
rinderpest, 38, 48, 81
Rossel, Gerda, 24
Royal Geographic Society, 109
rubber, 12, 61, 98–99

Sakarre, 84
savanna, 5
Semboja, 34
settlement
    fortified, 35
    highland, 20–21
    patterns, 87, 103
    refugee, 33
Shambaa (Washambaa pl.), 10, 27, 28, 30
Shebuge Magogo, 104, 106
Shita, 131–32, 142

Shume, 74–76, 78, 79, 82
Shume-Magamba Forest Reserve, 83, 152–53
Sikh Saw Mills, 156–57
silviculture, 75–76
sisal, 12, 46, 99–100
slavery, 32–34
soil erosion, 10, 13, 108–9, 112–13, 134, 146
    Standing Committee on, 109
Soil Erosion Control and Agroforestry Project, 157
soil fertility, 18, 92
sorghum, 116
South Pare, 8, 20, 22–23, 25, 28
squatters, 79, 82–83. *See also* forest: labor
Staples Plan, 129
Staples, R. R., 127
Storey, H. H., 65
Stuhlman, Franz, 59
sustained yield, 14
Swahili Coast, 23

Taita
    hills, 1, 9, 20–22
    mercenaries, 35
    refugees, 33
Tanganyika Forests and Lumber Company (TFLC), 78–79, 83
Tanganyika Standard, 54–55

tea, 90, 94
teak, 61
Tewa, Said, 152
Tewe, 37, 124
tobacco, 26, 37, 59, 65, 82–83
Troup, R. S., 77

Umba River, 22, 25, 99, 124, 146
Upare (Pare), 1, 9, 21–22, 25, 27. *See also* North Pare and South Pare
Urwald, 12
Usambara Scheme, 126, 139–47

Van Rensberg, H. J., 128
Vansina, Jan, 19
Village Development Council (VDC), 152
vitivo. *See* kitivo (vitivo pl.)
Vuga
    mission, 106
    subchiefdom, 106, 142

Wambugu. *See* Mbugu (Wambugu pl.)
Warburg, Otto, 58
Washambaa. *See* Shambaa (Washambaa pl.)
Washana (Pare smiths), 22
Wilhelmstal, 48
Wilkins and Wiese Co., 75
Woodcock, J. T., 52–55

Zimmerman, Albrecht, 59–60, 63

www.ingramcontent.com/pod-product-compliance
Lightning Source LLC
Chambersburg PA
CBHW031243290426
44109CB00012B/419